Contesting Identities

Contesting Identities

SPORTS IN AMERICAN FILM

Aaron Baker

UNIVERSITY OF ILLINOIS PRESS

URBANA AND CHICAGO

© 2003 by the Board of Trustees
of the University of Illinois
All rights reserved
Manufactured in the United States of America
C 5 4 3 2 1

⊗ This book is printed on acid-free paper.

Library of Congress Cataloging-in-Publication Data
Baker, Aaron.
Contesting identities : sports in American film / Aaron Baker.
p.   cm.
Filmography: p.
Includes bibliographical references and index.
ISBN 0-252-02816-3 (cloth : alk. paper)
1. Sports in motion pictures.
2. Motion pictures—United States.
I. Title.
PN1995.9.S67B35   2003
791.43'655—dc21   2002009061

For Mattheo and Natalia

CONTENTS

ACKNOWLEDGMENTS

This book got its start as an essay about football on television that I wrote in a graduate class at Indiana University. I would like to thank the professor for that course, Patrick Brantlinger, who introduced me to cultural studies and whose work has continued to influence my thinking about culture and society.

Other professors at Indiana University contributed to this project after it became a dissertation. Harry Geduld told me about movies that I needed to see and helped me understand the significance of several 1920s comedies for my argument. Murray Sperber offered inspiration by having the courage to take sports seriously, to see them in political terms, and to write in an accessible style. To the degree that this is a book about film, my greatest influence came from James Naremore, whose own ideas improved the following text significantly and who has shown me by example how enjoyable and enlightening good analysis of movies can be.

I wish to thank Indiana University and Arizona State University for generous grants that helped me travel to libraries and archives to do research for this book and to have the time to write it.

A number of colleagues, both at Arizona State University and at other universities, read part or all of the manuscript and offered useful suggestions for its revision, especially Daniel Bernardi, Todd Boyd, Charles Dellheim, Montye Fuse, Christine Holmlund, Jack Kugelmass, Peter Lehman, Keith Miller, Michael Oriard, Steven Pope, Kenneth Shropshire, and Vivian Sobchack.

This book might never have been completed without the patient support of its editor, Joan Catapano, who has shown unwavering belief in its value, offered good advice, and put a great deal of time and energy into getting it finished.

Most of all, however, I owe an immeasurable debt to Juliann Vitullo, who has read each of the various versions of this text, given me invaluable suggestions for revision, and put up with its long career.

• • •

Portions of chapter 1 previously appeared in "Sports Films, Identity, and History," *Journal of Sport History* (Summer 1998): 217–33.

Portions of chapter 2 previously appeared in two publications: "From Second String to Solo Star: Classic Hollywood and the Black Athlete," in *Classic Hollywood, Classic Whiteness,* edited by Daniel Bernardi, 31–51 (Minneapolis: University of Minnesota Press, 2001), © 2001 by the Regents of the University of Minnesota, and "Hoop Dreams in Black and White: Race and Basketball Movies," in *Basketball Jones: America, above the Rim,* edited by Kenneth L. Shropshire and Todd Boyd, 215–39 (New York: New York University Press, 2000), reprinted by permission of New York University Press.

Portions of chapter 4 previously appeared in "A Left/Right Combination: Populism and Depression-Era Boxing Films," in *Out of Bounds: Sports, Media, and the Politics of Identity,* edited by Aaron Baker and Todd Boyd, 161–74 (Bloomington: Indiana University Press, 1997).

Contesting Identities

INTRODUCTION: SPORTS FILMS AND THE CONTEST FOR IDENTITY

Since the start of the motion picture industry in the United States, sports have been a frequent subject for the movies. Hollywood has produced hundreds of films about sports for the same reason that synergistic ties have been established between American movies and other cultural forms, including theater, literature, fashion, television, advertising, and toys.[1] From the documentary-style "news films" of major prizefights and the World Series that were an important part of the early film industry to recent blockbusters such as *Space Jam* (1996), *Jerry Maguire* (1996), and *The Waterboy* (1998), collaboration with sports has helped sell the movies.

Such films, like other media representations of American sports, are therefore extremely "popular" in the sense that Stuart Hall uses the term to describe those cultural texts that are consumed by a large audience.[2] When Disney purchased Capitol Cities/ABC in 1995, ESPN, which proclaimed itself as the "largest provider of sports TV programming in the world" and included twenty-six television networks, a radio network, an Internet site, and "sports-themed dining and entertainment," was the most important asset in the acquisition. Executives from both ABC and Disney explained the value of sports as their "universal appeal" and ability to "offend no political position."[3] Yet the popularity of sports as represented by this lucrative symbiosis with the media does not depend exclusively on their appeal as commercial entertainment. Films and other media representations of sports are also popular in a second sense described by Hall: They function "in a continuing tension (relationship, influence and antagonism) to the dominant culture."[4]

This book employs both of Hall's definitions of popular culture to analyze how films about sports present competing discourses on class, race, gender, and to a lesser extent sexuality. It therefore challenges media executive wisdom regarding the apolitical nature of sports by examining how these films contribute to the contested process of defining social identities.

The methodology that I use here to analyze sports films works with the assumption that culture is a site of ideological conflict between dominant and subordinate groups over the construction of social identities. In order to maintain hegemonic control, dominant interests attempt to represent subject positions that they favor as serving the interests of all people in the society. When it comes to sports films, the overriding example of hegemonic representation is their repeated endorsement of the viability and usefulness of self-reliance—and therefore the irrelevance of a social identity based on one's membership in a group. Despite these efforts at ideological maintenance, contradictions often show up in the utopian logic of self-determination in these films, allowing us to see the larger structural determinants of social identities and even possible responses to how these forces can create disadvantage and injustice.

As I explain further in chapter 1, the use of history to achieve realism in sports films produces much of the contradiction and contestation. In their attempt to portray plausible athletes and sporting events, Hollywood films often include historical forces that complicate their narratives, which are otherwise focused on individual characters as causal agents. In chapter 1 I analyze several films, in particular *Knute Rockne—All American* (1940), *Gentleman Jim* (1942), *The Jackie Robinson Story* (1950), and *Soul of the Game* (1996), to illustrate how the inclusion of this historical complexity, especially as it pertains to discourses of social identity, complicates their utopian stories.

Chapter 2 begins with a brief overview of the exclusion and marginalization of African Americans from films about sports until the late 1940s. In the decade after World War II, blacks began to gain more substantial and even starring roles in sports films, but with the restriction that they continue to accept white control and represent an ideology of self-reliance and gradualism. These values have continued to inform filmic representation of African American athletes, even as blacks have become a dominant presence in sports such as basketball and football. In chapter 2 I analyze also how films about basketball made during the 1980s and 1990s use an African American athletic aesthetic to reaffirm an individualist notion of success best represented by Michael Jordan. As they seek to show an increase in black access to the American dream, these films attempt to discredit the other prominent notion of black identity in contemporary popular culture, that of gangsta nihilism and violence. However, in addition to his endorsement of American opportunity, Jordan, and the black aesthetic associated with the NBA, also emphasize improvisational pleasure that critiques the alienation demanded by an individualist ethos.

Chapter 3 contains an analysis of how, within the utopian narrative typical of American sports films, the heroic individual who overcomes obstacles and achieves success through determination, self-reliance, and hard work is most often male. The primary notion of masculinity in sports films is that this male protagonist defines and proves himself through free and fair competition modeled on American society, which claims that rewards go to the most deserving individuals. Differences in social position are therefore naturalized as evolutionary rather than as a result of a lack of competitive opportunities.[5] These films seldom acknowledge that women have had limited access to sports. Instead, the competition involving men that the films showcase provides an opportunity to validate the assumption of male superiority. When gender discrimination comes up, it is often portrayed not as a systemic flaw in sports competition or American society, but rather as just another ad hoc challenge that the strong and resourceful individual will overcome.

Industrialization, urbanization, immigration, and the assertion of the New Woman all contested the authority of white, bourgeois men, and sports films contributed to a response to such challenge by justifying claims of earned privilege. However, since the mid-1970s, sports films have begun to react to new social patterns, including multiculturalism and a second wave of feminism, and to changed modes of cultural representation—tendencies often classified under the heading of postmodernism. To maintain its appeal, sports films have made room for variations in ideal masculinity, showing it as less exclusively white, as available for appropriation by female athletes, and even as more overtly commodified and sexualized. Some recent films have therefore adopted new representational practices to complement traditional narrative constructions of sports heroism, including a music video–like flow of images aimed at younger viewers that often objectifies the athletic body.

Because of their inherent connection to the body, sports have traditionally played an important role in definitions of gender, especially masculinity. As a result, to some degree every sports film is about gender, whatever it has to say about other aspects of social identity. Chapter 3 is therefore longer than the others in this book, because of my effort to analyze the major tendencies in the representation of gender in sports films.

Hollywood films generally avoid representation of social identity, but class in particular suffers from such omission. While the recognition of social difference, if it gets shown at all, appears in sports films as an obstacle to be overcome by individual initiative, physical traits often serve as essentialized reminders of racial and gender identity. By emphasizing the value of sports as a catalyst for upward mobility, films such as *Pride of the Yankees* (1942), *Gentleman Jim, The Babe Ruth Story* (1948), *The Pride of St. Louis* (1952), *Somebody Up*

There Likes Me (1956), *Rocky* (1976), and *All the Right Moves* (1983) attempt to erase signs of membership in the working class and therefore dismiss the need for collective solidarity. Working-class origins may be invoked as a source of the athlete's physical strength and lack of pretention, but while this modesty explains his ability to work with others, an inclination toward teamwork is rarely valued in and of itself. Instead it functions to make the inevitable social ascension appear as if it couldn't happen to a better person.

Chapter 4 analyzes how, while self-determination is a common theme in boxing films, the historical record again intrudes on many of these stories. Historical contextualization appears in the form of the economic exploitation of boxer labor by those who run prizefighting, and through the fighters' own handicaps arising from their backgrounds of deprivation. Some boxing films therefore take the position that the most effective strategy for a working-class fighter requires the support of family and community. To the degree that these films represent effective collectivity, they establish class identity in both senses described by Raymond Williams: as including those persons "who are objectively in that economic situation," and as "a formation in which, for historical reasons, consciousness of this situation and the organization to deal with it have developed."[6]

As these four chapter summaries show, the analysis in each foregrounds a particular aspect of social identity but also examines the relationships between identities as useful in understanding their representation and definition. For example, chapter 3 shows how whiteness, heterosexuality, and ideas of middle-class self-definition are essential traits for the normative idea of masculinity in many sports films. Chapter 4 also makes clear how, especially as the demographics of professional sports in general and prizefighting in particular grew increasingly nonwhite after World War II, the relationship between race and class became more significant.

This book doesn't claim to offer a complete study of sports films. Rather it analyzes roughly ninety movies about sports that represent positions on the social identities (race, class, gender, and to a lesser degree sexuality) that are my main concern. Such interest in social identity has also influenced the historical boundaries of this book. Chapter 2, on race, focuses primarily on films made since World War II because, with the exception of a few silent films about Native Americans and prizefighter Jack Johnson, it has only been in that period that nonwhite athletes have been main characters in sports movies. Likewise, in chapter 4, I show that the notion of prizefighters as representative of working-class identity gets firmly established during the Depression, which is why the analysis there starts with the films from that era. Robert Sklar argues that the questions the Depression raised about American capitalism were an important impetus for Hollywood films to move toward a conservative ideology, what he calls "the mythmaking role of the movies."[7] The emphasis on individualism and self-reliance that came with that American mythology is central to the utopianism in so many films about sports. On a formal level, sports films since the advent of sound use audio (e.g., the sounds of athletic competition and the announcer voice-over so common in action sequences) as a component of a realist aesthetic aimed at creating historical legitimacy.[8] For these two reasons, this book emphasizes sound films. The one exception to this time frame occurs in chapter 3, in which the analysis of several silent films helps illustrate the forces of modernity that influenced normative masculinity.

I focus here primarily on commercial, feature films about boxing, baseball, football, and basketball—the sports that because of their proven commercial viability have been the subjects of the largest number of films.[9] Only nine of the movies analyzed here are not about those four sports. I use the term *sports* rather than *sport* because the former is more widely used to refer to the rule-governed, physical contests that are my concern here. Professional and college sports offer themselves as defining the highest standard of skill and organization, and for that reason I emphasize films about those levels of competition as sites where models of identity (and their complications) get presented.

A few other terms that I use require some explanation. Throughout the book, but especially in chapter 2, I employ the term *whiteness* to refer to a notion of identity defined as superiority over others lumped together as nonwhite. The term *nonwhite* itself has that problem of putting other racial groups in the United States—most prominently African Americans, Chicanos, Native Americans, and Asian Americans—together in a vague mass of otherness and defines people by what they are not. Nonetheless, I use it rather than the equally general "people of color" because the latter suggests that whiteness is not a racial identity, when it is important to show that it is.[10]

Richard Dyer's critical study of whiteness from which I borrow these terms offers a model for the analysis of identity in this book. Just as he has shown how whiteness is socially and culturally defined, I hope that the analysis of sports films in this book will critique the powerful mythology of self-determination by illustrating some of the values and practices that inform social identities.

Notes

1. Kristin Thompson describes the movies' relationship with vaudeville in *The Classical Hollywood Cinema* (New York: Columbia University Press, 1985), 163–66. Charles Eckert traces the establishment of a symbiotic relationship between Hollywood and the fashion industry in his essay "The Carole Lombard in Macy's Window" in *Fabrications:*

Costume and the Female Body, ed. Jane Gaines and Charlotte Herzog (New York: Routledge, 1990). Mark Crispin Miller has written about the increasing use of advertising within film narrative in his essay "Advertising" in *Seeing through the Movies,* ed. Mark Crispin Miller (New York: Pantheon, 1990). Finally, Robert Sklar sums up this synergy between film and other forms of culture when he states that "something akin to synergy has always existed in movie culture, from the medium's ties to vaudeville in its earliest days through its later relationships with stage plays, popular novels, short stories, radio and television." *Movie-Made America* (New York: Vintage, 1994), 339–40.

2. Stuart Hall, "Notes on Deconstructing 'The Popular,'" in *People's History and Socialist Theory,* ed. Raphael Samuel (London: Routledge and Kegan Paul, 1981), 231.

3. "The Trophy in Eisner's Big Deal," *New York Times,* August 6, 1995, sec. 3, pp. 1, 11.

4. Hall, "The Popular," 235.

5. Arthur Brittan, *Masculinity and Power* (London: Blackwell, 1989), 78.

6. Raymond Williams, "Class," in Williams, *Keywords* (New York: Oxford University Press, 1983), 68.

7. Sklar, *Movie-Made America,* 195–96.

8. Robert Ray, *A Certain Tendency of the Hollywood Cinema, 1930–1980* (Princeton, N.J.: Princeton University Press, 1985), 55–56.

9. Harvey Marc Zucker and Lawrence J. Babich state that approximately two thousand sports films had been made by the middle 1980s. I count at least forty more films about sports made for television, video and DVD, or theatrical release since that time. *Sports Films: A Complete Reference* (Jefferson, N.C.: McFarland, 1987), 3. I define a feature as a partially fictional narrative film of more than one hour in length, intended for exhibition in theaters, on home video or DVD, or on television.

10. My choice and definitions of these terms have been influenced by Richard Dyer's book *White* (New York: Routledge, 1997).

1   Sports Films, History, and Identity

Popular culture is like the study of labour history and its institutions. To declare an interest is to correct a major imbalance, to mark a significant oversight. But, in the end, it yields more when it is seen in relation to a more general, a wider history.

—Stuart Hall

Because they frequently draw upon real contests and athletes, sports films often claim historical status. While one might regard any film as historical in the sense that it offers what Robert Rosenstone calls "a document" representing "the social and cultural concerns" of the time when it was made, most sports movies that make explicit claims to historical meaning do so instead by portraying the past, although even these films look back in time through the lens of present concerns.[1]

Rosenstone identifies several characteristics shared by most of the latter type of explicitly historical films, whether dramatic features or documentaries. They generally tell history "as a story" using a strong element of closure that leaves the audience with "a moral message and (usually) a feeling of uplift."[2] *Hoosiers* (1986) does this by employing the climactic contest conventional to sports films to reestablish a moral order that rewards the hard work and determination of underdog protagonists. Even historical sports films that are more qualified in their optimism generally suggest that things have gotten or are getting better, although they may emphasize the price paid for such progress.

Two examples of the "progress doesn't come cheap" ending are *Knute Rockne—All American* (1940) and *Pride of the Yankees* (1942), both of which finish with the death of their biographical subjects. These two films show that the hard work of men like Knute Rockne and Lou Gehrig—from working-class, immigrant families—earned them fame and material comfort and made their deaths "in the line of duty" meaningful as they preserved the values that made such success possible. Released just before or during U.S. involvement in World War II, these movies validate military service by suggesting that sometimes the ultimate sacrifice is necessary to ensure a free and prosperous future. The preface to the Rockne biopic tells us that he is killed in a plane crash that cuts short his work "molding the spirit of . . . millions of young men and boys who are living by the high standards he taught."[3]

Sports films frequently represent this progressive view of history in melodramatic terms. Literary critic Peter Brook has said that melodrama is a common fictional mode of addressing disturbing social issues that are otherwise repressed.[4] In an essay on television movies, Laurie Schulze qualifies Brook's assertion by noting that "If melodrama involves itself with the excessive, its function consists, many critics have argued, in invoking desires or anxieties only to put them back into the box again."[5] This melodramatic containment is a common way for Hollywood films to present history—and sports films are no exception. Sports movies generally frame history as adequately represented by the individual desires, goals, and emotional dramas of the main characters, often in a biopic story. Such telescoping attempts to exclude the complexity of historical questions, and by the end of the film answers in the form of individual actions are fit into a single explanation, represented with a realistic mise-en-scène and an emotional resonance that undermine critical scrutiny. Nonetheless, as this chapter will show, some of these formal and thematic structures can function in other ways to produce a contradictory historical complexity.

On the surface, *Knute Rockne—All American* presents a personalized, melodramatic version of history. As I mentioned earlier, Rockne's life is shown as representative of the social mobility possible in America; how even a boy from a working-class, immigrant family can grow up to become a national sports hero. George Custen has commented that the first generation of Hollywood studio heads liked heroes whose traits resembled their own, which is why many biopics from the classic period use the narrative found in this film of "immigrant pluck rewarded by a benevolent America."[6] In his history of Notre Dame football, Murray Sperber says that when producer Mark Hellinger pitched the idea for the film to Jack Warner, "the movie executive liked it immediately."[7] Yet while *Knute Rockne—All American* ostensibly offers the biography of the Notre Dame coach as historical proof of the American dream, it inadvertently makes reference to the selective nature of such opportunity.

As *Knute Rockne—All American* opens, we are told that Lars Rockne brought his son, Knute, and the rest of his family from Norway "following the new road of equality and opportunity which led to America." The film unintentionally shows, however, that such opportunity did not extend to African Americans. Blacks appear only as minor characters in most sports films prior to the early 1950s, a marginalization that reflects their exclusion until just before that time from the highest levels of commercial sports. Despite their brief appearance in the film, the two black characters in *Knute Rockne—All American* qualify its affirmation of the American dream. In an early scene, when young Knute plays football for the first time in a sandlot game, an African American boy running the ball for the other team knocks him flat. The only other appearance of an African American character comes much later in the film, when Rockne, now the famous football coach at Notre Dame, returns to South Bend on the train after a tough loss. A black porter stops at the door of his compartment and asks Rockne if he would like his suit brushed off before they arrive. The presence of the porter ironically recalls the boy who had run over little Rock in the football legend's first experience with the game that was to make him famous. The difference in social position between Rockne and the porter suggests why the African American boy appears nowhere but in the one early scene. The promise of equal opportunity, which both blacks and whites were called upon to defend in the war, extended to some parts of American society and not others.

Even more recent revisionist sports films don't operate entirely outside these Hollywood conventions. As a filmmaker whose career has been distinguished by his attempts to avoid the melodramatic, ahistorical tendencies of Hollywood, John Sayles in *Eight Men Out* (1988) makes concessions to the dominant model of historical filmmaking that demonstrate its authority. In an interview with historian Eric Foner, Sayles explains that he had to wait eleven years from the time he wrote the first draft of the script to make *Eight Men Out,* because "I wanted to tell that story, *Eight Men Out.* Not *One Man Out* or *Three Men Out and a Baby.*"[8] Yet even Sayles could not entirely overcome the need to present history as what Rosenstone calls "the story of individuals."[9] He justifies this compromise with the assertion that audiences will understand and tolerate only a story told with at most three points of view: that of the protagonist, that of an antagonistic opponent, and that of an omniscient narrator. While the eight Chicago White Sox players associated with the fix of the 1919 World Series have different interests, and their opponents are both the gamblers and the owners who want to make an example of them, the film tries to center viewer identification on two characters: Buck Weaver (John Cusack) and Joe Jackson (D. B. Sweeney). The sympathetic treatment of Weaver and Jackson implies that if their actions—playing well in the World Series—didn't determine the course of events, they should have.

Despite this narrative focus on Weaver and Jackson, Sayles presents them as representative of larger interests. Although the other six players adopt the self-serving tactics of the gamblers and owners, the outstanding play of Weaver and Jackson both rejects the manipulative deal and exemplifies how the achievements of working people often go unrewarded and unrecognized. In the film's last scene we see Jackson four years after his expulsion from the major leagues, playing for a semi-pro team in New Jersey. A dramatic series of shots shows him hitting a long drive to right-center field, rounding first and second, and arriving safely at third base. These shots recall a tracking shot used earlier in the film to establish Jackson's hitting ability while with the White Sox. In both cases, we know that the spectacular skills shown are underrewarded, but during the latter scene we also hear a spectator tell another that Jackson was "one of them bums from Chicago . . . one of the Black Sox." With this comment *Eight Men Out* sums up the distortion in public memory that it hopes to rectify by showing the social and economic forces that affected players like Jackson and Weaver. To further this revisionist project, however, Sayles is not above using the tactics of conventional history films. The identification that *Eight Men Out* encourages with Weaver and Jackson, combined with the injustice of their treatment, follows the third of Rosenstone's rules of historical filmmaking by emotionalizing history—aiming for feelings of outrage and sympathy to increase viewer investment in it.

The primary focus on individual characters as the makers of history in most sports films fits with what Robert Ray has described as Hollywood's tendency to affirm "American beliefs in individualism, ad hoc solutions, and the impermanence of all political problems."[10] In Ray's view, "history's major crises," those situations in which individuals and groups feel the influence of larger social institutions and discourses on the choices about how they will define themselves, "appear in American movies only as 'structuring absences'—the unspoken subjects that have determined an aesthetic form designed precisely to conceal these crises' real implications."[11] Rosenstone describes such omission as a fourth practice in most historical filmmaking, its tendency to be "unproblematic and uncontested in its view of what happened and why."[12] Sayles refers to this reductionist approach when he says that the historical feature film has to avoid too many points of view or risk threatening the all-important emotional connection with its audience. He admits, however, that this limiting of perspective militates "against complexity," or what Rosenstone calls "alternative possibilities to what we see happening on the screen."[13]

Feature films about sports follow all these rules that Rosenstone, Ray, and Sayles describe, but they are especially fond of the idea that history is made by individuals. I can think of only nine feature films about sports history that are not biopics: *The Harlem Globetrotters* (1951), *The Bingo Long Traveling All-Stars & Motor Kings* (1976), *Miracle on Ice* (1981), *Hoosiers, Eight Men Out, A League of Their Own* (1992), *When We Were Kings* (1996), *Soul of the Game* (1996), and *Remember the Titans* (2000)—and even these focus primarily on two or three main characters. The overwhelming prevalence of sports biography films (more than seventy since 1940) demonstrates that the symbiosis between sports and movies is ideological as well as economic. Custen points out that the inclination of biopics toward the stories of a few, mostly white, men is an important part of a Hollywood version of history that is "ideologically self-serving" for those who have run the movie business.[14] Therefore, just as biopics are part of the promotion of self-reliance by classic Hollywood narrative when it uses what David Bordwell and Kristin Thompson call "individual characters as causal agents," sports also give the greatest recognition to star performance regardless of any gestures they might make to teamwork, fair play, and fan communities.[15]

At this point I want to briefly digress in order to make some general statements about the meaning of individual performance in media representations of American sports. Some of what I am about to say may sound dehistoricized, but I would argue that, since their inception in the later half of the nineteenth century, commercial sports have consistently been portrayed as disproving the idea of a socially constructed identity. Sports movies at least in part follow this representational tendency. Borrowing from the work of the Annales historians, Stephen Hardy has referred to such diachronic meanings as the "long residuals" of sports culture that have "crossed time and context."[16]

Like Hollywood, where ethnic minorities, women, and gays have played an important role, professional and college sports have given greater opportunity than the larger society to what Richard Dyer calls "structurally subordinate groups,"[17] especially working-class and nonwhite men. Nonetheless, sports fit squarely within a traditional American mythology that champions the promise of a unified self through individual achievement in order to deny the importance of social identity. Despite the recent growth of women's sports, such a self-reliant identity is still strongly associated with masculinity, so that movies about athletes, with a few exceptions, involve women only as they support male self-definition. Although they aim themselves more at women than most sports films do, Nike's ad campaigns centered on a slogan like "Just Do It" or "I Can" are prominent examples of the notion that sports offer an opportunity for uncomplicated self-definition; the emphasis on stars and the frequency of the sports biopic are more longstanding manifestations of this idea. Such belief in agency supports the utopian promise of sports: that once the contest begins, success depends primarily on one's determination and effort.

Movies and other media texts about sports at times digress with endorsements of teamwork and fair play to allay audience fears about the potential for athletic competition to devolve into social Darwinism. Yet ultimately the individualist mythology has a stronger appeal as utopian narrative, and it certainly best represents the interests of those who own teams, newspapers, networks, movie studios, and the other corporations that use sports to do business. Even when teamwork figures prominently in narratives about athletics, it doesn't reduce the value placed on individual performance. Rather, like the bourgeois nuclear family, the team operates as a social structure to foster the development of self-reliant individuals; self-effacing play therefore subordinates itself to the more recognized actions of the star. *Hoosiers* offers a good example of this ideological hierarchy. Although much of the film is a nostalgic parable involving a big-city basketball coach who learns the importance of teamwork and community in a small Indiana town, that thematic emphasis is subordinated in the film's climactic scene to the individual heroism of a game-winning basket by a star player. Along with the cultural specificity of the term "Hoosiers," this individual emphasis explains why the film was distributed outside the United States under the title *Best Shot.*

As part of their affirmation of the idea of meritocracy, professional sports continually remind us of the standard of living that star players achieve. While constant media reports of seven- and eight-figure annual salaries create the fan resentment one hears expressed on sports talk radio and finds in a film like *The Replacements* (2000), they also reinforce the belief that opportunity for economic advancement exists in American society. The blockbuster *Jerry Maguire* (1996) makes this more optimistic interpretation of big contracts its central theme. Moreover, it is no coincidence that as downsizing has reduced economic security for many Americans, the good fortune of a relatively small number of athletes who sign long-term, multimillion-dollar contracts has increasingly received media attention. The frequent calls for athletes to act as role models further bolsters the notion of personal success achieved by following the path of agency and self-reliance that sports stars are expected to define.

In what I have said about sports and movies I don't want to suggest that historical narrative should exclude the role of individual action. In fact, borrowing from Dyer's analysis of entertainment and utopia, I would claim that the idealized identity of professional athletes responds to real needs that viewers have and act upon: for greater economic means, for a sense of personal accomplishment, and for recognition from others.[18] What is less connected to social reality in many sports films is the overly simplistic explanations they offer for how star athletes achieve these successes.

Therefore sports films often present us with decontextualized celebrations of the achievements of star athletes offset by a realist aesthetic of reportage disavowing that the whole thing is staged for our consumption and reassurance. This realist style figures most prominently in action scenes involving footage of actual contests or set in stadiums filled with crowds of extras, employing authentic uniforms and equipment and often real athletes. The cinematic contests are frequently narrated by announcers in the style of television or radio coverage and shown with a continuity editing style that makes the sequence of shots seem motivated by the logic of the events rather than choices made by the filmmakers. For historical sports films this representational style has special resonance, because it recalls real events in sports "history": athletic contests that the audience has witnessed in the past. Heightened realism in scenes in which the star competes is especially important in validating an ideology of agency that assumes that individual performance in these situations counts most in making the athlete what he is.

As Dyer points out, the conservatism of utopian entertainment comes from the way it offers representations of a better life if we just follow the rules and try harder. In other words, not only does such utopian entertainment avoid suggesting specific ways to change the current social reality, it promises us happiness by adhering to the status quo. Yet Dyer adds that this utopian response only works if one ignores—as entertainment almost always does—how social identities such as race, class, gender, and sexuality complicate self-definition. On the contrary, the acknowledgment of social forces in the constitution of identity makes evident that the opportunity, abundance, and happiness in utopian narratives are not there for everyone to the same degree. Even when sports movies acknowledge the disadvantage of racism, sexism, or class difference (homophobia is still widely ignored), individual performance is generally held up as the best way to overcome their influence. Later in this chapter I analyze *The Jackie Robinson Story* (1950) as an example of how sports films endorse self-reliance as the best response to social disadvantage.

The more one regards sports films as historical because of their need for verisimilitude, and not just as utopian stories about individuals, the more they reveal what Mikhail Bakhtin called dialogism, or the combination of discursive positions within one text. Applying Bakhtin's ideas about literature to ethnic and racial representation in film, Robert Stam has described his goal as to "call attention to the voices at play in a text, not only those heard in aural 'close-up,' but also those voices distorted or drowned out."[19] Using this idea of textuality to approach historical sports films, one can see how their protagonists overcome external obstacles to succeed but are also formed in part by social forces and the choices they offer. For example, the 1942 biopic *Gentleman Jim* shows 1890s boxer Jim Corbett fighting his way to the heavyweight title yet at the same time negotiating between different conceptions of masculinity, social class, and race. Through his "scientific" boxing, mannered charm, and stylish appearance, Corbett renounces the working-class masculinity of his Irish-American family to define a more "respectable" type of prizefighter. His formation of this "gentlemanly" style at an elite men's club necessitates his acceptance of a bourgeois notion of masculinity that invalidates the ethnic, working-class identities of his father and two brothers as well as that of the man from whom Corbett takes the heavyweight belt, John Sullivan. Corbett's opportunity for self-advancement also requires that he avoid endangering the dominant discourse of white supremacy that Gail Bederman has shown intersected through the arena of prizefighting with constructions of masculinity in turn-of-the-century American society.[20] *Gentleman Jim* therefore refers indirectly to, but never mentions by name, the black fighter Peter Jackson, a top heavyweight of the period whom Sullivan, and Corbett once he became champion, refused to meet in the ring.[21]

Ironically, because it is so rule bound Hollywood's individualistic history inadvertently portrays the influence of social discourses on its representations of identity. Custen notes that the biopic "reduces individuals to . . . a mass-tailored contour for fame in which greatness [for the biographical subject] is generic and difference has controllable boundaries."[22] In contrast to these narrative limits, Cornel West asserts the importance of a more contextualized understanding of history and identity in his response to conservative explanations of the black underclass. West states that one should not, as some conservatives have tried to do, overemphasize the "themes of self-help and personal responsibility" by wrenching them "out of historical context . . . as if it is all a matter of personal will."[23] Instead, he counters, "How people act and live are shaped—though in no way dictated or determined—by the larger circumstances in which they find themselves."[24] Along similar lines, a more complete analysis of how sports films represent history can be developed by studying how they define the athlete's identity as always a matter of negotiating the discourses and institutions that make up his or her world.

Two films about Jackie Robinson's entrance into major league baseball, *The Jackie Robinson Story* and the HBO made-for-TV movie *Soul of the Game*, illustrate this dialogic tendency in historical representation by offering both the utopian individualism of the biopic and also a less monochromatic viewpoint. Both films show Robinson reluctantly accepting Dodger owner Branch Rickey's strategy that he turn the other cheek as he faces the racist abuse directed at him once he begins playing in previously all-white "organized baseball." Rickey's strategy was important in avoiding the interracial violence that would have created pressure to stop his "great experiment." By requiring that Robinson withstand the abuse Rickey could also demonstrate the black player's self-denial and deferral of gratification that many white Americans thought African Americans lacked. Sports historian Randy Roberts describes the widespread belief among white fans at the time of Robinson's debut that the black male was "incapable of organized team sports, where raw talent and brute strength were secondary to mental acuity, careful planning, and coordinated execution. . . . Imagine Sambo trying to master Knute Rockne's single-wing shift. . . . Nor could whites imagine blacks playing with the intensity of Ty Cobb, the dedication of Lou Gehrig. . . . Nature had designed them to laugh, sing, dance, and play but not to sacrifice, train, work, compete, and win."[25] By going it alone in pursuing the difficult task of proving himself, by shouldering the pressure and accepting the emotional and physical pain from all the racist abuse hurled at him, Robinson demonstrated that he was just as willing as any white person to pursue the path of hard work, self-reliance, and deferred gratification to ensure a better future.[26]

Perhaps because Rickey's assistant, Arthur Mann, co-wrote the script and oversaw the project according to his boss's specifications, *The Jackie Robinson Story* presents its title character in terms of the same integrationist strategy. Playing himself in the film, Robinson portrays the values of hard work, discipline, deferral of gratification, and self-reliance that he used to overcome white resistance to black opportunity. When they first meet, Rickey (Minor Watson) tells Robinson: "I want a player with guts enough not to fight back." After a graphic description of the racist abuse he will face, Robinson assures Rickey that he can turn the other cheek.

The Jackie Robinson Story's representation of Robinson aimed at acceptance by white viewers doesn't start, however, with his career playing for the Dodgers. The film's use of a white male voice-over, beginning with its first image of Jackie as a boy, through commentary spoken by a radio announcer during games in his first two seasons with Montreal and Brooklyn, and summarizing the larger meaning of his success as the movie ends, makes clear who is telling the story. This voice-over reminds the viewer of Rickey's paternalistic guidance and states clearly the film's ideology of cold war patriotism and self-reliance.

Soon after the opening shot of Jackie as a boy and the statement by the voice-over that "This is the story of a boy and his dream," we see a montage sequence in which Robinson's early adoption of a strong work ethic is represented through images of him shining shoes and delivering newspapers on his bicycle. Even the film's brief reference to Robinson's time in the military reinforces the lesson of hard work and achievement. No mention is made of Robinson's battle with Jim Crow in the army and his narrow escape from a dishonorable discharge. Instead we see a scene of girlfriend Rae Isum (Ruby Dee) showing a friend a picture of Jackie in his lieutenant's uniform and telling her that Jackie has been given a position "as some kind of athletic director" by the army.

Along with its emphasis on self-reliance, *The Jackie Robinson Story* individualizes Robinson's experience of racism to imply the appropriateness of his unique opportunity and self-sufficient responses to its roadblocks. Unlike *Soul of the Game,* which foregrounds the injustice of offering only Robinson and not other black players a chance to enter the major leagues, *The Jackie Robinson Story* doesn't specify that Robinson was one of several African American players that Rickey considered. This glaring omission works to separate Robinson from what Ben Rader calls the "pressures that were mounting to end America's apartheid" by the conclusion of World War II.[27] As historians such as John Hope Franklin and Manning Marable have shown, by the time Robinson joined the Dodgers the civil rights movement had already begun to challenge racial restrictions on employment and housing in American society. In fact, Marable makes the case that the cold war anticommunist hysteria represented by Robinson's testimony before the House Un-American Activities Committee (HUAC) shown at the end of *The Jackie Robinson Story* was a factor in slowing down the start of the civil rights movement.[28]

Breaking the color barrier in baseball was not just about Rickey's desire to help the Dodgers win pennants and Robinson's ability to compare favorably on and especially off the field with white players. As Rader explains, it was also prompted by Rickey's desire to draw on a rapidly growing popula-

Jackie Robinson reenacts his testimony before the House Un-American Activities Committee in *The Jackie Robinson Story* (1950).

tion of African Americans in Brooklyn as potential paying customers. New York mayor Fiorello La Guardia had already begun to court African Americans when in 1945 he established a special committee "to consider the city's race relations, including the apparent discrimination against blacks by the local Dodgers, Giants, and Yankees."[29] The nearly four and one-half million blacks who had migrated to northern cities since World War I Rader says "represented both potentially new baseball customers as well as a new political bloc." Between 1940 and 1950, the black population of Brooklyn alone nearly doubled.[30]

Disregarding such factors in Rickey's great experiment, *The Jackie Robinson Story* represents the racism directed at Robinson as occurring through individual acts of discrimination, implying therefore the appropriateness of his self-reliant responses. Even when we see more institutionalized patterns of racism, as when none of the schools that Robinson applies to after leaving UCLA offers him a coaching job, it is soon followed by the representation of a corresponding unbiased institution (in its patriotic fervor, the film portrays the army as this counterweight of opportunity). Like the individualizing of racism and Robinson's response, this depiction of equal-opportunity institutions suggests the limits of social determinism.

However, despite the ways in which the film tries to isolate Robinson's experience, his performance in the title role at several points counters this dehistoricizing tendency. One prominent instance occurs in the action scenes in which Robinson uses an aggressive, improvisational style of play perfected during his time in the Negro Leagues. Rader describes the black baseball of the Negro Leagues as "more opportunistic, improvisational, and daring than white ball. . . . Nothing summed up the uniqueness of black baseball more than its sheer speed . . . combined with the bunt [Robinson had an astounding forty-seven bunt hits his first year with the Dodgers], the hit-and-run play, the stolen base, and taking the extra base."[31]

In *The Jackie Robinson Story* we see at least three scenes of Robinson using this assertive, improvisational style. The first occurs when he is shown doubling and then stealing third and home while playing, appropriately enough, in the Negro Leagues. The lack of any voice-over narration of these feats suggests that it received no radio coverage, indicating a "bush league" status for black baseball. Yet even in two later scenes of Robinson playing for Montreal and Brooklyn, radio announcers who explain beforehand the significance of Robinson's play—how for example, "In baseball, it's not who or what you are, but can you play the game?"—become oddly silent as we see him in action.

In the Montreal scene, a radio announcer sets the scene but then says nothing as Robinson reaches first on a bunt, steals second, goes to third on the

Robinson's aggressive, improvisational style of play in *The Jackie Robinson Story*.

wild throw, and then—by faking a dash for the plate—forces the pitcher to balk him home. In the game that clinched the pennant for Brooklyn, Robinson doubles, steals third, and comes home on a wild throw to win the game. In both cases the lack of narration, so important in describing the significance of Robinson's experience elsewhere in the film, goes silent as if it is incapable of explaining what this style of play means.

While *The Jackie Robinson Story* shows briefly this distinctive black style, *Soul of the Game* makes it a more central concern. *Soul of the Game* focuses not just on Robinson but also on two other Negro League stars, Satchel Paige and Josh Gibson. All three players have a similar athletic aesthetic, which allows for feelings of freedom and the expression of stylized creativity at the same time that they compete. *Soul of the Game*'s attention to this style suggests that the limited opportunity organized baseball was willing to extend to African Americans had to do primarily with how most whites, and even Robinson himself at first, misunderstood this aesthetic. They saw it as indicative of the inability of blacks to work and achieve, to control their desire to "showboat," in order to focus on the task at hand. In contrast, *Soul of the Game* offers the view that the successful performance of players like Paige and Gibson was due to the composure and confidence they achieved through the balance they struck between competing and enjoying themselves as they played. Through its portrayal of black dancer Bill "Bojangles" Robinson (who owned the New York Black Yankees in the Negro National League) and its use of a jazz score by Terrence Blanchard, *Soul of the Game* connects this black baseball aesthetic with a larger African American cultural heritage of improvisation that responds to present conditions of performance as well as the needs of the finished work.

This aesthetic represented by Paige, Gibson, and Robinson functions in *Soul of the Game* to define not only racial difference but also the class relations between players and owners. While Robinson's use of a black style is made more efficient by his internalization of white obsession with structure, the showboating of black players like Paige is part of what the owners of white baseball regarded as "disorganized" about the Negro Leagues. What whites thought of as the disrespect that Gibson and Paige showed for the "product" (winning), through their fraternization and pauses in the action to engage in dozens humor, was a big part of the draw for Negro League games. Outstanding exhibitors of this showboating style, especially Paige, could therefore demand a greater financial return for their services. While the terms of remuneration for most African American players were not better than those for white players in the major leagues even under the reserve clause, the style of play in the Negro Leagues, with its emphasis on an immediate return in expressive pleasure, symbolically critiqued the alienation of blacks within the economic status quo.

As if to contain the alternative black discourse of Robinson's Negro League style of play, *The Jackie Robinson Story* ends quickly with a scene of Robinson testifying before HUAC in Washington. That he asks Rickey's advice about whether he should go, and that the Brooklyn executive strongly urges him to do so, marks this scene as another instance of white paternalistic guidance. Yet even in the testimony scene, the film can't entirely suppress different discursive positions. Robinson's statement before the committee refers to his awareness that American society offers opportunities such as he has had to only a few blacks, but he also puts forward the view that only by battling within the system can African Americans realize more of the potential rights of a democratic society. After Robinson states that "I am not fooled because I've had a chance open to very few Negro Americans," he adds, "but democracy works for those willing to fight for it." The white male voice-over then returns and disregards this criticism of the lack of opportunity for most blacks by asserting over a shot of the Statue of Liberty that America is "a country in which every child has the opportunity to become president or play baseball for the Brooklyn Dodgers."

Soul of the Game reassesses the integrationist strategy that predominates in *The Jackie Robinson Story* in the manner that Ed Guerrero says characterizes "the New Black Movie" of the 1990s.[32] While *Soul of the Game* also wants to cross over to a white audience, it examines the costs of integration by contrasting Robinson's breaking of the color line with the denial of opportunity to Paige and Gibson. By showing how they were initially passed over (Paige later played briefly in the major leagues), *Soul of the Game* highlights the selective opportunity that Robinson's experience (and integration as a whole) have represented.[33] This emphasis on limited opportunity articulates what Salim Muwakkil calls the contemporary "skeptical attitude . . . among African Americans across the ideological spectrum" toward integration, because of "its questionable benefits and its lack of mainstream [white] support."[34] *Soul of the Game* implies that while Rickey chose to commodify the African American sports culture that Robinson embodied, by denying opportunity to other black players he ignored (and confirmed) the critique of racial and economic inequality contained in that black style.

Soul of the Game portrays Robinson as the right player for white baseball precisely because he appears unaware of the social meaning of the way he plays. The film shows him when he arrives in the Negro Leagues as fiercely resentful of discrimination, but determined to adopt the values of the dominant white society in order to redress racial injustice. After a confrontation with Paige on the field because of his disdain for the pitcher's showboating ("You're not pitching, your putting on a bullshit show"), Robinson lectures the other players in the locker room about how he learned as an officer in the army "the discipline of managing your time, setting goals, taking the personal responsibility for seeing them through." Through his naive presumption that he is teaching the other players an important life lesson, *Soul of the Game* attempts to establish Robinson as an Uncle Tom who has yet to learn about the soul of the game his teammates play. In fact, it's doubtful that the real Robinson would have made such a positive statement about his experience in the army. Arnold Rampersad describes how most of Robinson's time in the service was spent waiting around and fighting its Jim Crow practices.[35] *Soul of the Game*'s representation of Robinson's flamboyant playing style therefore seems more accurate than its portrayal of his naivete. His carefully practiced skill in the Negro League style, along with the early experiences described by his biographers and in his autobiography, *I Never Had It Made*—which testify to his belief in self-reliance yet also describe the racism he faced—suggest that Robinson even at this age was probably aware of the complex relationship between personal responsibility and race.

For the time when it was made, *The Jackie Robinson Story* was a very liberal film. The film's screenwriter, Lawrence Taylor, found that no studio in Hollywood would back the project because of its black protagonist. Two major studios did express interest, however, if the story could be changed so as to focus on a white male character who teaches Robinson about baseball. Rampersad states that Taylor regarded such a change as "out of the question," but to a degree, that is what the picture wound up being.[36] On a practical level, such white patronage may have been necessary to get this film on the screen, just as Robinson's restraint the first three years he played for the Dodgers was necessary to avoid the interracial violence (at least between him and his aggressors) that would have been used to justify shutting down the great experiment. Like Robinson's breaking of the color line itself, *The Jackie Robinson Story* was a step forward in that it gave a black man an unprecedented opportunity to demonstrate his abilities in a major cultural venue, and it made evident the moral incongruity between American claims of equality and the racist resistance to such opportunity. Where the film's liberal thinking hinders its historical honesty is in its dogged insistence on showing racism as a problem best understood and responded to in individual terms. However, within the cold war climate in 1950 America, this emphasis on individualism was probably a necessary qualification of the complexity of social identity that Robinson's playing style and statement in the HUAC testimony scene bring to the film.

Writing in *The Nation* in 1995, Mark Harris credited Robinson's use of a black style of play that challenged the assumed supremacy of white baseball, and his strong political stands, as in part responsible for the substantial contractual gains seen by black ballplayers in the years since.[37] While what Harris says is true to a degree, it again replicates the individualist orientation of most cultural representations of sports and results in the same limited historical perspective. In fairness to Harris, his comments about Robinson are more thoughtful and well informed than many of the more conservative versions of a great-man-in-baseball-history viewpoint that appeared widely in the media in 1997, the fiftieth anniversary of Robinson's joining the Dodgers. Yet, from what I would regard as a more historicized perspective, Ken Shropshire has documented how African Americans have been denied management and ownership opportunities (both in baseball and throughout sports) that could open up the business to blacks on all levels.[38] Extending this analysis of race and sports to a global perspective, David Theo Goldberg makes a similar point when he states that "The mega salaries associated with the racialized bodies of sports hide from view the exploitative conditions marking racialized bodies elsewhere that precisely make such spectacular salaries possible."[39] The recent attention to Nike's exploitative labor practices abroad and advertising using college athletes has shown the contradictions in how the sports industry addresses but also contributes to racial inequality. The contrast between Harris's appraisal of the legacy of Jackie Robinson and that of Shropshire or Goldberg—or that I have described in *Soul of the Game*—demonstrates the difference that considerations of social identity make to the study of history.

Notes

1. Robert Rosenstone, *Visions of the Past* (Cambridge, Mass.: Harvard University Press, 1995), 3.

2. Ibid., 55.

3. *The Knute Rockne Story,* Warner Brothers, 1940.

4. Peter Brook, *The Melodramatic Imagination: Balzac, Henry James, Melodrama, and the Mode of Excess* (New Haven, Conn.: Yale University Press, 1976).

5. Laurie Schulze, "The Made-for-TV Movie: Industrial Practice, Cultural Form, Popular Reception," in *Television: The Critical View,* ed. Horace Newcomb (New York: Oxford University Press, 1982), 169.

6. George Custen, *Bio/Pics: How Hollywood Constructed Public History* (New Brunswick, N.J.: Rutgers University Press, 1992), 8.

7. Murray Sperber, *Shake Down the Thunder: The Creation of Notre Dame Football* (New York: Henry Holt, 1993), 464.

8. Eric Foner, "A Conversation between Eric Foner and John Sayles," in *Past Imperfect: History according to the Movies,* ed. Mark C. Carnes (New York: Henry Holt, 1995), 14.

9. Rosenstone, *Visions,* 57.

10. Robert Ray, *A Certain Tendency of the Hollywood Cinema, 1930–1980* (Princeton, N.J.: Princeton University Press, 1985), 31.

11. Ibid.

12. Rosenstone, *Visions,* 58.

13. Foner, "Conversation," 13; Rosenstone, *Visions,* 57.

14. Custen, *Bio/Pics,* 8. Custen defines a biographical film as "one that depicts the life of a historical person, past or present," 5.

15. David Bordwell and Kristin Thompson, *Film Art* (New York: McGraw-Hill, 1997), 108.

16. Quoted in S. W. Pope, "Introduction: American Sport History—Toward a New Paradigm," in *The New American Sport History: Recent Approaches and Perspectives,* ed. S. W. Pope (Urbana: University of Illinois Press, 1997), 6.

17. Richard Dyer, "Entertainment and Utopia," in *The Cultural Studies Reader,* ed. Simon During (London: Blackwell, 1993), 273.

18. Ibid.

19. Robert Stam, "Bakhtin, Polyphony, and Ethnic/Racial Representation," in *Unspeakable Images: Ethnicity and the American Cinema,* ed. Lester D. Friedman (Urbana: University of Illinois Press, 1991), 256.

20. Gail Bederman, "Remaking Manhood through Race and Civilization," *Manliness and Civilization: A Cultural History of Gender and Race in the United States, 1880–1917* (Chicago: University of Chicago Press, 1995).

21. Jeffrey T. Sammons, *Beyond the Ring: The Role of Boxing in American Society* (Urbana: University of Illinois Press, 1988); Michael T. Isenberg, *John Sullivan and His America* (Urbana: University of Illinois Press, 1988).

22. Custen, *Bio/Pics,* 26.

23. Cornel West, *Race Matters* (New York: Vintage, 1994), 22.

24. Ibid., 18.

25. Randy Roberts and James S. Olson, *Winning Is the Only Thing: Sports in America since 1945* (Baltimore, Md.: Johns Hopkins University Press, 1989), 27.

26. Benjamin G. Rader notes that "At the personal cost of persistent headaches, bouts of depression, and smoldering resentments, Robinson eased the way for his acceptance by publicly ignoring the racial slurs of the players on the other teams" (*Baseball: A History of America's Game* [Urbana: University of Illinois Press, 1992], 152).

27. Ibid.

28. Manning Marable, *Race, Reform, and Rebellion: The Second Reconstruction in Black America, 1945–1990* (Jackson: University of Mississippi Press, 1991), 31–32. Not only is Robinson's achievement best seen as part of a larger movement attempting to change the status of African Americans after World War II, his later disillusionment about race relations in the United States at the time of his death in 1972 parallels the trajectory of the civil rights movement from hopefulness and belief in integration in the latter half of the 1950s and early 1960s to despair about the willingness of white America to offer African Americans as a group the same rights and opportunities. In his 1972 autobiography, Robinson's pessimism echoes the disillusionment that fueled a move toward a more militant nationalistic strategy in the black community during the same period.

29. Rader, *Baseball,* 149.

30. Quotation, ibid. U.S. census figures as reported in Jerome Krase and Charles La-Cerra, *Ethnicity and Machine Politics* (Lanham, Md.: University Press of America, 1991), 248.

31. Rader, *Baseball,* 145–46. Keith Miller and Montye Fuse have written a very interesting essay about Robinson's use of this style, which they say was called "trickeration" in the Negro Leagues. "Jazzing the Basepaths: Jackie Robinson and Negro League Baseball," in *Contesting American Sports,* ed. John Bloom and Michael Willard (New York: New York University Press, 2002).

32. Ed Guerrero, *Framing Blackness: The African American Image in Film* (Philadelphia: Temple University Press, 1993).

33. Paige received his opportunity to play in the major leagues from Cleveland Indians owner Bill Veeck, who had much more progressive racial attitudes than the other men who ran white baseball.

34. Salim Muwakkil, "Letting Go of the Dream," *In These Times,* November 2, 1997, 13.

35. Arnold Rampersad, *Jackie Robinson* (New York: Knopf, 1977), 91, 96.

36. Ibid., 223.

37. Mark Harris, "Where Have You Gone, Jackie Robinson?" *The Nation,* May 15, 1995, 674–76.

38. Ken Shropshire, *In Black and White: Race and Sports in America* (New York: New York University Press, 1996).

39. David Theo Goldberg, "Call and Response: Sports, Talk Radio, and the Death of Democracy," in *Soundbite Culture: The Death of Discourse in a Wired World,* ed. David Slayden and Rita Kirk Whillock (Thousand Oaks, Calif.: Sage Publications, 1999), 39.

2 From Second String to Solo Star: Hollywood and the Black Athlete

With the exception of a few race films, African Americans appear only as minor characters (if at all) in feature-length movies about sports from the coming of sound through the beginning of the civil rights movement. A cycle of Hollywood films in the early 1950s that featured black athletes followed closely on the opening of previously all-white professional sports to African Americans just after World War II, but in stories of self-reliance and white paternalism that attempted to deemphasize social determinants of racial identity. Black participation in Hollywood movies has increased slowly and unevenly in the half-century since, and like their involvement in professional sports, it has been restricted to a limited range of performative and behind-the-scenes roles.

During the classic period, the majority of the infrequent appearances by black characters were in films about prizefighting, probably because it was the least exclusionary professional sport for reasons of race.[1] Like the representation of women in classic Hollywood films, the representation of blacks functioned in these narratives of white male self-definition through athletic competition as either supportive—but self-negating—helpers or occasionally (along with Mexican or Chicano characters) as opponents: obstacles that the protagonists overcome in order to realize their heroic identity.

Thomas Cripps explains that the restrictive roles for blacks resulted from the studio system's practice (monitored by the Production Code Administration) of circumventing controversy on issues of race. This evasion fit into Hollywood's tendency to avoid choice on matters of ideological debate so as to not risk offending its desired audience.[2] According to Cripps, the result was that "Hollywood's aversion to the racial contradictions in American life reduced African Americans to absent, alibied for, dependent victims of marketing strategies aimed at a profitable universality"; this conception of a mass audience was based on the assumption that the vast majority of viewers wanted reaffirmation of the racial status quo—or avoidance of racial difference entirely.[3] In the case of Hollywood sports films, such sidestepping of the contradiction between black disadvantage and the promise of American opportunity translated into narratives about the achievements of white male athletes, occasionally aided by, or at the expense of, African American characters. Until the message movies of the early 1950s, these sports films entirely avoided any portrayal of the denial of competitive opportunities to African Americans, even if the latter kind of story was as firmly grounded in historical events as those about the successes of white athletes.

Though generally utopian, at times classic Hollywood sports films emphasize race, but in order to distract attention from other issues of social identity. This occurs in two boxing films, *The Champ* (1931) and *Winner Take All* (1932), in which racial difference (here involving Latinos as well as blacks) is used to deemphasize the class antagonism of Depression America. As I analyze in more detail in chapter 4, both *The Champ* and *Winner Take All* include fights between their white protagonists and Mexican boxers that displace class difference into nationalist conflicts. While Mexican fighters function in these stories as the racial other, blacks fit into minor roles within the white protagonist's circle of supporters. In *The Champ,* Dink (Jackie Cooper), the son of the prizefighter protagonist, has a black companion (Jesse Scott) who helps keep the father sober and away from the gaming tables. In *Winner Take All* a black trainer named Rosebud (Clarence Muse) warns Jimmy (James Cagney) about relationships with other women who will lead him away from his boxing career and new family. Despite Jimmy's wanderings, after he realizes that his fast-lane friends have deceived him and decides to return to fighting and family, he finds Rosebud and partner Peggy still in his corner. Such multiracial support groups would become a convention of the sports film, turning up in *Body and Soul* (1947) and *The Harder They Fall* (1956), as well as *Rocky III* (1982), *Field of Dreams* (1989), and *White Men Can't Jump* (1992); most of the time these groups allow female and black characters to contribute to the success of the white protagonist without challenging traditional gender roles or the racial status quo.

While *The Champ* and *Winner Take All* employ racial difference to distract from class antagonism in American society, another 1930s boxing film, *Golden Boy* (1939), reverses that displacement and portrays class solidarity between black and white fighters resulting from their common experience of exploitation. After killing a black fighter in the ring, and then seeing the strength and unity of the dead boxer's family despite their loss, *Golden Boy*'s protagonist, Joe Bonaparte (William Holden), realizes that he has become as destructively ambitious and isolated as the gangster who manages him. Bonaparte therefore decides to give up prizefighting and return to the support and responsibility of his own family and neighborhood. While it represents the costs of American individualism, *Golden Boy* still follows classic Hollywood's practice of using African American characters for the purpose of defining its white protagonist.

The moral and material motivations for changing the portrayal of blacks in Hollywood movies came about as a result of World War II. A desire to "enunciate a strong position on democracy" in contrast to Fascism, and the inability to wage total war without the inclusion of black Americans, prompted concessions in a number of areas, including Hollywood. In 1942 studio heads promised Walter White, executive secretary of the NAACP, to "improve the quality and quantity of black roles."[4] One example of such improvement was the 1947 boxing film *Body and Soul*.

Like *Golden Boy*, *Body and Soul* uses the corruption and exploitation of professional boxing to indict capitalism. *Body and Soul* screenwriter Abraham Polonsky and star John Garfield both liked the Clifford Odets play adapted in *Golden Boy*.[5] In fact, Odets had written the Joe Bonaparte role for Garfield, but the director of the original Group Theater production, Harold Clurman, turned Garfield down as too inexperienced for the part.[6] Within its anticapitalist critique, *Body and Soul* also includes *Golden Boy*'s assumption of proletarian brotherhood between working-class ethnic and black boxers in the face of a corrupt fight business that cares little for the welfare of its performers.

Unlike the black boxer in *Golden Boy*, who has no lines, appears only briefly during a fight, and is clearly a device of white characterization, Ben Chaplin (Canada Lee) in *Body and Soul* is a major figure in the story. During the time in which the Garfield character, Charley Davis, fights his way up to a title shot, Ben is the middleweight champ. Although Ben has cut a deal with a promoter/gambler named Roberts to get his shot at the championship, the film never questions his ability as a boxer, and after he aggravates an injury during the fight in which Charley takes the title, we see that a relationship of mutual respect and concern develops between the two boxers. Michael Rogin argues that the victory of the white fighter over the African American in *Body and Soul* constructs a model of working-class ethnicity defined in part by ideas of white supremacy. Yet it's also true that Ben's courage moves him to the "moral and dramatic center" of the film as he teaches the Garfield character the importance of integrity in withstanding the exploitation of the fight game.[7] While Ben therefore contributes to the moral formation of the white lead, the size and importance of Lee's role in *Body and Soul* was a step forward for black representation in Hollywood. "Obviously it was Garfield's movie," states Cripps, "but . . . Canada Lee as Ben . . . provided the ethical bridge between the complaisant Charley and the resolute Charley."[8] Writing in the *New York Times,* Bosley Crowther pointed out the importance of the Ben character in *Body and Soul,* noting: "It is Canada Lee who brings to focus the horrible pathos of the cruelly exploited prize fighter."[9]

The anti-Communist pressure that would soon create problems for left-wingers like Polonsky and Garfield also strongly influenced the first Hollywood sports films with black leads. *The Jackie Robinson Story* (1950), *The Harlem Globetrotters* (1951), and *The Joe Louis Story* (1953) are films that take the position that hard work and self-reliance, guided by paternalistic whites, was the way for young black athletes to gain access to the highest level of professional sports. Like other message films in the decade after World War II, these three films employ location settings, some nonprofessional actors, and generally modest production values in a manner indebted to Italian neorealism. Such a restrained representational style fit the assumptions about integrationist strategies that made these films acceptable in the conservative political climate of that time. Nevertheless, as we saw in the analysis of *The Jackie Robinson Story* in chapter 1, this realism also allowed them to represent less monochromatic views about race.

The Joe Louis Story covers the events of the title character's career up through his last fight, a loss to Rocky Marciano in 1951. Like the 1938 race film *Spirit of Youth, The Joe Louis Story* maintains the carefully controlled public image that had been constructed for Louis to avoid memories of the controversial previous African American heavyweight titleholder, Jack Johnson, and therefore overcome white resistance to a black champion. In both films the Louis character is soft-spoken, polite, modest, and obedient to authority, whether it be his mother, his handlers, or the white sportswriters and boxing promoters with whom he must interact once he becomes champ. Both films show a scene in which Louis asks his mother for her permission before becoming a prizefighter, and both regard Louis's first big loss (to German heavyweight Max Schmeling in 1936) as a youthful mistake that only reinforces his work ethic and desire to succeed.

When *The Joe Louis Story* opened in November 1953, the African American newspaper the *Chicago Defender* reported that "before a line of the script was written, Joe was closeted for over a month with producer [Sterling] Silliphant and script-writer [Robert] Sylvester," and that Louis had "plenty to do with making the film" in his capacity as "chief technical advisor."[10] Yet, consistent with the modest, unassuming image Louis had maintained his entire career to appeal to a white audience, the film itself bears no marks of his control. A white sportswriter character narrates in flashback much of the film's representation of Louis's life, and the credits list Mannie Seamon, the ex-champion's white trainer, as the film's technical adviser.

The Harlem Globetrotters also depicts the need for an African American protagonist to advance his interests, and those of his race, as they are defined by whites. Nelson George points out that from the time of the team's origins in the 1920s the African American artistry of the Globetrotters' style of basketball laid the groundwork for the spectacular athletic aesthetic that dominates the NBA today. George also notes, however, that the management of Globetrotters' owner, Abe Saperstein, offers "a definitive example of white paternalism and Black male submission."[11] Saperstein was of course himself a member of an oppressed ethnic minority, and his involvement with the Globetrotters was not unlike that of the moguls in Hollywood, where, as Neal Gabler has remarked, "There were none of the impediments imposed by loftier professions and more firmly entrenched businesses to keep Jews . . . out."[12] The lack of interest that WASP businessmen showed in African American sports in particular opened up possibilities for Saperstein and basketball and baseball promoter Eddie Gottlieb, who could get better bookings and financial deals than were available to black management.

The Harlem Globetrotters tells the story of a former All-American player named Billy Townsend, who after joining the Trotters makes clear that he is more concerned with his own stardom than the success of the team. Although he helps the Trotters win the opening matchup of an important three-game series against the New York Celtics, before the second contest Townsend sneaks out of the hotel to get married and aggravates an old knee injury when he runs into a garbage can on the sidewalk. Gamblers see Townsend hurt himself and pass the information on to the Celtics, who exploit his reduced mobility by pressuring him whenever he gets the ball. When Saperstein finds out about the injury after the game, he releases the young star, telling him that he does not understand how to be a team player, nor does he appreciate the importance of the Trotters winning to the pride of his race. His own pride hurt by his release, Townsend signs a lucrative contract with another team, contingent upon his resting the injured knee until the following season. In the interim, Townsend (an honor student in college as well as an All-American) takes a job teaching chemistry at a small African American college. There he sees the racial pride that the students and faculty take in the Trotters, and he begins to feel guilty about losing the opportunity to set a successful example for other young blacks. Just before the decisive third game with the Celtics, Townsend gives up his lucrative contract and returns to help the Trotters win.

The Harlem Globetrotters represents Abe Saperstein as concerned above all with the welfare of his players and with the symbolic importance of the team as a source of pride and inspiration for African Americans. The year before the film was released, however, according to George, the real Saperstein's handling of a Trotters player named Nat "Sweetwater" Clifton demonstrated a more self-serving management style. Joining the team in 1947, Clifton, like Billy Townsend, was a stylish and talented former college star who made a strong addition to the Trotters' lineup alongside Goose Tatum and Marques Haynes. During a barnstorming tour in the summer of 1950, Clifton confronted Saperstein after he discovered that the white players who made up their opposition during the series were getting paid more money. Knowing that the New York Knicks were interested in adding an African American player to their roster, Saperstein soon afterward sold Clifton's contract to the NBA club.[13]

Clifton's experience with Saperstein demonstrated that the Trotters' owner, unlike his character in the 1951 film, was not always most concerned about the welfare of the Trotters or their importance as a symbol of racial pride. In fact, in the case of Nat Clifton, the real Saperstein seemed willing to sacrifice some of the team's ability to win when it came into conflict with his desire to keep labor costs down. The deferred gratification and gradualism that the Saperstein character in the film asks the young star to accept therefore appears a strategy less calculated for black advancement than for maximizing owner profit.

The use of real locations and nonprofessional actors, which forms part of the neorealist formal style of these three films, was not new to movies about sports. Actual stadiums and athletes playing themselves had long been a rhetorical strategy of such films, a way of presenting their viewpoint as grounded in real people and places. Yet this realist style also allowed these films about black athletes to align with the message movies that had come out of Hollywood in the late 1940s such as *Gentleman's Agreement* (1947), *Pinky* (1949), and *Home of the Brave* (1949). Through this formal likeness with other socially engaged movies, the self-reliant ethos in these three sports films gains validity by offering a similar, apparently well-intentioned, response to social problems—here the conflict between racism and the democratic values of opportunity for all—seen within a "realistic" view of the world.

Writing about *The Jackie Robinson Story* in the *Chicago Defender*, A. S. "Doc" Young called it "not a fantastically lavish production . . . just a straight forward, uncolored story about Jackie's trials, tribulations and successes."[14] The stylistic modesty that Young refers to here and that characterizes also *The Harlem Globetrotters* and *The Joe Louis Story*—the lack of color film and the absence of lavish sets or sweeping camera work, the general avoidance of visual spectacle like that found in an opulent musical like *Singin' in the Rain*

(1952)—this formal reserve underlined an integration strategy of gradualism and self-denial as the most effective one for black advancement.

Yet, at the same time, the realist aesthetic in *The Jackie Robinson Story* and *The Harlem Globetrotters* also documents examples of a black cultural style at odds with such promises of future return for present sacrifice. In the latter film real game footage shows the basketball skills that made the Trotters famous, especially center Goose Tatum's accurate low-post shooting and guard Marques Haynes's ball handling. Haynes's speed, dribbling, and passing skills influenced Los Angeles Lakers' star Earvin "Magic" Johnson, who has cited the Globetrotter guard as the inspiration for his "Showtime" style of improvisational play.[15] With its emphasis on combining the pleasure of creative flair with competitive efficacy, this improvisational style qualifies the deferred gratification prescribed for African Americans in a white-controlled economy.

Hoop Dreams in Black and White: Race and Basketball Movies

> I can play basketball, that's the bottom line. I can play East Coast, West Coast, Space Jam on Mars. I can play it.
> —Brent Barry

> Who knows but that, on the lower frequencies, I speak for you?
> —Ralph Ellison

Since the early 1980s the NBA has become an important part of an increasingly spectacular, globalized, and racialized American popular culture. Broadcast revenues for the league rose 1,000 percent between 1986 and 1998 (the NFL and Major League Baseball saw much smaller percentage increases during that time), as the NBA's bursts of action highlighted by dunks and three-point shots fit smoothly into the fast-paced flow of spectacle that has come to dominate television and increasingly the movies. During this period, Michael Jordan replaced Muhammad Ali as the best-known American athlete worldwide. A big part of the NBA's greater appeal both here and abroad came from its spectacle of black style headlined for most of this period by Jordan; because over 80 percent of the NBA players are African American, the league exemplifies "the status of 'difference' as *the* commodity in postmodernity."[16]

In the remainder of this chapter, I will analyze how feature film representations of a black style of basketball modeled on the NBA offer an alternative narrative about the experiences of African Americans in this country and also how these representations reinforce the racial status quo. In the latter sense such films reaffirm the values of whiteness that still dominate American culture despite the commodification of blackness and present what Stuart Hall calls "a difference that doesn't make a difference of any kind."[17] While African Americans have clearly been the primary victims of the justification of racial discrimination that I'll analyze, this biased thinking can affect whites as well, and so it is in the interest of whites to recognize how it functions in media texts like these films. The overemphasis on individual exceptionalism in the representation of African American star athletes contributes to what bell hooks calls a "spirit of defeat and hopelessness" among poor and working-class blacks so that they "have no belief that they can attain wealth and power on any playing field other than [as elite athletes in professional] sports."[18] Yet absorption with such black athletic excellence can also lead to belief in the inherent physical limitations of whites. Another point I will make in analyzing these films is how they at different points both ignore and respond to economic inequality that crosses racial lines.

Although I will attempt to link them to a larger intertexual media framework that is contemporary American popular culture, my analysis here focuses mainly on several movies about basketball made during the period of the NBA's ascendancy. Because they incorporate the new difference, yet are still strongly bound by formal and thematic conventions that have been used for decades to privilege the values of whiteness, Hollywood films provide a good locus for analyzing competing discourses of racial difference. Many of these films are not specifically about the NBA; they instead feature "amateur" players or the playground game. Yet even if they are not explicitly about the NBA, these movies often have it in their utopian imaginations as the promised land, or they make reference to the constructions of blackness featured there. They therefore share with other media representations of the NBA a dialogue about racial identity.

In his description of an ad offering a Michael Jordan video in return for subscribing to *Sports Illustrated,* John Edgar Wideman refers to the NBA's interest in a white audience:

> In this ad, which saturates the prime time on the national sports network [ESPN], a gallery of young people, male and female, express their wonder, admiration, awe and identification with Michael Jordan's supernatural basketball prowess. He can truly fly. The chorus is all white, good looking, clean cut, casually but hiply dressed. An audience of consumers the ad both targets and embodies. A very calculated kind of wish fulfillment at work. A premeditated attempt to bond MJ with these middle-class white kids with highly disposable incomes.[19]

This ad exemplifies how, with Jordan leading the way, what sold the NBA to white consumers during the 1980s and 1990s was what Nelson George calls a "Black [athletic] aesthetic."[20] This aesthetic features constructions of black masculinity that correspond roughly to traditional positions about identity in the African American community. On the one hand there is Jordan's creative improvisation, grounded in black cultural tradition, yet also distinctive in the degree of its crossover appeal and its use as proof that (some) blacks have access to the American dream. Almost as widely commodified, but with a less sanguine view of race in America, has been its flip side, the hypermasculine menace and intimidation represented in professional basketball by Charles Barkley and others, their "gangsta" personae overlapping to some degree with what certain rap performers have offered for most of the same period. Much of the time these different versions of blackness are presented to a white audience in a solipsistic, apolitical manner at least as old as the rock and roll craze of the 1950s. Writing in the *New York Times* in 1993, Peter DeJonge describes this white interest in a packaged, unchallenging version of black identity: "In the last decade, the N.B.A., long considered too black to attract a mainstream audience, has prospered by giving middle-class whites, desperate for some semblance of a connection to black America, a series of unthreatening yet bigger than life cartoon superheroes called Magic, Michael, Charles and Shaquille."[21]

While these two versions of athletic blackness might appear natural and obvious—one a recipe for maximizing creativity and style, the other an exam-

Gangsta menace in *Space Jam* (1996).

ple of the tough self-assertion necessary in a competitive world—they also have meanings that make them political. The pleasure of creative improvisation claims an immediate compensation that many African Americans have worked for but not received. The gangsta persona can be about frustration over racial disadvantage as well as hard masculinity. Moreover, some media representations of the gangsta life become political as they encourage whoever consumes them to adopt what Cornel West calls a "market morality [that] stigmatizes others as objects for personal pleasure or bodily stimulation."[22] Functioning this way, the gangsta identity—like the Globetrotters' clowning misconstrued to reinforce the notion that black men are physical but simple— reaffirms the racial status quo rather than contests it.

The civil rights movement awakened in some whites an interest in identity grounded in greater cultural specificity (often ethnicity), rather than a racial subjectivity based primarily on their assumption of superiority over nonwhites. Werner Sollors says that this has reached the point at which "casting oneself as an outsider may in fact be a dominant cultural trait. . . . Every American is now considered a potential ethnic."[23] But since assimilation has made the connection to ethnic heritage difficult for many, especially younger European Americans, blackness in popular culture offers a ready substitute; its respect for the body presents a welcome alternative to the deferred gratification of middle-class life.

A nostalgic basketball film like *Hoosiers* (1986) shows a time before black culture became a common response to white anxiety over identity. Instead it celebrates small-town Indiana basketball and the values of homogeneity and community cohesion. An all-black team from the city becomes the threatening Other that must be defeated in the climactic contest in order to reaffirm the traditional white values that matter in this film. Conversely, more contemporary stories such as *Grand Canyon* (1991) and *White Men Can't Jump* demonstrate the widespread white interest in black culture. Both films contain scenes in which African American men use basketball to help white men figure out who they are.

In addition to these movies that overtly link basketball to race, other recent films about the sport try to erase any emphasis on social identity with stories that endorse utopian belief in color blindness, equal opportunity, and the viability of simplistic moral judgments about individual responsibility as the solution to all problems. Basketball films of the last two decades therefore demonstrate a dialogism, not only between the denial of racial difference in stories of self-reliant gradualism and the emphasis on difference implicit in improvisational pleasure, but also with the more direct critique of American society presented by the gangsta identity.

Michael Jordan figures in several of these films, starring in *Space Jam* (1996), appearing in *He Got Game* (1998), and invoked by *White Men Can't Jump, Hoop Dreams* (1994), and *The Air Up There* (1994). His importance to these stories doesn't just come from being widely regarded as the best basketball player ever; Jordan also has a social significance that goes beyond the basketball court. Writing in the *New Yorker* in 1998, Henry Louis Gates Jr. describes him as representing one of the two "forces that contend for the soul of contemporary America." For Gates, Jordan is not only the best on the court, but also the "greatest corporate pitchman of all time" and therefore the supreme representative of the trend toward "'winner-take-all' markets, visible in every economic and cultural realm but epitomized by the star system of the NBA." Gates describes the rival trend as "the fragmentation of culture into ever narrower niches, from the proliferation of cable channels to the supposed balkanization of the canon"—such that, within the context of basketball and juxtaposed with Jordan, this description could refer to the outsider alienation of his NBA alter ego, the gangsta player.[24]

Gates therefore starts off his essay by placing Jordan very high up the ladder of fame, fortune, and social significance. He subsequently goes back to chronicle Jordan's "modest origins," the "working class childhood in Wilmington, North Carolina (father a foreman at a General Electric Plant; mother in customer relations for the United Carolina Bank)," and down-to-earth, accessible demeanor, "the manner—direct and artless—is familiar," so as to cast Jordan's success as proof that the American dream still exists. To ignore his down-to-earth and generous manner would leave Jordan as Mr. Winner-Take-All, vulnerable to association with the greed that coincided with the period of his stardom and led to the great wealth disparity in the United States.[25] Star athletes are frequently attacked in the media for their large salaries and egos as a way of displacing that glaring issue. However, Gates isn't naive about this success; he doesn't claim that it is available to all or even most African Americans or that Jordan himself hasn't suffered from a certain degree of alienation. Nonetheless, Gates offers Jordan's combination of ordinariness with the extraordinary fame and wealth he has achieved as an endorsement for the All-American claim that there is the possibility for anyone to succeed. NBA Commissioner David Stern sings the same tune of social mobility, describing Jordan as "the kind of person you'd like to have as a friend, and who just happens to be the most fiercely competitive athlete of his time,"[26] and Gates, remembering that in a global marketplace the promise of opportunity is also for overseas consumption, calls Jordan "an international symbol of America."[27]

In an attempt to remove race from the story in which Jordan stars, his agent, David Falk, states that "people don't look at Michael as being black."

"They accept that he's different because he's a celebrity," he explains.[28] Falk here wants to convey a naive belief in color blindness that tries to wish away racism in America. Stating that "people" (whites) don't regard Jordan as black fits the utopian assumptions of much of Jordan's media representation, suggesting that he proves race is no longer an insurmountable barrier in American society. I would doubt that whites ever forget Jordan is black. In fact, they may choose to regard his race as what makes the story all that much more uplifting and inspirational; his celebrity proves for them how personal initiative and achievement can overcome even the obstacle of racial discrimination.

Falk played a major role in developing the film *Space Jam* as a star vehicle for Jordan, and its representation of his rise to success coincides with the race-blind utopia the agent describes. The film opens with a scene of Jordan as a boy, shooting baskets late at night outside his family's North Carolina home. His strong, patient father comes out to get him to go back to bed, and when the younger Jordan asks "You think if I get good enough I can go to college?" he reassures the boy, "If you get good enough, you can do anything you want to." The opening-credits montage that follows shows Jordan's career up through 1996 as if to reinforce that statement. We see Jordan's unimpeded rise to success from boyhood, through high school and college basketball to the championships with the Chicago Bulls. This climb seems fueled by the hard work and determination evidenced in the late-night practice session; Jordan's elevation in his spectacular moves to the basket appears in the credits as a metaphor for his rise to success and therefore implies that such achievement can occur simply through acts of physical effort.

Another part of placing Jordan in the raceless utopia wished for by a white audience involves making him familiar to us. Repeated references to him as simply "Michael" (shortened further in the "Be like Mike" Gatorade ad) suggests that we somehow know Jordan. This familiarity plays on the assumption regarding race in the media that Benjamin DeMott describes as the friendship imperative. In DeMott's view, interracial friendships are widely represented in American popular culture as effortless and common, offering personal relations as a way of overcoming racism without the need for social movements or government action.[29] Calling Jordan by just his first name suggests that even as we consume him in a mediated, commodified form we somehow achieve that friendship and contribute to the social harmony it creates.

White Men Can't Jump, The Air Up There, and *Above the Rim* (1994) also emphasize interracial friendship as important to the success of individuals of both races, while at the same time using it to reaffirm conventions of black representation. As I mentioned earlier, *White Men* portrays basketball as a venue in which a black character (Sidney Deane) helps a white character (Billy Hoyle) find himself. Hoyle arrives in Los Angeles with his girlfriend Gloria on the run from gamblers to whom they owe money. He then uses his unassuming appearance (specifically his lack of height and his geeky style) to hustle Sidney Deane in a game at Venice Beach. Sidney in turn decides to put the "the white boy can't play" assumption to work for both of them, and together they hustle black opponents on playgrounds around South Central.

While his trash talk and temper in early scenes seem to portray the angry "don't give a fuck" attitude of a gangsta-style player, Sidney turns out to be more representative of Jordan's improvisational creativity and confidence than Barkley's belligerence. Michael Eric Dyson has described Jordan's playing style as using three skills that have long had special importance in African American culture. The first is improvisation, the ability to spontaneously develop an effective response to a situation, which Dyson says is learned through the "the honing of skill by the application of discipline, time, talent and energy." The second skill Dyson calls the stylization of the performed self: the ability to mark what one does with an individual flair. Earlier in his career Jordan defined his distinctive style through what Dyson calls his "repertoire of dazzling dunk shots." His game later became less athletic but was still punctuated by moves to the basket that no one else could do. The third practice that marked Jordan's game was his use of "edifying deception," achieved by convincing himself, and everyone else, that he was the best. As Dyson points out, the main way that Jordan initially achieved this deception was by creating the myth that he could outjump anyone, that he could literally hang in midair—hence his nickname, "Air Jordan."[30] With a less high-altitude game, but the accomplishment of several NBA titles, Jordan's psychological advantage became his reputation of being able to outplay any opponent at a crucial moment.

The Sidney Deane character in *White Men* plays a Jordan-inspired brand of ball in his playground games, supremely confident as he improvises in drives to the basket to elude taller opponents and creates distinctly stylized moves. To accommodate his white partner, Sidney's con game with Billy employs deception predicated on gaining an advantage over opponents not through convincing them the pair is unbeatable, but rather that they aren't competitive. The underestimation of Jordan's disproportionately white "supporting cast" with the Chicago Bulls functioned in a similar manner.

In contrast to Sidney, Billy starts off the film playing a textbook game. Todd Boyd has described this kind of white basketball as one "in which adherence to a specific set of rules determines one's ability to play successfully and 'correctly.'"[31] Just as basketball functions as a metaphor for racial identities, the textbook style suggests a white ideology that accepts the rules of the game, broadly defined. On the court, playing by the book means that Billy avoids the traits that mark the style that Sidney employs. Billy's game is not improvisational but rather about mastering conventional moves and executing them. He therefore stresses controlling the ball, getting position, and hitting the high-percentage shot. At times, Billy's passes show some flash, but they merely hint at his potential for improvisation before he reverts to the textbook game.

Although Billy and Sidney win and make money working their hustle, their difference in style and in ideas of racial identity causes friction between them. A conversation in Billy's car articulates this cultural barrier. When Billy plays Jimi Hendrix on the tape deck, Sidney tells him that he may "listen" but that he doesn't "hear" the music. Sidney's point here is that Billy doesn't appreciate the improvisation in how Hendrix played the guitar. In Sidney's view, which is based on what Stuart Hall calls "the metaphorical use of musical vocabulary" that characterizes black popular culture, Billy may listen to Hendrix, yet his lack of interest in an improvisatory game on the basketball court implies that he doesn't appreciate this style's broader cultural significance.[32]

Billy responds by voicing to Sidney his belief in the superiority of his textbook, do-only-what-you-need-to to win, view of the game. He tells Sidney, "You're just like every other brother I've ever seen on the playground. You'd rather look good and lose than look bad and win." Billy's comment represents a view commonly expressed in media discourse about the supposed ineffectiveness of a black, "playground" style of basketball. *White Men Can't Jump* proves this critique wrong, however, by repeatedly showing that Billy, with his textbook style, is incapable of adapting to new challenges as they arise.

For most of the film Billy makes bad decisions in reaction to situations that he encounters, whereas Sidney improvises viable responses to his own and also to Billy's problems. When Gloria leaves Billy because he loses all their money, Sidney figures out a way to repair the couple's relationship by getting her a chance to fulfill her dream of appearing on the game show *Jeopardy*. Through such effective responses, the film suggests that Sidney's confidence and improvisation can be as useful off as on the basketball court.

Even though *White Men Can't Jump* makes clear that Billy—like Sidney—has also been forced to learn about hustling because he comes from a working-class background, the white character's style of play on the court conveys that he has yet to critique the bourgeois assumptions of a textbook game. The textbook approach is one that believes in the rules and defers individual pleasure (such as that found in improvisation and stylization) in order to win. It isn't until a climactic, big-money game against a legendary playground team that Billy begins to employ the black aesthetic that Sidney has modeled for him. Billy realizes that the competition in this instance is so formidable that he has to adopt an improvisatory style to create something new. Taking an alley-oop pass from Sidney, he defies the statement of the title, gets up, and dunks the ball.

While *White Men Can't Jump* reverses the racist stereotype voiced by Billy and represents Sidney's style of playing basketball as part of an effective identity, the film also conforms to Hollywood's pattern of using black characters to define white masculinity. By setting up the kind of easy friendship DeMott describes, *White Men Can't Jump* implies that through respect for and loyalty to an African American, a white character can overcome racism. In addition to subordinating him to the role of defining Billy, the film decontextualizes Sidney's strategies by defining black achievement "in terms of individualism and exceptionalism."[33] While *White Men* shows numerous black characters playing an improvisational, stylized brand of basketball, and there is an a capella vocal trio that recalls the grounding of improvisation in music, no other African American character is as capable as Sidney. Conversely, in the scene in which their con is first shown, Sidney's virtuoso performance as hustler and player contrasts with the violent behavior of a defeated black opponent who angrily goes to get his gun. The latter character fits within the limited range of identities that American cinema has traditionally offered to blacks, in this case their common portrayal "either as victims or soulless predators who, because of fatal moral and character flaws, cannot possibility transcend the limits of their condition."[34] Such black "loser" characters appear in many films like this one as foils against which protagonists (both black and white) define their exceptional abilities; yet rarely do these films offer any explanation for criminality or disadvantage. By default, we are asked to assume that individual shortcoming is the reason.

These formulaic characterizations of African Americans operate also in *Above the Rim*. The movie's main character, Kyle (Duane Martin), is an exceptional high school point guard who hopes to win a scholarship to play at Georgetown University. Though less prominent than Billy in *White Men,* a white character, Kyle's high school coach Rollins (David Bailey), is again crucial to the success of the black protagonists in *Above the Rim.* Not only has the coach patiently endured Kyle showcasing his skills and not involving the rest of the team, he also brings in an ex-star player, Shep (Leon), to help keep the young player from making the wrong choices. As the film portrays Kyle's situation, he must choose between realizing his potential for success and adopting the gangsta life of Birdie (Tupac Shakur), a local drug dealer. Once again, this narrative conflict plays upon the exceptional/pathological, Michael Jordan/gangsta character duality that dominates media representation of black basketball in particular and African Americans in general. What *Above the Rim* adds to this Manichean dualism of black identity is a third equally well-worn character, the outsider hero, Shep, Birdie's estranged brother who returns to the neighborhood to overcome his tragic past and help Kyle follow the path of self-reliance to success.

Although it doesn't hide the fact that he deals drugs, the film initially presents Birdie as charismatic and—because of his new clothes, his expensive vehicles, his night club, and the attractive women around him—"successful" in the material terms that Kyle dreams about achieving through an NBA career. Birdie skillfully cultivates Kyle to play on his team in a neighborhood tournament, motivated by how the success of an aggressive gangsta style on the court will validate his "business" activities. While Kyle at first seems unaware of how to conduct himself in order to land the scholarship offer from Georgetown that he covets, Birdie is strategic and in charge. As part of his sales pitch, Birdie introduces Kyle in his club to an agent eager to represent him and to an attractive young woman. When Kyle and the young woman kiss and embrace too passionately, however, Birdie intervenes: "Alright, Alright," he tells them, "I'm gonna get my club closed down." Later, when Kyle quits the team after he sees how ruthless and violent Birdie can be, the gangsta springs a carefully laid trap, telling the young star that he will reveal his acceptance of gifts and ruin his amateur eligibility if he doesn't let Birdie's team win.

Because the first half of the film emphasizes the similarities between the gangsta's highly rationalized criminal activity and the "legitimate" business world, in its second half *Above the Rim* emphasizes Birdie's sadistic side to distinguish his actions from the ladder to success that it has Kyle climb. When Birdie betrays Kyle, however, we should remember that there are plenty of "legitimate" but no less manipulative agents, like the one shown earlier in the nightclub who "represent" young stars. To arrive at its utopian message, the film must discredit this similarity, along with Birdie's politicized critique of the dead end of "an honest day's work," summed up by his taunting of Shep about his job as a security guard at the high school. Birdie therefore becomes a sadistic killer, the scar on his cheek linking him to earlier movie gangsters as he slices up a homeless man who disrespected him. However inconsistent such vindictive violence is with Birdie's previous careful, highly rational behavior, it allows the film to discredit the gangsta's cynicism about the efficacy of an honest job and the possibility of success for working-class blacks in American society.

Conversely, the Shep character is an important part of the film's inspirational message. While Kyle had selfishly showboated and been willing to throw the tournament after Birdie's threat, Shep takes the court for the coach's team in the championship game and models for the younger player the hard yet "clean" game that will get Kyle a Georgetown scholarship. Shep's game is clean because it supports the rules of the existing social structure: Like the image of Michael Jordan celebrated by the media, he reinforces the idea that individual excellence can carry the interests of the group, he is respectful of white authority as represented by Coach Rollins, and he uses the physical force that Birdie's team gangstarizes, but only on behalf of masculine self-assertion, rejecting the angry statement such aggression makes about racist disadvantage.

Above the Rim celebrates Shep and Kyle as exceptional, "better" than the other young black men in the film because these two individuals follow the rules of determined self-interest and respect for authority necessary to gain access to the few opportunities available. Kyle gets his scholarship at Georgetown once he tones down the self-gratification of his game and stops resisting the control of his coach. Shep as well benefits from his seemingly altruistic behavior; the film ends with the suggestion that he will accept the coach's offer to succeed him at the high school, a valued position in a community where basketball is highly regarded and the drug trade flourishes from a shortage of good jobs.

Whether in rap music and cinema or in representations of black basketball culture, the toughness and self-sufficiency of the gangsta character are more appealing for a crossover audience than its statement about the nihilism created by racism. *Above the Rim* therefore emphasizes these traditional masculine characteristics in Kyle and Shep, meanwhile rejecting the racial critique implicit in Birdie's drug business and denial of the rules of the game in how his team plays. As with the murder of the homeless man, the film shows the gangsta life leading to irrational violence when, after Birdie's team loses, he sends his enforcer Monroe to shoot Kyle. Birdie's angry and eloquent justification of his criminal life to Shep earlier in the film gets lost once the shooting starts. The film focuses our attention instead on the destructiveness of violence, but no attention is paid to the roots of this behavior in social disadvantage. For *Above the Rim* to acknowledge such a contributing factor to the violence would compromise the utopian logic it puts forward as the solution to what is lacking in the lives of these young black characters. Movies like *Above the Rim* and most other media representations of basketball generally avoid careful engagement with the moral and social complexities that confront working-class African American men. They prefer instead more simplified constructions of masculinity that affirm the dominant values of competitive toughness and self-sufficiency channeled within a utopian optimism and not as part of a racialized social critique.

Space Jam also depoliticizes the gangsta response to disadvantage, casting it as both comical and driven by the desire to enslave and exploit others in contrast to the self-reliant and generous success represented by Michael Jordan. The story in the film involves five diminutive aliens, abused and intimidated by their tyrannical boss, who arrive on earth to enslave the Warner Brothers cartoon characters and take them back to perform at an outer space amusement park. The cartoon characters offer to play a basketball game for their freedom, but when the aliens show up with gangsta identities stolen from NBA players, the Looney Tooners do some kidnaping of their own, abducting Michael Jordan to help them win. Although Sean Bradley, one of the NBA players robbed of his "talent," is white, his presence seems an obvious attempt by the film to distract from the racialized character assumed by the alien "Monstars." The Monstars take the floor to the sounds of "Hit 'Em High," performed by rappers Busta Rhymes, Coolio, LL Cool J, and others, and dominate the first half, led by the aliens, who have adopted the identities of Charles Barkley and Larry Johnson, two NBA players strongly associated with the working-class cynicism and aggressive physicality of the gangsta identity. The subsequent victory by Jordan and the Toons in the big game reiterates a utopian view of basketball and criminalizes and ignores the racial critique of the gangsta style.

Jordan and the Critique of Style

> What drove me back . . . was I truly loved the game. I missed the enjoyment that it gave to me.
>
> —Michael Jordan about his return to the NBA

In his *New Yorker* feature, Henry Louis Gates anoints Jordan as the ultimate representative of corporate success, yet he also reports instances of what can only be called the superstar's alienation, his disaffection with the economic system within which he has been such a hot commodity. For instance, Gates tells us that for eight years, as he led Chicago to NBA titles and his popularity grew to its unprecedented level, Jordan was undercompensated by the Bulls, stuck in a contract that paid him a salary below what other, lesser players were making in the NBA marketplace. Adding insult to injury, Bulls owner Jerry Reinsdorf refused to acknowledge this past unfairness, grumbling that he was sure he would regret the $30 million contract he signed with Jordan for the 1997–98 season. Gates quotes Jordan's response to Reinsdorf: "All these years where you knew I was underpaid and you been making money and your organization's moved from a fifteen-million-dollar business when you bought it to a two-hundred-million-dollar business—all those years have gone down the drain because you have for once paid me my value. And you regretted that! That hit me so deep inside—the sense of greed, of disrespect for me."[35]

Because Jordan has earned so much money, and has achieved such praise for his achievements, to regard him as alienated initially seems absurd in comparison to millions of working people who have so much less. Yet, if even Michael Jordan has experienced denial of fair return for services rendered, that is evidence of just how typical such inequity is in an economic system that presents him as a testimonial figure. Within this context, his expressive, improvisational style on the court becomes not just an example of competitive, entrepreneurial achievement—creativity as the word is used in corporate marketspeak for IBM computers ("Solutions for a Small Planet")—but as a critique of alienation within a capitalist economy. His style that emphasizes pleasurable creativity while competing asserts the importance of finding for himself a return of expressive gratification without regard for whether the owners of the various venues in which he has performed (the Bulls, television, advertising, the movies) will compensate him fairly for the profits he generates for them. Clearly from his comments about Reinsdorf and the importance of his pleasure from playing, Jordan understands this return he must create for himself.

In Gates's essay, Jordan commented that he doesn't know why his popularity continued to grow and didn't drop off more quickly, as it does for so many stars who enjoy only a brief time at the center stage of media attention.[36] One explanation may be that he symbolizes a utopian promise about the continued viability of the American dream and about greater African American access to it. On the other hand, however, Jordan's appeal may be grounded in the satisfaction he derives from work, which appeals to millions of people who do not find their jobs as meaningful. This dissatisfaction comes from an increasing lack of employment security and from inadequate salary increases and benefits, but also as a result of the growing shortage of time workers have for their personal and family lives. Writing in 1991, Juliet Schor reported that Americans were working more than in 1970, contributing to more stress on their families, marriages, and health.[37] Jordan's apparent ability to deal with the tremendous pressures of his career, and even to make that work experience expressive and enjoyable, has been an important element of his appeal.

It is important to point out, however, that even if, despite his skill for expressive pleasure, an unfair return may alienate him from his work, Jordan's situation is still in a sense utopian. That he has made the move from player to owner only emphasizes how atypical Jordan's experience has been. As attractive as his creativity and style may be, not everyone has a job that allows for such pleasures. In *Hoop Dreams,* we see Arthur Agee and his friend Shannon listening to music and dancing while working at Pizza Hut, but that scene seems an overly favorable view of the otherwise monotonous jobs that millions do in the service economy. It is also another instance, in addition to the choice of blue-chip high school athletes as its subjects, of how *Hoop Dreams* tries to understate the disadvantage facing black youth in places like the Chicago neighborhoods of Cabrini Green and West Garfield Park. Falk may therefore claim that audiences don't see Jordan as black, but his career speaks directly to the situation of African Americans. As a model of mainstream success, he represents the gains of the post–civil rights talented tenth; in academics, Henry Louis Gates is another example of such improved possibilities for a limited group of African Americans. Yet as Jordan also offers a strategy of resistance to alienation, he speaks to the plight of the black working class, whose decline in wealth in recent years makes evident the continued importance of style and an improvisational aesthetic that provide a return for performance, even if not always in material terms.[38]

In several recent films about basketball, such an improvisational style of play allows the characters employing it a return for efforts otherwise not rewarded. In *White Men Can't Jump,* Sidney's game may supplement his family's income during slow times in the building trade, but even more important to him is the expressive pleasure he gets from it. One reviewer of the film has noted that, for both Sidney and his protégé, Billy: "the primary object of their basketball hustling is the irresponsible delight it gives them. The money they win buys them time, it keeps the heat off at home, and enables them to live the playground life for a little longer."[39] This description refers indirectly to the lack of adequate work for both men, but also to how the expressive, improvisational basketball that Sidney plays, and models for Billy, creates meaning and pleasure that they keep and don't exchange for a wage.

An awareness of such meaning and pleasure from basketball informs the following story that Sidney tells Billy when they first meet on Venice Beach: "Michael Jordan came down to the beach one time . . . took him to the hole, baby! You believe that? Took Michael Jordan to the hole! Michael said to me, he said, 'Hey, you should play summer pro league.' I said 'No! Shit might mess up my game.'" This anecdote expresses Sidney's view of the pro game as about playing basketball for money, where winning in the terms of the larger white society matters so much that it becomes difficult to hold onto the stylized game that counts for him as much as a payday. In Sidney's story, he regards Jordan as a symbol of mainstream success, a black man who has made it by the white man's rules. Yet rather than just mainstream success, what makes Jordan special has been his ability to maintain a difficult balance of white approval and individual identity while in the media limelight by using what Todd Boyd calls a fusion of the "formal" (textbook) and "vernacular" (black) styles.

• • •

When it's played the way it's spozed to be played, basketball happens in the air, the pure air; flying, floating, elevated above the floor, levitating the way oppressed peoples of this earth imagine themselves in their dreams, as I do in my lifelong fantasies of escape and power, finally at last, once and for all, free.

—*John Edgar Wideman*

The narrative conventions of racial representation that still dominate American popular culture strongly influence most films about black basketball, populating them like athletic contests with winners and losers: exceptional individuals (Sidney in *White Men Can't Jump,* Jordan in *Space Jam,* Kyle and Shep in *Above the Rim,* Saleh in *The Air Up There,* the Whoopi Goldberg character in *Eddie* [1996], Jesus in *He Got Game*), and moral misfits (Birdie in *Above the Rim,* Raymond the sore loser with the gun in *White Men,* Denzel Washington's character in *He Got Game,* the gangstarized aliens in *Hoop Dreams,* or Arthur Agee's father and William Gates's brother in *Hoop Dreams*). Despite such stereotypes that reduce black identity to self-reliance and moral strength or the lack thereof, the action sequences of these basketball films show the skills that make such exceptionalism possible, yet they often foreground as well styles that question such an easy prescription for success.

Above the Rim and *Rebound: The Legend of Earl "The Goat" Manigault* (1996) both present action scenes set on the playground in Harlem where Holcomb Rucker for decades ran a summer league so famous that top pro and college stars would come to meet the local talent. According to Nelson George, "At Rucker you played fly, flashy style (or at least tried to); otherwise you were just taking up space."[40] In *Rebound,* set during Rucker's era, and *Above the Rim,* about a contemporary tournament reviving his memory, we see scenes in which a spectacular, improvisational game, and the aggressiveness of the gangsta style, question the conventional moral simplifications of their narratives.

In the early games of the tournament near the conclusion of *Above the Rim,* a lengthy montage presents numerous players, almost all of them black, playing a fast-paced game of quick crossovers, no-look passes, and spectacular jams. The narrative function of this montage is to follow Kyle's and Birdie's teams as they win their way to an eventual showdown. Yet inadvertently the film qualifies its moralizing message about Birdie the bad guy and Shep and Kyle as heroes for following the rules. This montage shows that there are so many players with outstanding skills one can't help but wonder what makes Kyle, and later Shep, the best players on the court. Such a plethora of talent in this neighborhood tournament suggests that this story is not just about the importance of following the rules and succeeding, but also about how few of these young men get a chance to move up. Except for a white point guard on an opposing high school team, no mention is made of any other player besides Kyle from the neighborhood winning a scholarship to big-time college ball and possibly a pro career.

In *Rebound* we see several scenes in which the title character in this biopic, Earl "The Goat" Manigault, demonstrates the high-flying game that made him a playground legend in the early 1960s. The most spectacular of these scenes shows Manigault "double dunking," jamming with his right hand, catching the ball with his left and redunking it. If the bane of many young black players today is the power of the NBA dream despite the long odds, for Manigault in *Rebound* the creative pleasure of playing means everything because he never entertains such fantasies. When playground supervisor Rucker attempts to encourage Manigault to continue in school, assuring him that he has the ability to play college ball and then go to the NBA, Manigault dismisses such advice. He responds: "The NBA? Come on man! They ain't going to take me. You know they only take two brothers to a team if that." Despite his talent (Rucker calls him the best player to ever grace his court), the film shows how an insecure black college coach obsessed with playing textbook basketball later ruins Earl's chances to showcase his skills and make it to the NBA. The ending of the film retains the tension between Rucker's message of self-reliance as a ticket to success and Earl's stylistic critique. After breaking a heroin addiction, Earl gets the scornful approval of the dealer who controls the neighborhood to clean up Rucker's playground and restart the league in which presumably style will continue to count—even while dreams of the NBA are also born.

Through this emphasis on improvisational and gangsta styles, *White Men Can't Jump, Above the Rim,* and *Rebound* acknowledge the structural barriers that limit the opportunity that Michael Jordan is often used to symbolize. Although they dismiss gangsta cynicism and violence as destructive, an exaggeration of what Cornel West calls the selfish "market calculations"[41] that have contributed to the lack of opportunities for young African Americans in the first place, these films recognize, with their stylistic critique of utopian success, that the gap between promise and reality is a major factor in such nihilism.

While he notes how an essentialized notion of black identity has been useful for avoiding the domination of a discriminatory (white) mainstream popular culture, Stuart Hall also points out the problems that result from a dehistoricized and uncritical understanding of African American culture. Hall says that black popular culture can be better understood as overdetermined, constituted from "two directions at once," not as either black or American but both black and American.[42] The identities presented in the film representations of basketball I've analyzed communicate such a hybrid notion of blackness in that they offer both the expressivity of a Michael Jordan, which has given him access to mainstream success, and the denial of opportunity that fuels the anger of the gangsta. However, to the degree that Michael Jordan is offered to us as simply a utopian figure, as someone whose success proves that social mobility is available to everyone, he doesn't meet Hall's criteria for insight about African American identity. Such utopian interpretations of Jordan ignore the disadvantaged experience of many African Americans as well as his expressive critique of the alienation that white culture continues to insist on as a prerequisite of equality.

Notes

1. The sports historian Steven A. Riess reports that there were 1,800 black professional fighters in the 1930s, and by 1948 nearly half of all contenders were black. See *City Games: The Evolution of American Urban Society and the Rise of Sports* (Urbana: University of Illinois Press, 1989), 116.

2. Robert Ray, *A Certain Tendency of the Hollywood Cinema, 1930–1980* (Princeton, N.J.: Princeton University Press, 1985), 55–69.

3. Thomas Cripps, *Making Movies Black* (New York: Oxford University Press, 1993), 5.

4. John Hope Franklin, *From Slavery to Freedom: A History of Negro Americans,* 6th ed. (New York: Knopf, 1988), 389; Thomas Cripps, *Black Film As Genre* (Bloomington: Indiana University Press, 1979), 42.

5. Cripps, *Making Movies Black,* 211.

6. Robert Sklar, *City Boys: Cagney, Bogart, Garfield* (Princeton, N.J.: Princeton University Press, 1992), 82.

7. Michael Rogin, *Blackface, White Noise: Jewish Immigrants in the Hollywood Melting Pot* (Berkeley: University of California Press, 1996), 211–20; Cripps, *Making Movies Black,* 212.

8. Cripps, *Making Movies Black,* 212.

9. Quoted in ibid.

10. *Chicago Defender,* November 7, 1953, 19, and November 14, 1953, 18.

11. Nelson George, *Elevating the Game: Black Men and Basketball* (New York: HarperCollins, 1992), 42.

12. Neal Gabler, *An Empire of Their Own: How the Jews Invented Hollywood* (New York: Anchor Books, 1988), 5.

13. George, *Elevating the Game,* 100.

14. *Chicago Defender,* May 20, 1950, 17.

15. George, *Elevating the Game,* 52–53.

16. Jay Coakley reports these revenue increases in *Sport in Society: Issues and Controversies* (St. Louis: Times Mirror, 1998), 378. Todd Boyd has made the point that basketball is "a game perfectly suited to the fast paced visual culture [of] television." See *Am I Black Enough for You: Popular Culture from the Hood and Beyond* (Bloomington: Indiana University Press, 1997), 117. Quotation in Gitanjali Maharaj, "Talking Trash: Late Capitalism, Black (Re)Productivity, and Professional Basketball," *Social Text* 50 (Spring 1997): 101.

17. Stuart Hall, "What Is This 'Black' in Black Popular Culture?" in *Black Popular Culture*, ed. Gina Dent (Seattle, Wash.: Bay Press, 1992), 23.

18. bell hooks, "Neo-Colonial Fantasies of Conquest: *Hoop Dreams*," in hooks, *Reel to Reel: Race, Sex, and Class at the Movies* (New York: Routledge, 1996), 79.

19. John Edgar Wideman, "Michael Jordan Leaps the Great Divide," *Esquire*, November 1990, 210.

20. George, *Elevating the Game*, 240.

21. Peter DeJonge, "Talking Trash," *New York Times Magazine*, June 6, 1993, sec. 6, pp. 34, 38.

22. Cornel West, *Race Matters* (New York: Vintage, 1994), 26–27.

23. My analysis here was influenced by Frank P. Tomasulo's writing about his experience as an Italian American in "Italian Americans in the Hollywood Cinema: Filmmakers, Characters, Audiences," *Voices in Italian Americana* 7, no. 1 (1996): 69. The quotation is from Werner Sollors, *Beyond Ethnicity: Consent and Descent in American Culture* (New York: Oxford University Press, 1986), 31, 33.

24. Henry Louis Gates Jr., "New Worth: How the Greatest Player in the History of Basketball Became the Greatest Brand in the History of Sports," *New Yorker*, June 1, 1998, 48.

25. Relying on the work of New York University economist Edward Wolff, Ralph Nader in 1998 wrote a letter to Microsoft chairman Bill Gates asking his assistance in responding to the wealth disparity in the U.S. such that the top 1 percent in this country own more that the bottom 90 percent. "Nader Urges Gates to Tackle Wealth Disparities," Associated Press wire story, July 28, 1998.

26. Stern quoted in Gates, "New Worth," 51.

27. Ibid., 61.

28. Falk quoted in ibid., 53–54.

29. Benjamin DeMott, *The Trouble with Friendship: Why Americans Can't Think Straight about Race* (New York: Atlantic Monthly Press, 1995), 1–6.

30. Michael Eric Dyson, "Be like Mike?: Michael Jordan and the Pedagogy of Desire," in Dyson, *Reflecting Black: African-American Cultural Criticism* (Minneapolis: University of Minnesota Press, 1993), 67–69.

31. Boyd, *Am I Black Enough for You*, 115.

32. Hall, "What Is This 'Black,'" 27.

33. Herman Grey, *Watching Race: Television and the Struggle for "Blackness"* (Minneapolis: University of Minnesota Press, 1995), 156.

34. Ibid., 156–57.

35. Quoted in Gates, "New Worth," 51.

36. Ibid., 58.

37. Juliet B. Schor, *The Overworked American: The Unexpected Decline of Leisure* (New York: Basic Books, 1991), 1–15.

38. Edward N. Wolff states that "The racial distribution of wealth deteriorated in the 1980s from an already unacceptable level. Relative income of African American households held steady at about 60 percent of white income in the 1980s, but the relative wealth position of most black families deteriorated. Historically, black wealth always has been much lower than that of whites, the legacy of slavery, discrimination, and low incomes. Between 1983 and 1989, a bad situation grew worse. In 1983, the median white family had eleven times the wealth of the median nonwhite family. By 1989 this ratio

had grown to twenty. Middle-class black households did succeed in narrowing the wealth gap with whites, but most nonwhite families moved even further behind." See *Top Heavy: The Increasing Inequality of Wealth in America and What Can Be Done about It* (New York: New Press, 1995), 2.

39. T. Rafferty, "Boys' Games," *New Yorker*, June 6, 1992, 80–82.

40. George, *Elevating the Game,* 74.

41. West, *Race Matters,* 26.

42. Hall, "What Is This 'Black,'" 29.

3 From He Got Game to We Got Next: Gender in American Sports Films

In an important sense there is only one complete unblushing male in America: a young, married, white, urban, northern, heterosexual, Protestant, father, of college education, fully employed, of good complexion, weight, and height, and a recent record in sports. . . . Any male who fails to qualify in any one of these ways is likely to view himself—during moments at least—as unworthy, incomplete, and inferior.

—Irving Goffman

Historical analysis of masculinity in American society requires consideration of both the version that dominates at a given time and the social identities that compete with it. Sports films provide an interesting site for such analysis because they often foreground dominant masculinity, yet they also show how it has been refigured (and sometimes doesn't stand up) over time in response to changes in American society. From the 1880s through the end of the twentieth century, the effects of industrialization, professionalization, deindustrialization, changing forms of media representation, and the increased assertion of women and nonwhite and gay men have forced dominant masculinity to define itself in new ways. In an attempt to portray athletic events in a realist style, the makers of sports films have responded to these social changes in their portrayal of masculinity—by demonstrating its strength through service to others, by showing nonwhite men and women who embody its traits, even by presenting a white masculinity inflected with qualities associated with nonwhite athletes.

Within the utopian narrative typical of American cinema, one particular version of ideal masculinity has been represented repeatedly in sports films. This heroic individual overcomes obstacles and achieves success through determination, self-reliance, and hard work. He controls his own destiny by succeeding in free and fair competition offered as representative of an American society that promises rewards to the most deserving individuals. Differences in social position are therefore naturalized as evolutionary rather than as a result of a lack of competitive opportunities.[1] Sports films seldom acknowledge that women have not had as much access to athletic competition.

Instead, the competition among men that they show validates the assumption of male superiority. When gender discrimination comes up, whether in the few films about female athletes or in stories about less traditionally masculine men, it is often portrayed as just another ad hoc challenge for the strong and resourceful individual rather than as a systematic flaw in sports competition or American society.

The competitive opportunities offered to male athletes in most sports films justify patriarchal authority by naturalizing the idea of men as more assertive and determining, while women generally appear in the secondary role of fan and dependent supporter. A few sports films show assertive women, some of whom are athletes, pursuing a feminist desire for control of their career and relationships; in *Pat and Mike* (1952), *Bull Durham* (1988), and *Tin Cup* (1996), those strong women even verbally deconstruct masculinity. Several films about female athletes present a disjuncture between scenes in which they demonstrate their ability to appropriate qualities associated with masculinity (especially physical strength and self-confidence) and a narrative that pushes them toward compromise with conservative ideas of gender.

Heterosexuality is the preferred choice for male athletes in sports films because it not only assumes control in relationships with women but also denies the homoeroticism that, from a homophobic perspective, creates fear of being controlled by other men. While movies about sports may show the use of ideal masculinity to overcome barriers resulting from class, race, or gender, they still almost entirely avoid depicting lesbian and especially gay characters using athletics for self-definition. To acknowledge homoeroticism within the context of athletic activities that involve men touching each other, sometimes with not much on, would call the very idea of masculinity based on heterosexuality into question. The homophobic stereotype that equates gays and lesbians with weakness (the former too feminine, the latter an inferior imitation of masculinity) shows up in even the most sexually tolerant of sports films, *Personal Best* (1982), in which the main character's transition from loser to winner follows her shift from a lesbian relationship to heterosexuality. By emulating the competitive strength of her male lover, she becomes able to win.

Although elsewhere in this book I focus on sound films (for reasons I explain in the Introduction), to analyze adequately the way in which masculinity has been portrayed in sports movies, it is necessary to include films from the silent era. Silent films portray more directly the contextual forces of modernity that contributed to the formation of the core notion of masculinity that has predominated in sports movies. To illustrate the importance of understanding this formative process for more recent sports films, consider *The*

Natural (1984). Not only does *The Natural* contain the conventions of gender found in many sports films and therefore illustrate the prevalence and durability of a certain idealized athletic masculinity, it also takes a look back at some of the historical causes for this model of normative identity established during the period when silent films were made.

Like most Hollywood films, *The Natural* tells an apparently self-contained story, about a baseball player named Roy Hobbs (Robert Redford), whose physical "gift" for the game and determination enable him to overcome the conventional obstacles of manipulative women, dissipation, gamblers, and aging to arrive at the nostalgic, agrarian image of white male self-determination central to the national pastime. What the film invokes in passing, but prefers to downplay in favor of Hobbs's individual heroism, are the forces of modernity that had been redefining American masculinity for more than half a century when the story opens in 1939.

Early in *The Natural,* the plot flashes back in time to show us Roy Hobbs sixteen years earlier as a teenager, leaving his family's farm for a tryout to pursue his dream of playing in the major leagues. By 1923 when the scene takes place, professional baseball, played on large expanses of dirt and grass with wooden bats and animal-hide balls and gloves, had already become a nostalgic, agrarian response for many men to the redefinition of traditional masculinity occurring as the United States became increasingly industrialized and urbanized. While 80 percent of American men were farmers at the beginning of the nineteenth century, by 1880 only half the nation's labor force worked in agriculture.[2] New technology helped increase harvests, but overproduction kept prices down so that by the 1890s—despite attempts at gaining government assistance—the situation for farmers was one in which "crop prices were always falling, railroad rates rising, and banks foreclosing."[3] At the end of the century, as Michael Kimmel puts it: "Family farmers were, of course, far from extinct, but their decline was dramatic."[4] By the 1920s, for the first time, the national census showed a majority of Americans living in urban areas.[5]

Urban life only magnified the loss of control over work for many native-born men. The period from 1870 to 1910 saw a dramatic drop, from 67 to 37 percent, in the proportion of self-employed middle-class men.[6] Wage work was directed by managers and supervisors, new technology increased the speed of production, and ideas of scientific management justified the demand that workers function like machines.[7] Kimmel sums up these changes in work and masculinity when he writes that "Industrialization, technological transformation, capital concentration, urbanization, . . . all these created a new sense of an oppressively crowded, depersonalized, and often emasculated life. Manhood had meant autonomy and self-control, but now fewer and fewer

American men owned their own shops, controlled their own labor, owned their own farms."[8]

Besides the changes in working conditions, native-born men in the United States also faced an increase in competition as a result of immigration, the migration north of African Americans from the rural South, and the greater self-assertion of women. Twenty-three million immigrants came to the United States between 1880 and 1914, while from 1910 to 1930 the black population of northern cities almost tripled.[9] The African American move north was in general motivated by the economic opportunities provided by industrialization, but black men in particular sought to escape "the emasculation of Jim Crow laws"—clearly an objective that would challenge the privilege of white men in the North.[10]

During this same period from the 1880s until the Depression, women, especially if they had the means to do so, began pursuing greater equality. By 1900 educational and professional opportunities for white, middle-class women "had expanded dramatically," due in part to the women's colleges that had opened since the end of the Civil War. At the turn of the century women made up more than half the high school graduates in the United States, and "80 percent of the colleges, universities and professional schools in the nation admitted women."[11] In their history of the American family, Steven Mintz and Susan Kellogg claim that, during the first decades of the twentieth century, women's educational achievements even "began to approximate those of men."[12] Immigrant men also challenged the prerogatives of white bourgeois men, especially through labor conflict and in the political arena, and their arrival in the United States indirectly aided the New Woman by making possible an expansion in business and industry that created more service and public sector jobs for female workers.

In response to these challenges to their economic self-determination and social authority, middle-class white men found that sports offered a means of reaffirming an empowered masculinity. Elliott Gorn and Warren Goldstein state that the increasing popularity of participation in and spectatorship of sports at the turn of the century "was part of a vigorous reassertion of masculinity."[13] While urban society and industrial or bureaucratic work made it more difficult to attain the social privilege they expected, bourgeois men found in sports a culture that at least "symbolically negated fears of emasculation" by offering a space that they, or someone with whom they could identify, controlled through traditional "physical excellence . . . and individual heroism." Middle-class American men increasingly looked to the working class for a new idea of manhood that required that they "reject their genteel heritage in favor of new forms of action."[14] While in the 1860s the ideal body

for a middle-class man was lean and wiry, by the 1890s greater muscularity—
the product of strenuous exercise—was in vogue.[15]

Athletic Masculinity and the Movies

This notion of ideal masculinity with its roots in a response to modernity has
been frequently represented in films from the silent era to recent blockbusters like *Any Given Sunday* (1999) and *The Replacements* (2000). Its most recent
portrayals, however, respond more directly to multicultural challenges arising from the countercultures of the 1960s and new forms of media representation structured less as Aristotelian narrative and more as a rapid flow of
images. By necessity, the presentation of ideal masculinity in such postmodern sports films has had to include variations on dominant masculinity that
present greater inclusiveness and new forms of appeal.

The controversy over movies showing Jack Johnson, the first African
American heavyweight champion, demonstrated the power of middle-class
white masculinity and the role of sports films in its maintenance. Soon after
winning the title in 1908, Johnson was demonized in the white press, ostensibly because he offered a model of empowerment to African Americans as a
group, but also because he represented the antithesis of acceptable masculinity. Numerous historians have documented the perception of Johnson's threat
to white privilege, and Dan Streible has traced the reception of the popular
films of Johnson's title fights, showing how they were viewed as a threat to
"prevailing beliefs in the superiority of the white race."[16] This threat led to the
banning of prizefight films in 1912 when Congress passed the Sims Act, which
Streible places within "a larger social movement . . . to control the social aspirations of black citizens."[17]

Johnson challenged white superiority using its own assumption that his
Caucasian opponents were the best representatives of their race. As Gail Bederman puts it, "by the time Jack Johnson became champion in 1908, many
middle-class men had come to accept boxing champions like Jim Jeffries [a
former white heavyweight champ whom Johnson beat in 1910] as embodi-
ments of their sense of manhood."[18]

Besides challenging social Darwinist claims of white superiority, Johnson
also represented the fears of white men about how their own identities were
changing. In particular through his well-publicized indulgence in a life of overconsumption, Johnson raised concerns about how what Jackson Lears calls a
"therapeutic ethos" was becoming more influential on middle-class men.[19]

An important aspect of nineteenth-century masculinity had been restraint, the ability to check one's appetites and desires. Bederman describes

this important trait of manhood as emphasizing "control over impulse, . . .
[the] ability to control powerful masculine passions through strong character and a powerful will as a primary source of men's strength and authority
over both women and the lower classes. By gaining the manly strength to
control himself, a man gained the strength, as well as the duty, to protect and
direct those weaker than himself: his wife, his children, or his employees."[20]

Lears describes the shift to a therapeutic ethos as one that took place gradually between the 1880s and the 1920s, affecting mostly the educated classes
in Western Europe and North America. It involved a move away from the restraint and denial so strongly valued in nineteenth-century masculinity,
which had been characterized by belief in hard work, saving money, civic responsibility, and a strict morality. Instead, greater emphasis was now placed
on leisure, spending, and individual fulfillment. Because he spent freely,
Johnson became an easy target for the press to position him as an example of
black self-indulgence and therefore to displace onto him the effects that the
new culture of consumption was having on many whites. Bederman describes
how Johnson took pride in his buying power yet also sought to portray himself in terms of the traditional ideal of masculine domestic responsibility by
presenting his white wives not "as pathetic victims of Negro lust, but rather
as "respectable women whose husband was successful and manly enough to
support them in comfort and luxury."[21]

Several sports films from the teens through the Depression era represent
sports as a response to the loss of restraint created by the new consumer ethos.
They also show sports as an antidote for the feminization of the culture caused
by the loss of traditional forms of physical work and the increasing assertion
of women. *The Pinch Hitter* (1917) tells the story of a young man who uses college baseball to wean himself from a strong emotional attachment to his late
mother and move toward the traditional strong, self-reliant masculinity of his
farmer father. *Brown of Harvard* (1926) also employs college sports to instill the
discipline necessary to avoid the dangers of overconsumption and the depen-
dence created by "feminine" emotions. In *The Drop Kick* (1927), Jack Hammill
(Richard Barthelmess) uses college football to avoid the seduction of a widow
who, having driven her coach husband to suicide, almost ensnares Jack in her
life of overspending and sexual promiscuity.

In *The Pinch Hitter*, Charles Ray plays Joel Parker, a shy young man from a
small town in New England. The film's concern about the feminization of
masculinity and the importance of sports to reverse that tendency comes
through in its contrast of Joel with his father, Obediah (Joseph Dowling), a
crusty patriarch who represents a preindustrial masculinity defined by hard
physical work and the self-reliance of farm life. Obediah can't understand why

his son has no interest in the family farm and is obsessively attached to his deceased mother. Because he had promised it to his late wife, the father sends Joel to Williamson College, but consistent with Puritan beliefs in thrift and the positive effect of a "strenuous life" on one's character, he refuses to give the boy any extra money to spend at school. Joel's male classmates make fun of him as a rube and weakling, but the young woman who runs the local soda shop, Abbie Nettleton (Sylvia Bremer), tries to build Joel's self-confidence by encouraging him to go out for the Williamson baseball team.

Joel performs so badly that the coach makes him a mascot rather than put him on the team, his presence a warning to the other players to avoid falling to the level of Joel's lack of manliness. Nonetheless, injuries force the coach to put Joel in to pinch-hit in the last inning of an important game, and after getting behind no balls and two strikes, a nervous Joel looks over to Abbie for encouragement. The title card interprets the look she sends back to him: "Her eyes spell in one word—confidence! Confidence in him!" Bolstered by Abbie's support, Joel hits a home run to win the game for Williamson.

Brown of Harvard sets up a similar story about the fear of feminization and the role of college sports to reaffirm masculinity through individual excellence. The title character, Tom Brown (William Haines), is a young man from a wealthy family who by wanting for nothing has become selfish and undisciplined, forgetting the Victorian emphasis on restraint and hard work that the new strenuous masculinity aimed to reinvoke. Tom goes out with his buddies rather than spend time with his mother and father the evening before he goes off to Harvard, and after arriving in Cambridge, he immediately falls in with a group of young men interested only in drunken parties. *Brown of Harvard* shows the homoerotic danger of this dissipated life through the character of Jed Doolittle (Jack Pickford), Tom's roommate and constant companion, who not only has no aptitude for the rough sports that form the right kind of masculinity, but also directs loving glances and gentle gestures toward young Mr. Brown. To further emphasize the homoerotic danger such homosociality can create, Tom fails to attract much interest from Mary (Mary Brian), the daughter of a Harvard professor with whom he has fallen in love.

Mary gives her attention instead to MacAndrews (Francis X. Bushman), a sturdy and stoic young man who avoids wild parties in favor of diligent study and hard work in crew practice and on the football field. The low point of Tom's errant ways comes when a hangover prevents him from performing in a crew race in which he had been asked to spell an injured MacAndrews. When he learns of his son's problems, Tom's father urges his son to give up parties, dedicate himself to sports, and fight for Mary's attention.

Coincident with the protagonist's subsequent change in attitude, *Brown of Harvard* kills off Jed, who contracts pneumonia when he leaves his sickbed to run through the cold rain to give Tom a message from the football coach. Jed's death resembles what Vito Russo calls "the obligatory suicide" that has often been "the fate of screen gays."[22] To further emphasize the sexual danger that Tom has narrowly escaped, we see him just before the rain scene, gently rubbing balm on Jed's chest. Tom proves himself in the big game, helping his team score a last-minute touchdown to beat Yale. He therefore wins Mary's affection by no longer lying about with other men drinking and singing, but instead by embodying the right kind of disciplined, competitive, and heterosexual masculinity.

The Drop Kick emphasizes the danger to normative masculinity of jazz age overconsumption and female sexuality. Eunice's overspending drives her football coach husband to steal $10,000 from athletic department funds, resulting in his dismissal, disgrace, and suicide. Her desire for Jack, the team's captain, represents the danger of a similar fate for him: at the moment when her husband shoots himself in the backyard of their home, Eunice and Jack lie kissing on her bed.

In contrast to Eunice's dangerous sexuality and self-indulgence, Jack's girlfriend, Molly, demonstrates a virginal restraint that models the discipline Jack must show to save himself. Many sports films employ a reserved female character like Abbie in *The Pinch Hitter,* Mary in *Brown of Harvard,* and Molly in *The Drop Kick* to support the male athlete's deferred gratification by offering her affection as the prize for adhering to it. Distracted by guilt over what he believes to be his responsibility for the coach's suicide, Jack plays poorly for much of his team's big game but pulls himself together at the last moment to make a long drop kick and win the contest. Jack's strong and supportive mother (she has introduced him to Molly) makes public the coach's suicide note, showing that he didn't kill himself because of Eunice's relationship with Jack, and allowing the star player and Molly to reunite.

The use of college football to mold strong masculinity shown in these three films was part of a bourgeois response to the challenges of modernity. Prior to the Civil War, college life made little room for sports, or any extracurricular activities for that matter, as student time was taken up primarily with prayer and the study of a classical curriculum to prepare young men for a career in law, the clergy, or belles lettres.[23] By the turn of the century students had begun to break from the strict control of faculty, organizing extracurricular activities, especially sports like football, which had become a central part of social life at American colleges. Yet ruling-class leaders favored college sports not so much as leisure-time diversion for students as an effective way of teaching young men the discipline, teamwork, and leadership skills needed to reinforce the social boundaries that separated them from working-class men.[24] In the 1890s Theodore Roosevelt—who had himself been active in boxing, rowing, and wrestling while at Harvard—championed athletic training as a means of shoring up the supremacy of Anglo-Saxon men in the face of immigrants and radicals. As Gorn and Goldstein put it, college sports "made the new Darwinian worldview palpable."[25]

Wiley Lee Umphlett lists or analyzes more than twenty films about college athletes from the 1910s through the 1930s and comments that "athletic activity was . . . integral to the plot of the college-life movie of this era."[26] While melodramas from this period such as *The Pinch Hitter, The Drop Kick,* and *Brown of Harvard* show college sports as an important activity in building bourgeois masculinity, romantic comedies like *College* (1927) and *Horse Feathers* (1932) use a very physical brand of humor to endorse the immediate pleasures of the body rather than patriarchal control built upon deferred gratification. *College* asks whether sports really instill masculine discipline and responsibility or encourage inflated egos and arrogance. It also questions whether the objective for men who prove themselves in sports should be marriage and family founded on male responsibility. The Marx Brothers anarchic comedy *Horse Feathers* answers both those questions with a loud raspberry.

In the first scene of *College,* Ronald (Buster Keaton) gives a speech as valedictorian at his high school graduation, emphasizing the importance of learning and deriding sports. His message falls on deaf ears, however, and Ronald's awkward appearance along with mistaken references to "Ty Ruth and Babe Dempsey" support this hostile reception—characterizing him as a dreamy young man who doesn't know much about what he's criticizing. When Mary, the young woman whom Ronald adores, calls him a "weak-kneed teacher's pet," he decides to abandon his stated principles, go to college, and become an athlete. Like another silent parody of college athletics, *The Freshman* (1925) by Harold Lloyd, most of the comedy in *College* comes from the main character's failure at sports (here baseball and track and field) in gags that nonetheless display a high degree of grace and agility. Even during his anti-sports speech Ronald is not at all "weak-kneed"; he sways from side to side while addressing his audience, his body leaning over in an impressive display of balance and strength.

Yet the narrative in *College* initially associates sports not with Ronald but with Jeff Brown, a member of the same graduating class, introduced before the ill-fated address as keen for exercise but otherwise not very smart. Because of his athleticism, Brown initially has Mary's attention, but he demonstrates none of the qualities that sports promise to instill: self-discipline, a taste for hard work, and individual achievement that serves the needs of the group.

Instead we see him throughout the film trying to hold onto Mary's interest by ridiculing Ronald for his lack of athleticism. Brown's derision comes from his own insecurities, his worry that Ronald is smarter than he is, and that Mary, notwithstanding the influence of normative definitions of masculinity, will prefer Ronald because he adores and respects her rather than trying to bend her to his will.

Gerald Mast has written that, unlike those of another very talented and physical silent film comedian, Charlie Chaplin, Keaton's films generally avoid statements about social issues.[27] Indeed, *College* doesn't attribute Brown's fear of intellect and his controlling behavior directly to his involvement in athletics; we never actually see Jeff participating in sports, and his derision of Ronald occurs in reaction to the latter's bumbling attempts to play baseball, throw the javelin, and run track. On the other hand, during the scene in which Ronald tries his hand at baseball, *College* shows men's sports as allowing the kind of physical coercion with which Brown will later try to force Mary into marriage. After Ronald makes a series of errors in the field and running the bases, his teammates, and even the coach, knock the Keaton character around and expel him from their game.

Moreover, when Ronald demonstrates the running, jumping, hitting, and throwing skills that he was unable to master in sports to rescue Mary from Brown, the film follows that scene with a montage showing that it isn't simply celebrating him as a true sports hero. The montage instead questions the value of marriage and family as the rewards that sports films often promise for winning. Consider Mast's description of the last sequence: "In *College,* after Buster has successfully mastered athletics, his bullying rival, and his lady's affections, Keaton ends with a strange series of dissolves—Buster and wife with kids, the two as a pair of old folks, and then their tombstones in the cemetery. Though Keaton may have meant to imply their living 'happily ever after,' those two tombstones cast doubt on the whole value of the task he has mastered and the prize he has won."[28] Through these references to old age and death *College* questions the desirability of family as a man's (and a woman's) reward for athletic success. Although sports films often present physical activity as just a means to this end, the shots of "happily ever after" are more static and not nearly as pleasurable as what Keaton's brilliant physical comedy offers to his audience as humorous entertainment, and to him as expressive performance.

Within the context of *College*'s representation of a society that places great value on sports, this ending dismantles the normative masculinity created by athletics. *College* instead suggests better uses for the body: protecting others from the tyranny of an overbearing ego built upon athletic masculinity; for the audience the laughter created by Ronald's unexpected disruptions of a patriarchal world—which at the end of the film substitute for the earlier comedy premised on his failure to measure up as an athlete; and for the performer himself, the pleasure of controlling one's own body.

In the Marx Brothers' film *Horse Feathers,* physical comedy again critiques the dominant masculinity defined by college sports. The new president of Huxley College, Quincy Adams Wagstaff (Groucho Marx), hears from his son that "A college needs something else besides education, and what this college needs is a good football team." Following his son's advice, Wagstaff hires two "ringers" (Harpo and Chico Marx), creating in the process an anarchic situation at Huxley that undermines its mission of using athletics to form disciplined minds and bodies for young men of privilege.

Even though *Horse Feathers* is an early talkie, and Groucho and Chico base their comedy primarily on the skillful use and misuse of language, Harpo performs the kind of physical comedy that "substitutes the language of the body for speech."[29] Moreover, as in *College,* the comedy of the body in *Horse Feathers* deconstructs an all-too-serious narrative world of privilege and pretension established early in the film using language, as for example in the former president's introduction of Wagstaff as his successor. In *College,* Ronald's speech constructs a similar pretension by criticizing the overemphasis on sports in 1920s America, only to inadvertently reaffirm dominant beliefs when his views are dismissed as "weak-kneed."

The bodily humor of Chico and especially Harpo in *Horse Feathers* deconstructs college athletics by offering alternative uses for physicality. Because rival Darwin has already hired the ringers that young Wagstaff had in mind, Huxley is left with Chico and Harpo. They are also physical men; it's just that what they have in mind is sex, not football. Mast describes the sexuality of Harpo's physical humor: "Where Groucho's seductiveness (such as it is) takes the form of talk, Harpo is much less subtle. He simply chases and grabs [as we see him do with Chico in the classroom scene in *Horse Feathers*], wrapping his arms around whatever attractive lady happens to pass. . . . This intimate physical contact is violently antisocial, violating social codes of distance, propriety and masculinity."[30]

As a result, the Marx Brothers in *Horse Feathers* mock college football's claim to develop an ideal masculinity of strength, discipline, and self-determination, instead pursuing alcohol, sex, and laughter at every opportunity. What matters for Groucho, Chico, and especially Harpo is not how college and football offer the chance to acquire the values and social contacts for future success, but the opportunities for the immediate physical pleasures of drinking, humor, and sexual contact. College life therefore becomes an orgy of the hedonistic impulses described by Lears's therapeutic ethos. Even the real ring-ers playing for Darwin contribute to this critique of ideal masculinity as they represent a common practice of teams being bought rather than made through hard work. These mercenary players show how college football has often functioned less as an arena for fair play and masculine self-development, and more as a business devoted to selling that myth.

Depressed Fighters

In contrast to *Horse Feathers,* several other 1930s films return to the conserva-tive masculinity in the silent melodramas that celebrate college sports by emphasizing the danger of overconsumption and sexual women. *The Champ* (1931) tells the story of a prizefighter played by Wallace Beery who dies in part because of his profligate life of gambling and alcoholism. Jimmy Key (James Cagney) in *Winner Take All* (1932) falls for a seductive society woman, Joan Gibson (Virginia Bruce), who toys with him because his "primitive" physical-ity entertains her. Other Depression-era prizefight films, such as *Keep Punch-ing* (1939), *They Made Me a Criminal* (1939), and *Knockout* (1941), likewise em-phasize the importance of avoiding overspending and sexual women to maintain a strong, responsible masculinity.

Yet while they emphasize the importance of restraint, these Depression-era prizefight films also leave in doubt the ability of the boxer, even with the support of others, to live up to an ideal masculinity. All these films end with the boxer apparently putting aside his profligate ways to win the big fight and act responsibly for those who depend on him. Moreover, the nuclear family or familylike group in these films offer a social structure in which female char-acters contribute to the pugilistic construction of masculinity without threat-ening traditional gender roles. To attract the female moviegoer, sports films have often included sizable roles for women in stories focused on the athlet-ic exploits of male performers. A *Variety* reviewer commented on this strate-gy in writing about another 1930s fight film, *Kid Galahad* (1937), calling the Louise character played by Bette Davis "the thread that holds the story togeth-er" and that "will make *Galahad* acceptable to the women."[31] Barbara Stan-wyck plays such a supportive role in *Golden Boy* (1939), doing double duty as the reliable partner for two male characters. While engaged to boxing man-ager Tom Moody, she helps him persuade Joe Bonaparte to fulfill his poten-tial in the ring. After she falls in love with Bonaparte, however, she redirects her supportive efforts to convincing Joe to return to his family.

But while *The Champ, Winner Take All, They Made Me a Criminal, Knock-out,* and *Kid Galahad* define strong masculinity as the ability to provide for one's family, none of the stories ends with that ability confirmed. Andy in *The Champ* dies from injuries suffered in his last fight. At the end of *Winner Take All* it's not clear why Peggy should believe Jimmy won't stray again. *They Made Me a Criminal* concludes with the boxer character a fugitive from the law. A heartbroken Johnny in *Knockout* tries to commit suicide in the ring and gives up fighting when his girl agrees to take him back. And while the prizefighter protagonist returning to the farm at the end of *Kid Galahad* recalls the masculine self-determination of agrarian life, New Deal agricultural assistance directed to big landowners makes it at best a nostalgic response.

Only *Keep Punching* and *Golden Boy* don't doubt the boxer protagonist's ability to provide, but the latter film instead questions whether the crucial trait of successful masculinity should be the ability to make money in violent competition against other working-class men. Joe Bonaparte leaves his family because he feels that his father's desire for him to play the violin will limit his ability to demonstrate his manhood by making money. But when this aggressive ambition results in the death of an opponent in the ring, he regrets his choice and returns home to his family, friends, and violin. That the family in *Golden Boy* is not emotionally and financially dependent on the success of the male boxer indicates an unwillingness in the film to equate normative masculinity with the violent competition of prizefighting.

Golden Boy therefore raises a question that most sports films carefully avoid about the relationship between individual masculine distinction in sports and the benefits of that stardom for the team, family, community—whoever in the narrative has a stake in the athlete's success by virtue of supporting him. In *Golden Boy,* Joe's family and neighbors show a lack of enthusiasm for his success as a fighter; the father in particular maintains a strong disdain for his son's boxing even after Joe proves his ability in the ring. This lack of support represents a profound doubt about whether the victory of an individual athlete benefits the group. As we have seen in the other 1930s prizefight films discussed here, such collective benefit is hoped for but not affirmed. Even sports films that unequivocally endorse dominant masculinity as being in everyone's best interest assume this payoff often without justifying its value. In the following section, analysis of several of these more conservative films will show how this assumed benefit takes two forms: material rewards that the star athlete brings to his teammates, family, and other supporters, and a psychological boost from identification with his success. The latter benefit offers a model from within the story for spectatorship of sports films, although not always the narcissistic identification with the male gaze that Laura Mulvey analyzes. Instead, it fits with what Ava Rose and Jim Friedman describe as the invitation from sports media texts to membership in a special social group connected to the athlete(s), a place as "one of the guys."[32] Yet such initiate identification assumes that athletic excellence matters most, thereby reducing the status of the spectator to that of consumer rather than producer of value. Within the stories in sports films, the "team" that supports the star athlete may be given some of the material benefits from "his" achievement, although rarely with much acknowledgment that they earned them. They may also receive a psychological boost from membership in a winning team, yet there as well they usually aren't credited with making the group a desirable association.

Wartime Biopics and Martial Masculinity

Because they are also about working-class, ethnic athletes, several biopics made during the 1940s at first appear to resemble the Depression-era boxing movies. Warner Brothers, which had produced many of the earlier prizefight films, was also an important studio for sports biopics, releasing two of the first made: *Knute Rockne—All American* in 1940 and *Gentleman Jim* in 1942. What is distinctly different about the ideological positions in these stories of famous athletes and coaches is how, while the subjects are from immigrant, working-class families, their hard work and determination allow them to assimilate and achieve success without significant impediment. The wartime sports biopics entertain much less doubt about the viability of strong American masculinity. Because these films seek to celebrate the achievement of a famous individual, and some of them make the argument that the United States is a place of opportunity worth fighting a war to preserve, they show no fear that a strong masculine identity will be compromised by social or economic forces such as the Depression. In these stories, participation in sports is more than a psychological substitute for real masculine authority; it creates an opportunity to demonstrate reliable leadership.

The heroes of these 1940s biopics exemplify an ideal masculinity founded on ambition, determination, hard work, and sacrifice for the team, family, and community. Yet careful examination of these biopics also shows that, to the degree that they include the real events of their subjects' lives, historical contradictions intrude on their utopian narratives of opportunity. These films inadvertently show how race and class difference have been factors in who got opportunity and who did not, how patriarchal social structures support the success of the athletic hero, and how the protagonists choose sports for their life's work in reaction to the restrictions placed on traditional masculinity by the social and economic forces of modernity.

Despite the contradictions of history, on balance this World War II cycle of sports biopics strongly endorses the promise of the United States as the land of equal opportunity in which even working-class boys from immigrant families can achieve the American dream. At the beginning of *Knute Rockne—All American,* we read that Lars Rockne brought his son, Knute, and the rest of his family from Norway "following the new road of equality and opportunity which led to America." Frank Cavanaugh, the coach in *The Iron Major* (1943), tells his wife Florence that he is going to fight in World War I because "we're lucky enough to live in America, and that's a privilege that has to be fought for." In another sports biopic of the period, *Pride of the Yankees* (1942), Lou Gehrig's German immigrant mother explains to him that she and his father left Germany for the United States because "America [is] a wonderful country where everyone has a chance." And finally *Gentleman Jim,* which recounts the story of 1890s heavyweight boxing champion James Corbett, has wealthy San Francisco socialite Virginia Ware tell the film's title character: "There really aren't two sides of the tracks, . . . there's only the lucky and unlucky. Those that happened to have grabbed the right moment and those that don't." Corbett certainly does not miss his chance at equal opportunity, which comes in the ring and also when he marries Virginia, whose father made his fortune in silver mining and banking.

While this World War II cycle of biopics celebrates sports as the avenue by which young men from modest origins learn the values and skills that help them make it in American society, they also define a notion of masculinity that ignores class barriers. The rise of big business and the bureaucratization of the American workplace at the end of the nineteenth century created a demand for professionals, managers, clerks, and salesmen.[33] Each of the subjects of these biopics starts out in pursuit of such a position: Jim Corbett takes a job in a bank, Knute Rockne obtains a degree in chemistry and works in a lab, Frank Cavanaugh earns a law degree, and Lou Gehrig studies at Columbia to be an engineer.

All four soon find that these positions require long years of study and apprenticeship; sports provide a remedy to these limitations and therefore seem more masculine. Corbett selects boxing, but not the slugfests between professional brawlers idolized by the Irish male subculture of his cab driver father and longshoreman brothers; instead, he gains membership at the elite WASP Olympic Athletic Club, where he adopts the amateur ideal of boxing as a vigorous, manly sport that strengthens and toughens young men "from good families."

At the end of the nineteenth century, men with enormous wealth (even if recently acquired) established elitist athletic clubs in most American cities. Like the members of the Olympic Club in *Gentleman Jim,* these men gave lip service to the importance of fair play and the classlessness of sport. Their interest in gaining a competitive advantage over their business rivals in other clubs motivated them to grant membership to ethnic working-class youths such as Corbett, but only if the youth was not "black, a recent immigrant or too crude in social demeanor."[34] In the Warners' film, Corbett's style of dress, his speech, and his controlled "scientific" boxing indicate his adoption of the notion of bourgeois masculinity that such organizations defined.

In place of definition by class, these early 1940s biopics emphasize sports as the way to acquire a strong, self-determining masculinity—in most cases further enhanced with a national identity defined by the common purpose of the war effort. *Knute Rockne—All American,* which premiered in the fall of 1940, after fighting had begun in Europe but a little over a year before the United States became involved in World War II, and *The Iron Major,* released after Pearl Harbor, both employ the essentialist idea that war is a natural part of masculinity. Bob Connell calls this sort of association the "connection between admired masculinity and violent response to threat [that] is a resource that governments can use to mobilize support for war."[35] As we have seen, *Knute Rockne—All American* made a case for the value of the American system, offering what the *Variety* reviewer called a "timely" and "inspirational reminder of what this country stands for."

But while *Knute Rockne—All American* essentializes male violence, it doesn't directly advocate American military involvement in the war.[36] A group of fellow coaches asks Rockne to speak before a national commission investigating charges of professionalism in college football, and he defends the sport as offering an outlet for masculine aggression:

> Games such as football . . . they're an absolute necessity to the nation's best interest. Every red-blooded young man in any country is filled with what we might call the natural spirit of combat. In many parts of Europe and elsewhere in the world this spirit manifests itself in continuous wars and revolutions. We've tried to make competitive sport serve as a safer outlet for the spirit of combat. . . . In American life today . . . we're getting soft, inside and out, we're losing that forceful heritage of mind and body. These men and I . . . we've tried to build courage, initiative, tolerance and persistence.

This characterization of Rockne describing the male inclination to fight, what he calls "the natural spirit of combat," modifies what the real Rockne had publicly stated about football as training for war. More than a decade earlier, in a magazine article entitled "Football . . . a Man's Game," Rockne, adapting Wellington's famous statement that the battle of Waterloo had been won on the fields of Eton, wrote that "any future war in which America may participate will find its victory secured on American football fields."[37] Probably because the studio was aware that in May 1940 polls showed 64 percent of Americans still opposed U.S. involvement in World War II, it qualified Rockne's association of football with war, hinting at the sport's role in preparing men for battle, but also offering it as a preferred substitute.

By the fall of 1940, however, one month after the release of the Rockne biopic, and with London besieged by the Nazi blitz, American public opinion began shifting in favor of the United States entering the war. In November another Gallup poll showed a response evenly split, with 50 percent now in favor of helping England even if it meant going to war.[38] Seemingly aware of this shift, Warner Brothers emphasized the patriotic theme of the film in the South Bend premiere, which featured Kate Smith singing "God Bless America" and FDR's son delivering a message from the president.[39]

The nationalist tone for the premiere of *Knute Rockne—All American* reflects changes in the final version of the film to emphasize a more bellicose masculinity. Screenwriter Robert Buckner disagreed with this emphasis in a letter about Warner Brothers' choice of the title, *Knute Rockne—All American,* calling it "jingoistic [and] flag waving."[40] While Buckner's final script had Rockne in the scene before the commission agree that football as "a safer outlet for the spirit of combat" is a kind of "pacificism," that word never made it into the film.[41]

The Lou Gehrig biopic, *Pride of the Yankees,* like *Knute Rockne—All American* and *The Iron Major,* defines sports in the historical context of World War II and portrays masculinity in martial terms. Unlike Babe Ruth, whom *Pride of the Yankees* represents as selfishly indulging his consumer appetites, Gehrig (Gary Cooper) does not rebel against the authority of Yankee managers Miller Huggins and Joe McCarthy. We see Gehrig attentively taking advice from Huggins about how to become a better fielder, and in a newspaper photo with his arm around McCarthy when the latter became the Yankee manager in 1932. In its opening dedication, *Pride of the Yankees* connects Gehrig's "courage and devotion" in the face of a deadly disease to the "valor and fortitude" of "the thousands of Americans on far-flung fields of battle."

World War II sports biopics celebrate male heroes for their strength, courage, self-discipline, hard work, and dedication to a cause; meanwhile, female characters who display similar qualities get little or no recognition. Instead, women in these films appear as the dependent beneficiaries of male economic success. Once Jim Corbett succeeds as a prizefighter, he buys his mother a sealskin coat and a house in the exclusive Nob Hill section of San Francisco. Just before his tragic death, Knute Rockne treats his wife Bonnie and his children to a Florida vacation. Lou Gehrig becomes a star and purchases his parents a house in suburban New Rochelle. Gehrig's strong and assertive mother, who worked so hard as a cook to put him through college, becomes his full-time fan, listening to his games on the radio and watching him play at Yankee Stadium.

Because the war years were a time when there would be less available to buy, these representations of consumerism, like the prizefight performances of strong masculinity in the Depression-era films, were more endorsements of the American dream than references to its actual existence. If the promise offered to men in these biopics was opportunity for upward mobility in return for the duty to defend it in wartime, women were assured the commodities that symbolized improved social status in exchange for their acceptance of helpmate roles. As Charles Eckert has stated, such an offer to women was central to movies by the late 1930s, when "the Hollywood studios had come to occupy a privileged position in the advertising industry . . . [through] products associated with stars in film and radio." In what Eckert calls "an economy suddenly aware of the importance of the consumer and of the dominant role of women in purchasing of most consumer items," sports films, whose narratives were assumed to appeal mostly to male viewers, needed to consider such strategies for appealing also to female viewers. Bette Davis, besides her role in attracting women viewers for *Kid Galahad,* appeared in a number of movie magazines, along with other 1930s female stars, "as mannequins modeling clothes, furs, hats, and accessories that they would wear in forthcoming films."[42]

Consumerism at odds with wartime sacrifice also functions to contrast the athletic hero in these films with the working-class males of his family. Jim Corbett buys his drunkard father and brawling brothers a bar in which they drink and brag about his prowess in the ring, and the senior Gehrig is similarly relegated to a marginal position of consumption, watching the spectacle of his son's middle-class masculinity. Ironically, this association with an idealized representation of masculinity is the same pleasure offered to male spectators of commercial athletics, who purchase a demonstration of physical strength and assertive self-determination generally denied to them in the industrial and postindustrial workplace.

Company Men and Rebels

In the decade after the war, American masculinity was defined in terms of what Michael Kimmel calls "two negative poles":[43] the suburban breadwinner at one end and the outsider rebel at the other. Frequently this split between normative and outsider masculinities was understood in terms of class identity. The greaser, beatnik, or communist missed out on the country's postwar affluence, and the company man, husband, and father worked to take advantage of how, according to Marty Jezer, "for the first time in history, a society had achieved the potential of producing a sufficient quantity of goods to provide every citizen with adequate comfort and economic security."[44]

Three sports films from this period represent masculinity in terms of this opposition, favoring the hard-working breadwinner who fits in and is productive. Like the war-era biopics, *The Babe Ruth Story* (1948), *The Pride of St. Louis* (1952), and *Somebody Up There Likes Me* (1956) offer their subjects as further real-life examples of the need to follow the direction of those with authority. Conversely, two noir fight films from this period, *Body and Soul* (1947) and *The Set-Up* (1949), criticize the exploitation of working-class athletes and reject the values of good and bad masculinity founded on a belief in the opportunity for self-definition that its protagonists never enjoy.

The Babe Ruth Story and *The Pride of St. Louis* both focus as much on off-the-field barriers that impede masculine performance and the need for parental guidance to overcome those problems as on the extraordinary athletic accomplishments of their subjects. *The Babe Ruth Story* shows the title character growing up in a rough Baltimore neighborhood with a tavern owner father who fluctuates between ignoring his son and treating him roughly so that he winds up in the care of Father Matthias at a Catholic home for delinquent boys. As an adult, Ruth demonstrates a great talent for baseball but lacks discipline. The film shows his overeating and drinking interfering with his performance on the field, justifying the discipline imposed by Yankee owner Jake Ruppert and manager Miller Huggins. To that point the film conforms to accepted knowledge of Ruth's fast-lane lifestyle and attempts by the Yankees to keep him performing, much as credible biographers such as Robert Creamer have reported. Yet *The Babe Ruth Story* goes on to make a more general statement about how management acts in players' best interests. By using the actions of Ruth's maternal wife, Claire, and Father Matthias to further contain the slugger's wild behavior, the film equates the authority of team owners with the parental and pastoral guidance of these two characters. This equation becomes explicit when Ruth tells a young player who urges him to take legal action after the Yankees dump him and the Boston Braves renege on an agreement, "No kid. That would be like suing the Church."

The Pride of St. Louis presents the story of another extremely accomplished ballplayer, Dizzy Dean, who like Ruth is portrayed as childish and self-indulgent. Also as in the Ruth biopic, *The Pride of St. Louis* justifies team control of the wayward player with another maternal wife character who makes it seem parental and reasonable. Both biopics therefore function less as historical narratives than as family melodramas, in the sense that Thomas Elsaesser describes such films as often showing "the failure of the protagonist to . . . shape the events and influence the emotional environment, let alone change

the stifling social milieu."[45] A prime example of how these two movies characterize their working-class subjects as childlike occurs in the Dean biopic
when, after he threatens to strike over the Cardinals' requiring him to stay
with the team on a day off, his wife Pat compares her husband's behavior to
"a child stealing cookies five minutes before dinner." "You can't always have
things the way you want them," she tells him, "unless you insist on twisting
and bending and forcing everything out of its natural shape."

While Ruth and Dean are prompted to fit in before suffering too much of
the pain of destructive rebellion, the Rocky Graziano biopic *Somebody Up There
Likes Me* shows that even confirmed rebels can still reform. Director Robert
Wise uses a noir visual style similar to that in his earlier prizefight picture, *The
Set-Up,* but with less critical content. In *Somebody Up There Likes Me,* the Graziano character overcomes his youth as angry urban delinquent and ex-con
to fit in and become middleweight champion and family man. Joan Mellen
sees this film as being "in the service of the conformity of the 1950s. It dictates
to men that they should enlist all their strength in a quest for success within
the established order."[46]

It Happens Every Spring (1949) doesn't feature a real-life athlete whose re-
bellious reputation needs recuperation, but it does emphasize respect for authority as part of ideal masculinity. The nervous intensity of the film's central character, Vernon Simpson (Ray Milland), demonstrates the dominant
masculinity of this period as "individualism within corporate life, urgently
trying to belong."[47] A chemistry professor, Simpson seeks a profitable application for his research so that he can marry Debbie Greenleaf (Jean Peters), the
daughter of the president of the college where he works. Simpson inadvertently discovers a chemical that repels wood and decides to capitalize on it by
pitching for the St. Louis Cardinals, putting the substance on the ball to make
his deliveries unhittable. This plan goes off course when he takes St. Louis to
the World Series, and his fiancée and her parents learn of his pitching. Although Simpson fears that because of his deception President Greenleaf won't
give him his job back and he'll also lose Debbie, he finds when he returns to
the college that the Cardinals have endowed a research laboratory with him
as director. Simpson's ability to make a productive application of his research
for both the Cardinals and the college demonstrates his understanding of the
right kind of company man masculinity. In fact, the film is so enamored with
this notion of success that it never concerns itself with the ethical problems
of what Vernon does to pitch so effectively or how the college gets the lab.

In contrast to the middle-class notion of masculine success defined in these
four postwar films, *Body and Soul* and *The Set-Up* celebrate men who rebel, justifying it as necessary resistance to those with power who seek to exploit them.

Charley Davis in *Body and Soul* and Stoker Thompson in *The Set-Up* stage their rebellion in the ring, winning fights they had been told to lose. Therefore, like the Depression-era films, these movies hold up the hope that success in the ring with the support of faithful friends and family can overcome constraints on the protagonist's masculine self-determination. As I show in chapter 4, both films use noir lighting, camera movements, and mise-en-scène to undermine such heroism built precariously on an emotional victory and the assistance of a few loyal supporters. These two movies therefore qualify the utopian masculinity found in most sports films by showing that even athletic success may not be enough to make the man. Nonetheless, it wouldn't be until *Fat City* (1971) and *Raging Bull* (1980) decades later that direct acknowledgment would come of what fight films—at least since the 1930s—had hinted at: that no matter how strong a fighter might be, his attitudes, behavior, and the larger circumstances around him can present an unbeatable combination.

Variations within Dominant Masculinity

Until very recently, a common assumption linking the few sports movies with Native American, African American, and Latino athletes as major characters has been the expectation that they accept a qualified masculinity. Rather than self-definition, nonwhite male athletes in sports films have compromised and fit in with a white-controlled society because of the belief that such cooperation produces progress for—or at least a positive image of—their race.

As part of the establishment of this pattern of racial representation, the discourse about white masculinity that had such a strong impact on the reception of movies showing Jack Johnson's prizefights also influenced other silent-era sports films about nonwhites. Daniel Bernardi notes how American films from the mid-1890s through the 1910s fit the social Darwinist "notion that Anglo Saxons, first, and the rest of Caucasians, second, were superior to all other 'races.'"[48] This assertion of racial superiority was defended with claims of white male restraint and self-control; in contrast, African American, Mexican, Native American, and Asian men appear either as childlike, subordinating themselves to their "betters," or else showing no control over their appetites for gambling, alcohol, sex, and violence.

Ward Churchill has observed that for as long as African American men have been shown in the movies as thieves and sexual aggressors, American Indian men have been similarly misrepresented—despite a very low level of rape in their cultures and the fact that they were the ones who had the most taken from them.[49] In general, the only other characterization of American Indian men has been as noble savages, about whom Daniel Francis says that strict acceptance of "their individual fate and of the ultimate demise of their people [has] endeared [them] . . . to white audiences."[50]

Both these characterizations occur in two silent-era films about American Indian athletes: *His Last Game* (1909) and *Strongheart* (1914). Charles L. P. Silet and Gretchen Bataille attribute the presence of American Indians in films after 1890 to a European American desire to assert the superiority of white culture by contrasting it to a notion of "savagism" associated with Native Americans.[51] By the end of the nineteenth century the violent subjugation of Native Americans had been fully accomplished, making them a safe subject for representation in films produced by whites; with Indians securely "in their place" on reservations, whites assumed that images of savagism were unlikely to generate the kind of revolt feared from African Americans inspired by a figure like Jack Johnson. The combination of physical assertion and acceptance of white authority used to characterize Native American athletes in *His Last Game* and *Strongheart* bring together these essentialized views of American Indians past and present.

Set in Arizona, *His Last Game* tells the story of Bill Going, the star player for a baseball team of Choctaw Indians, who kills a gambler in a fight but is allowed by the sheriff to play one last game against the Jimtown team before his execution. As such a synopsis makes clear, *His Last Game* represents a "civilized" system of due process that is far from fair and equitable. The white gambler offers Going a bribe to throw the game against Jimtown and then tries to drug the Native American ballplayer when he turns down the offer. In response, Going angrily initiates a fight and kills the gambler in self-defense once the latter pulls a gun. The circumstances of the fight would seem to allow Going something less than a capital offense, yet *His Last Game* omits Going's trial and sentencing in order to avoid the contradictions created by race in the legal system. Instead, the film emphasizes how, from his experience as a ballplayer, Going has adopted some of the values of white Protestant masculinity: he has learned the physical discipline to resist alcohol and has absorbed enough of the ethic of fair play to reject the offer of a bribe. His attack on the gambler, however, demonstrates that Going has yet to assimilate fully to "civilized" values.

In his last game, Going's outstanding pitching and hitting lead his team to victory over Jimtown. This performance proves that he understands and accepts the ideology that baseball promotes: he rejects gambling's attack on competition by winning the game, instead affirming the rules of masculine achievement that a fixed contest undermines. As if to reward the adoption of these values, a judge grants Going a reprieve of his death penalty, but notification of the stay of execution does not arrive until after the sentence has been carried out. This ending ironically invalidates the superiority of white law founded on masculine restraint and reason by showing the "savagery" of capital punishment, which here takes a life just as impulsively and irrationally as the Native American did in his fight with the gambler.

Strongheart is another film about a Native American athlete who tries to adopt white middle-class masculinity. Developed by the theatrical company Klaw and Erlanger from a play written by William C. DeMille, *Strongheart* was shot in 1913 using American Biograph studio space and personnel, including D. W. Griffith, who supervised the production. Griffith stock company veteran Henry B. Walthall stars as the title character, who meets two wealthy New Yorkers, Frank Nelson (Antonio Moreno) and his sister Dorothy (Blanche Sweet), during their vacation in the Dakotas, where Strongheart's tribe lives. Strongheart is so impressed with what Frank tells him about white culture that he decides to attend the Carlisle Indian School in Pennsylvania and then Columbia University. Like the other red-blooded young men at Columbia, Strongheart plays football, but he is implicated in a plot with gamblers to give another team the signals. He clears his name by proving that a teammate is the true culprit.

Strongheart has less success in his relationship with Dorothy Nelson. After his arrival in New York he and Dorothy fall in love, but when they inform her brother of their relationship Frank strongly disapproves. Strongheart's respect for the white man's culture forces him to give Dorothy up; a title card explains this imperative when it states that "Strongheart begins to feel the law of race."

It's here that *Strongheart* displays the marks of Griffith's influence. Throughout his filmmaking career, Griffith extended the cinematic discourse of social Darwinism by portraying nonwhites as a threat that strong white men overcome. Even when nonwhites are shown in his films as respectful and supportive, Griffith presents them as unable to fully assimilate when that involves interracial relationships. Another of Griffith's Biograph films, *The Call of the Wild* (1908), tells a very similar story of an American Indian who studies at a white school, plays football, and falls in love with a white woman but cannot stay with her. Alongside narrative situations in which whites defend themselves from savage attacks (as in *Birth of a Nation* 1915), the failed romance provides a second justification for the nonwhite "servitude, segregation and punishment" that characterize Griffith's films.[52] The last shot in *Strongheart* shows the title character back with his tribe, standing before a landscape of tall trees and a rushing stream. By representing Strongheart in this environment, the film naturalizes his choice to go back to his people, depicting it as a decision that has returned him to the setting in which he belongs.

While the images of Native American masculinity in *Strongheart* (repeated in its 1925 remake *Braveheart*) follow the sports film convention of portraying a woman's desire (here that of Dorothy Nelson) for the star athlete, they don't produce for the Indian athlete who is the object of that desire the same patriarchal authority enjoyed by white men. Instead *Strongheart* and *Braveheart* present American Indian men as models of the strong physicality that white men sought to reclaim. Philip Deloria describes a "'natural' physicality and strength," a self-composure and "balance" that were common in white perceptions of Indian masculinity at the time. He places this image of Indian masculinity within the larger "crisis" of American manhood to which sports was an important response during modernity: "Indians fit neatly into the nostalgic, antimodern image of professional and college sports. If athletes in general were emblems of post-frontier masculinity . . . 'Indians' could be objects not simply of racial repulsion but also—as they reflected nostalgia for community, spirituality, and nature—of racial desire . . . not only enactments of manhood and identity but spectacles of a lost time of 'natural' physicality and strength."[53]

In films such as *His Last Game, Strongheart,* and *Braveheart,* this image of natural, physical masculinity offers white viewers comforting ideas of gender and race in the face of unsettling social and economic changes. The respect that the American Indian protagonists show for white authority in the form of "law" allows these stories to contain the strength of their main characters and present them as models for a reenergized white masculinity.

Regardless of such appropriations of American Indian athleticism, "the idea of 'sport'" was not something entirely imposed upon native people from outside. Deloria points out that lacrosse "dominated the eastern region of Indian America for centuries," colonial commentators recorded the playing of "Indian football," and, like the sports developed by whites, "Indian contests had rules, traditions, and multiple layers of cultural meaning, with performances at once signifying status or rank, individual ability, religious observance, and group identity."[54] Moreover, Deloria adds that when Native Americans adopted (often from white missionaries) "American-style" football, baseball, and basketball, they modified these sports to fit existing cultural traditions (e.g., as part of "a refigured warrior tradition"). Another way in which Native American athletes played white sports was to use them to gain "an entrée into American society—a chance to beat Whites at their own games . . . get an education . . . an occasion for fun and sociality."[55] Just as African American athletes today often sell a similar notion of physical masculinity to middle-class white consumers, the American Indian men portrayed in these films look to derive something for themselves from the identities they model for whites. Also like black sports stars now, these Native American athletes face long odds in trying to make this transaction work for them. *His Last Game* limits the reward for Going's skill on the field to a reprieve that arrives too late to save his life. *Strongheart* ends with a vague promise that knowledge of white culture will benefit the tribe, while in *Braveheart* there is a more tangible return as the title character uses his time as a football star at a white college to learn what he needs to know about the legal system and win back fishing rights for his people. As Deloria states, while "American society valued them [Native American men] all the more for not becoming 'White,' [m]any Indian men refused that distinction, . . . using 'primitive' sports to acquire an 'assimilatory' education." At least for the Braveheart character that education produces worthwhile results, allowing him to "beat Whites at their own [here both legal and athletic] games."[56]

After World War II white interest in Indian masculinity eroded, the result of a decreased tolerance for even such controlled difference. What Deloria calls "total cultural hegemony" was imposed by federal policy aimed at destroying reservations and tribal political identity. As a result, "by the late 1940s, native people, who had little desire to eradicate their distinctiveness, found themselves viewed as recalcitrant and backward rather than 'pure' and 'primitive.'"[57] One sees this hegemonic attitude in *Jim Thorpe—All American* (1951), which shows its title character as "recalcitrant" for not accepting the decision of the Amateur Athletic Union in 1913 to take away his Olympic Gold Medals because he had played semipro baseball—enforcing codes of amateurism designed to keep bourgeois white men from having to face the best working-class competition.

Like the Native American athletes in silent-era films and in the Jim Thorpe biopic, the Ben Chapin character in *Body and Soul,* Jackie Robinson and Joe Louis in the biopics about them, and the Chicano boxer Tomás Cantanios (Lalo Ríos) in *The Ring* (1952) lack the discipline and autonomy central to the favored masculinity in most sports films. The black athletes in these films and even to some degree the young fighter in *The Ring* have athletic ability, but they must accept the control of white mentors because of a lack of strategic skills. Ben takes money from a crooked promoter that limits his choices, Robinson can only play if he accepts Rickey's direction, Louis overspends, and teenage Tomás has little idea how to navigate in the dangerous waters of professional prizefighting. The advice of their mentors directs them toward compromise with social authority, even when that brings insults and threats for Robinson, acceptance of economic exploitation for Joe Louis and Ben, or produces no measurable success for Cantanios.

By 1970 this portrayal of a nonwhite athlete controlled by a white mentor became increasingly inconsistent with the militant turn in the politics of racial identity. But, just as the sports films about black athletes in the decade after World War II both promote and contain the ideas of the civil rights movement that was gaining steam in those years, so *The Great White Hope* (1970) makes reference to black nationalism, but with a protagonist who is ultimately shown as not able to realize its goal of self-determination.

The Great White Hope features James Earl Jones as Jack Jefferson, an assertive African American heavyweight champion whose battles with white prejudice are based on the career of Jack Johnson, and who like Johnson lacks the self-discipline to protect his career. In his 1967 review of the Washington production of Howard Sackler's play *The Great White Hope* from which the film is adapted, Clive Barnes, writing in the *New York Times,* commented on the specter of Muhammad Ali haunting the production: "In these liberal times we can accept a black heavyweight champion, but can we accept a Black Muslim heavyweight champion? It is a question that seems to lurk like a silent ghost in the very corridors of Mr. Sackler's play."[58]

Although Jefferson's harassment by U.S. authorities in the film resembles Ali's prosecution for refusing induction into the U.S. military, rather than treat the racial and class issues that Ali raised, *The Great White Hope* moves in a safer direction by offering black masculinity as a catalyst for sexual revolution. Jefferson's problems with the legal system occur because of his personal relationship with a white woman, Eleanor Backman, rather than, as was the case with Ali, because he actively critiqued racism and colonization. *The Great White Hope* defines Jefferson's individual transgression as against a racism manifested in sexual repression—the film therefore demonstrates what Douglas Kellner and Michael Ryan call the counterculture's interest in liberating itself from square sexual behavior.[59] The equation in *The Great White Hope* of boxing with sex is underlined by several scenes in which Jones appears barechested, either in bed with Eleanor or training for the ring. Because of his relationship with Eleanor, Jefferson, like his real-life referent, has to flee the United States and gives up his title.

Robert Ray has noted that during the late 1960s and early 1970s the increasing ideological fragmentation of American society extended to the movies. As a result, "in their self-righteousness and refusal to admit competing possibilities," liberal films like *The Graduate* (1967) or *Bonnie and Clyde* (1967) and conservative movies like *Patton* (1970) or *Dirty Harry* (1971) appeared to polarize audiences, asking them to choose which values they would go to see represented on the screen. In fact, this polarization was less substantial than it appeared, as the two kinds of films shared the mythology of individualism, and Ray points out that "the wide popularity of both sets of movies" suggested that "far from choosing between them, most filmgoers went to both."[60] *The Great White Hope* pursues this inclusive approach, aiming itself at a left-wing audience sympathetic to racial injustice, and yet also placing great emphasis on that part of the countercultural critique, its attack on sexual repression, which would turn out to have the broadest appeal to the American belief in self-fulfillment. Like the corporate version of African American hip-hop culture, which has attracted the attention and dollars of young white males more for its "hard" sexual masculinity than for its racial politics, the emphasis in *The Great White Hope* rests on essentializing a sexual black masculinity rather than on making a statement about the history of discrimination against African Americans. *The Great White Hope* therefore illustrates how, because African Americans had by 1970 come to dominate the heavyweight class in prizefighting, films about boxing would represent them, but more important, it foregrounds widespread assumptions about African American masculinity that presented the least challenge to dominant conceptions of race.

By the 1990s the prominence of nonwhite, especially African American, men in the professional sports—exemplified in particular by the unrivaled stardom of Michael Jordan—reached the point where sports films began to make room for a less monochromatic ideal masculinity. Jordan himself in *Space Jam* (1996), African American protagonists in *White Men Can't Jump* (1992), *Above the Rim* (1994), *Love and Basketball* (2000), and the Chicano father/boxing trainer played by Jimmy Smits in *The Price of Glory* (2000)—all exemplify the qualities long associated with star white athletes: hard work, deferral of gratification, self-reliance, and responsibility to others.

While sports films have often been somewhat evasive about how the victories of a star athlete or coach benefit the group, six recent movies take greater care to defy the stereotype of nonwhite athletes as self-indulgent and therefore emphasize the specific social value of their performances. Michael Jordan in *Space Jam* and the Shep character in *Above the Rim* save others from violent exploitation. In *White Men Can't Jump, Love and Basketball,* and *Price of Glory,* the African American and Latino protagonists take good care of wives and children. Wesley Snipes in *White Men Can't Jump* even guides his white playground game partner to self-realization. Denzel Washington in *Remember the Titans* (2000) plays a high school football coach who helps a newly integrated team of white and black players overcome their prejudices about race.

Even before this recent elevation of nonwhite athletes to the status of ideal masculinity, their increasing presence in professional sports and the expressiveness and stylization they often employ had begun to influence white athletes. Vivian Sobchack cites an example of this influence when she refers to how, from the late 1950s through the 1970s, Major League Baseball saw an "increasing incorporation (both figuratively and literally) of non-Anglo players."[61] Several sports movies since the 1970s acknowledge this change by presenting a racially in-between masculinity, embodied in characters regarded as white—and who retain the utopian self-determination central to whiteness—combined with an expressive physicality associated with nonwhites.

The tremendous popularity of a film like Rocky (1976) can be explained as in part the result of how it offers this racially in-between but still recognizably white masculinity. In the 1970s movies about Italian Americans were part of a wave of both scholarly and popular interest in the cultural roots of the so-called "white ethnics."[62] The even broader appeal of The Godfather (1972) and Rocky, however, resulted in part from how they also fit into what Micaela di Leonardo describes as the larger society's postcounterculture ideas about identity. In contrast to stereotypes of WASPs as "too cold," bloodless, repressed, and selfish, and of blacks as "too hot," wild, promiscuous, and overly dependent, the Italian American men in these movies appeared—like baby bear's porridge—"just right": expressive, physical, and connected to family and community, yet strong and self-determining.[63]

Although the trajectory of the narratives in all five Rocky films is toward greater whiteness for its protagonist marked by material wealth and respectability, the Stallone character's success as a fighter always necessitates returning to his racial in-betweenness involving a white ethnicity shaded by an unselfconscious physicality. One of the cleverest ideological sleights-of-hand in Rocky is how, at a time when the number of well-paid blue-collar jobs in the United States had begun its unchecked slide, the film equates its title character's faith in the body with his realization of ideal masculinity founded on economic empowerment and social mobility.[64]

While Rocky achieves a heroic whiteness with just the right amount of forceful physicality, Raging Bull portrays its main character, Jake LaMotta, as controlled by, rather than in control of, bodily drives and desires. Raging Bull shows that LaMotta's success in the ring resulted from his very physical style. However, LaMotta misuses that same aggressive physicality in his private life outside the ring to repress his own sexuality and emotions, and those of others around him, because he sees them as impairing his ability to control his world. Consumed with this need for dominance, Jake views the sensuality of his wife Vicki, as well as the physical and verbal expressiveness of his brother Joey and the social relationships it promotes, as dangerous challenges to his masculine autonomy.

Raging Bull depicts LaMotta's frustrating battle for self-determination as a struggle against blackness. The fighter believes autonomy and control can be achieved by mastering his appetites, demonstrating his dominance in the ring (in particular over the stylish African American fighter Sugar Ray Robinson), and moving from the Italian American neighborhood where he grew up to bourgeois spaces on Pelham Parkway and later in Miami. Yet as the film represents these battles through expressionist imagery and a heavy reliance on shots from LaMotta's point of view, it suggests that his dark vision of the world comes from a distorted understanding of what is holding him back. In the scene of his fourth bout against Sugar Ray Robinson, we see through LaMotta's eyes the African American fighter loom menacingly just before finishing off the title character with a fierce beating that goes unopposed. Using such a visual style, this scene externalizes both LaMotta's failure to achieve the whiteness he desires and his insistence on pain and punishment as penitence for his inability to fully control his own identity.

Hard, Fast, and Beautiful: Female Masculinity and Women's Sports Films

> Despite unyielding barriers to full female participation, modern athletics have been a receptive site for gender innovation.
> —Susan K. Cahn

Most of the relatively few feature films about women athletes limit their achievements by enclosing them within much the same notion of self-negating femininity found in sports movies about men. The narratives in these movies center on how women can participate in sports yet retain a femininity defined primarily by their support for the needs of others, especially men and children. With just a couple of recent exceptions, women's sports films therefore operate inside what Judith Butler calls "The limits of the discursive analysis of gender [that] presuppose and preempt the possibilities of imaginable and realizable gender configurations within culture." Butler describes how this limiting discourse returns to "binary structures [of gender] that appear as the language of universal rationality."[65] Women's sports films have often shown female athletes who, through sports, develop "imaginable and realizable" gender identities that move beyond the "universal rationality" of men as the only strong, active "stars" and women as weaker supporters, or "team players." Such strong, accomplished women athletes evade the dominant assumptions about the distinctness of masculinity and femininity, at least until the stories—as they often do—pull them back into the "binary structures" of gender and away from their transgendered identities.

Although some post–Title IX films such as *Personal Best* and *Pumping Iron*

II (1985) to various degrees challenge this gender containment, it recurs with a vengeance in as recent a movie as *A League of Their Own* (1992) about the All-American Girls Baseball League (AAGBL). In a study based on interviews with former players, Susan Cahn notes that, during the league's existence from 1943 to 1954, some women in the AAGBL "blurred the sexual and gender cat-egories that governed everyday life." They did so by adopting on the field the athletic skills and mannerisms of male players and, off the field, pants, short hair cuts, and lesbian sexuality regarded as "mannish." In addition, Cahn says that the players with such masculine traits often combined them with "more traditionally feminine qualities of affection and tenderness, . . . an attitude of 'caring and sharing.'"[66] Director Penny Marshall's film shows some of this transgender mixture but ultimately discounts it by focusing on the more feminine main character Dottie (Geena Davis) and a narrative shift from the women's play on the field (which some AAGBL players saw as a pale imitation of their skills) to Dottie's choice to give up baseball and dedicate herself to her husband and family.[67]

To analyze how some women's sports films in places transgress dominant notions of femininity requires the recognition of revised gender categories, or what Eve Sedgwick calls "nonce taxonomies."[68] Put another way, these films ask the question posed by Judith Halberstam: "If gender has been so thoroughly defamiliarized, . . . why do we not have multiple gender options?"[69] However, most of these films return to a gender binary because on balance they are governed by a patriarchal logic that knows that, as Halberstam acknowledges, "the suppression of female masculinities allows for male masculinity to stand unchallenged as the bearer of gender stability and gender deviance."[70]

A brief analysis of four films about female athletes, *Hard, Fast, and Beautiful* (1951), *Pat and Mike, Personal Best,* and *Pumping Iron II* will illustrate in greater detail how versions of athletic female masculinity get represented, but then to various degrees contained, either by a maternal imperative or through the uncritical acceptance of other traits of a traditional femininity that limit women's achievement in sports.[71] In contrast, *Girlfight* (2000) and *Love and Basketball* break with this pattern by emphasizing a version of the female masculinity that Halberstam describes. While they retain the assumption of heterosexuality, these two films take a more feminist position than earlier sports movies about women by showing female athletes who surpass their male partners in competitive success and therefore refuse to be the only ones who compromise.

Written by Martha Wilkerson and directed by Ida Lupino for RKO, *Hard, Fast, and Beautiful* is a cautionary tale about the danger of women pursuing their own interests rather than nurturing others. When young Florence Farley (Sally Forrest) shows an aptitude for tennis, her mother, Millie (Claire Trevor), arranges for her to play in tournaments in Philadelphia, New York, Wimbledon, and Europe. As Florence wins matches, her loving but passive father and her dedicated boyfriend, Gordon, are pushed aside while she and her mother pursue their ambitions of fame and material rewards.

The 1931 John Tunis novel that furnished the story for *Hard, Fast, and Beautiful* ends with the tennis player daughter on her own and self-sufficient. RKO producer William Fadimar in a 1950 memo stated the need to change that ending to fit dominant ideas at the time about femininity as defined by marriage and not career: "The screen play demands and requires a happy ending in which the heroine relinquishes any idea she might have had of turning professional and decides to marry the boy she has always loved."[72]

Despite her success on the court, Florence becomes dissatisfied with playing tennis; she blames it for destroying her family and chooses instead a "normal" life by giving up the sport to marry Gordon. Millie's subsequent opposition to the marriage appears motivated by the fear that it would prevent her from continuing to benefit from Florence's athletic achievement. This use of Millie's divisive ambition to undercut the value of women's success in athletics is emphasized in the film's last scene, where we see the mother, rejected by her daughter for being greedy and selfish, left alone in an empty, dark tennis stadium.

Like *Hard, Fast, and Beautiful*, *Pat and Mike* cautions against excessive female ambition manifested through participation in sports, although it does allow for a woman to be a professional athlete and have a successful personal life, provided she has the guidance of a good man. As the film begins, the problem for Pat Pemberton (Katharine Hepburn), a talented golfer and tennis player, is the hole in her self-confidence caused by a lack of support from her fiancé, Collier Weld. Weld's insecure need to control Pat and have her play the role of "the little woman" supporting his career makes him trivialize her ambitions, even laughing derisively when she becomes nervous and plays poorly at her first professional tennis match.

Pat's confidence receives a boost, however, when promoter Mike Conovan (Spencer Tracy) takes on the management of her career. Conovan is also romantically interested in Pemberton, but unlike Weld, he shows that his attraction to Pat does not depend on limiting her athletic skills when he comments, "You are one beautiful thing to watch . . . in action." To make Conovan's handling of Pat seem her best option, the Tracy character shows Pat more respect than she gets from the selfish fiancé, or from the gamblers who back her financially but insist that she lose a golf tournament so that they can bet against her and clean up. One of the gamblers, Spec Cauley, demonstrates that he shares the boyfriend's conservative attitudes about gender when he comments "Golf is what I call a nice game. I mean it's dignified and fresh air, men and women both. Now you take them lady wrestlers, now that's somethin' I can't stomach, that's somethin' that shouldn't oughtta be allowed." Combined with his desire to sacrifice Pat's chance to compete, Cauley's endorsement of the "dignified" femininity of golf over the muscles and aggressive self-assertion of wrestling sums up the attitude found in *Pat and Mike, Hard, Fast, and Beautiful* and most films about women's sports: women can participate in athletics, but only to the degree that it doesn't impede, and better yet supports, conservative ideas of femininity and thus the greater importance of male control.

While he is less threatened by her success as an athlete, Mike's plan for what Pat should be and how it will advance his interests is in some ways no different from that of Weld or the gamblers. When two of the gamblers later confront Pat and Mike and threaten force if they don't comply with their plan, Pat demonstrates her own wrestling abilities by subduing them while Mike looks on in amazement. Seeing Mike's discomfort with her latest display of physical skill, Pat asks him, "What have I done?" "Too much," he responds. "I built ya up into some kind of a Frankenstein monster. . . . I like everything to be five-o, five-o. I like a he to be a he and a she to be a she." Faced on the one hand with Weld's derision and attempt to make her give up sports altogether, and the gamblers' request on the other that she lose on purpose, the film offers as balanced and responsible Mike's desire that Pat assume a middle ground between the strength and self-determination of which she is physically capable and his preference for a more conventional reliant and self-sacrificing femininity.

Susan Cayleff has commented that *Pat and Mike* recalls multisport athlete Babe Didrikson's marriage to George Zaharias, a former professional wrestler who would go on to promote his wife's athletic career.[73] In fact, the similarities between the relationship of the film's title characters and the marriage of Didrikson and Zaharias go beyond the women's athletic skills and the men's promotional roles. Babe Didrikson Zaharias was one of the best female athletes in the first half of the twentieth century, winning two gold medals in track and field at the 1932 Olympics and later becoming a successful golfer. Yet, like Pat, to escape the sexist attacks of men (especially sportswriters) threatened by her athletic abilities, she revised "her early reputation for masculine build and bravado . . . as she took up golf and carefully cultivated a feminine image."[74] Her marriage to Zaharias contributed to this compromise for Babe Didrikson, just as the romance with Conovan does for Pat.

Even production-history anecdotes involving director George Cukor, Hepburn, and screenwriter Garson Kanin show that *Pat and Mike* initially was about female athleticism but wound up as something else. In his biography of Cukor, Emanuel Levy notes that the director had always been impressed with Hepburn's "physical prowess . . . how she swam in his unheated pool in the dead of winter." Levy also quotes Hepburn as saying: "The film is based on the fact that I could do all those athletic things. . . . Gar [Garson Kanin] and I were good friends; he wrote it for me."[75] While, true to those comments, *Pat and Mike* begins as a showcase for Hepburn's athleticism, it eventually turns into a movie highlighting Spencer Tracy's regular-guy humor about Pat's attractiveness ("There ain't much, but what there is is cherce") and his common-sense reformation of her from a "Frankenstein monster" into a lady golfer.

However much *Pat and Mike* makes such containment of female athleticism appear to be in the woman's best interest, the experience of its real-life model, Babe Didrikson, was much more coercive. After her success at the 1932 Olympics, press coverage, especially that of well-known sportswriter Paul Gallico, attacked Didrikson, labeling her a "muscle moll" and criticizing her as representative of the dangerous tendency by some female athletes to display traits of masculinity. Didrikson's short hair, preference for pants and plain shirts, and especially her "sheer competence in the male realm of competitive sports" elicited the homophobic fears of sportswriters, in particular Gallico, whose muscle moll label for Didrikson, according to Cayleff, "came dangerously close to the mythic mannish lesbian."[76]

Didrikson's response to these attacks was to adopt a more feminine appearance. She exchanged the pants and plain shirts for dresses, put on make-up, and let her hair grow. One of her friends on the women's golf tour, Betty Hicks, described this change in the following manner: "She was not feminine by our culture's peculiarly warped definition of it, though she did acquire certain layers of the veneer of femininity. She painted her fingernails, curled her hair, put on high-heels, and wore lace-trimmed dresses."[77] Cayleff states that Babe Didrikson in the early 1930s embodied a combination of male and female qualities, but "lacking real economic or political power," she and other "members of the intermediate sex" could not "legitimize their difference." "Little wonder" concludes Cayleff, "that Gallico's and others' prose wounded Babe deeply and helped precipitate her fierce public rejection of all things 'masculine.'"[78]

Rather than represent the sexism and homophobia that Didrikson had to contend with, like most sports films about women, *Pat and Mike* excludes lesbian relationships as a possibility. The film also discounts the need for close ties between women because it suggests that the right kind of heterosexuality functions as an adequate source of fulfillment for the female athlete.[79] Babe Didrikson Zaharias's experience again provides a qualification of those assumptions. In the last years of her life, as the marriage to George Zaharias proved increasingly inadequate both physically and emotionally, Didrikson became involved in an intimate relationship with a young golfer named Betty Dodd that lasted until Babe's death from cancer in 1956. A posthumous TV biopic, *Babe,* made in 1975 under the close editorial control of George Zaharias, disregards the importance of this relationship, and no character representing Betty Dodd appears in that film.

In the wake of the second wave feminism of the 1960s and 1970s, women's sports and the films about them did and did not change. In the 1970s, 1980s, and 1990s, a feminist "language of equality, opportunity and rights," along with a growth in interest in fitness in the United States, fueled a rapid growth of sports for women.[80] Title IX of the Federal Educational Act, passed in 1972, established a legal basis for women's claims to equal athletic access within public educational institutions by prohibiting any exclusion or discrimination in programs receiving federal money. Susan Cahn notes that prior to Title IX, "at a typical midwestern university in the Big Ten Conference, men's athletics received thirteen hundred dollars for every dollar spent on the women's program."[81] The impact of Title IX, and the push for increased support for women's sports in general, were quickly felt; by the end of the 1970s the number of women competing in intercollegiate athletics had doubled. At the high school level the gains were even more dramatic, as girls' participation in sports increased almost sevenfold between 1971 and 1991.[82]

The growth in women's sports also created complications. Corporations have attempted to commodify the increase in women's interest in sports, and, like fan spectatorship, the resulting consumer products function as a substitute for an empowered athletic identity as well as the means with which to achieve it. Access for women has also been impeded by educational officials who have delayed the implementation of Title IX and in professional sports by corporate backers who have often demanded a "sexy" feminine image to make the performance of women athletes more sellable.[83] As the NCAA realized the federal government's intention to enforce Title IX, it began a push to take over women's college sports by offering television revenue in return for greater administrative control. Such merging of women's and men's sports programs has resulted in greater male control both at the administrative and coaching levels.[84] One justification for this increase in male control has been the need to prevent lesbians from assuming positions as coaches from which they could influence younger women. The prevention of lesbian involvement is regarded by male administrators as essential to generating mainstream appeal and attracting sponsorship with images of women athletes as heterosexual and feminine.[85]

While *Pat and Mike* tried to repress the homophobia that Babe Didrikson faced, twenty-five years later *Personal Best* represented lesbian sexuality, but only to show it as incompatible with success in athletic competition. The film tells the story of two female pentathletes, Tory Skinner (Patrice Donnelly) and Chris Cahill (Mariel Hemingway), who meet at the 1976 Olympic trials, become involved in a sexual relationship, break up, but then meet again at the 1980 trials, where Chris helps Tory earn a spot on that year's Olympic team.

The pressbook for *Personal Best* underlines the film's realism, stressing that it is about women's sports, not a lesbian relationship. It points out that certain scenes were shot on location at the 1980 Olympic trials in Eugene, Oregon; that nineteen world-class athletes appear in the film; that writer/director Robert Towne relied on the technical advice of athletes to ensure accuracy in the action sequences; that Mariel Hemingway trained for a year to prepare for her role; and that Towne chose costar Patrice Donnelly for her athletic skills as much as for her acting potential.[86]

As part of its realist aesthetic, *Personal Best* also represents the material benefits of Title IX on women's sports by showing Tory and Chris training with a team of female track and field athletes at Cal-Poly, San Luis Obispo. Yet along with the funding, facilities, and sophisticated training methods these women have access to, we also see the male control that they have to accept to get such support. *Personal Best* shows a liberal tolerance for lesbian sexuality, portraying the relationship between Chris and Tory as accepted by their coaches and teammates and building a closeness between the two pentathletes after they are no longer sexual partners. But while the film accepts the social possibilities of lesbian sexuality, it also assumes that heterosexual men know best how to win, and if women athletes want the social acceptance and validation that winning brings, the price they have to pay is compromise with them. It's for this reason that both Tory and Chris accept the verbal abuse of their coach Tingloff. He is a proven success at "motivating" women athletes to succeed in competition.

Chris's move to a heterosexual relationship has a similar motivation. After her breakup with Tory, Chris gets involved with Denny, a former Olympic swimmer. Because he knows about Chris's past, Denny assumes that she won't tolerate a more traditional male-controlled relationship. His desire for Chris therefore prompts him to allow her to determine the pace of their involvement, and he quietly supports the goals she identifies rather than trying to determine her actions. But in addition to how he helps recuperate heterosexuality from the overbearing Tingloff, Denny is also attractive to Chris because, as is consistent with a more traditional masculinity, he knows how to win. He has earned two gold medals as a swimmer, and when Chris is not performing well in the 1980 Olympic trials, Denny tells her that if competing against the other women bothers her, she should focus instead on competing against herself. By urging Chris to ignore the distance from other women that competition promotes, Denny implies that, if her goal is the social recognition of individual achievement, she should compete against that part of herself that wants to connect with them.

Therefore, instead of endorsing lesbian identity, *Personal Best* moves toward a slightly revised version of heterosexual relations. Chris and Tory break up as the result of an accident in practice in which Chris injures herself after Tory unknowingly moves a takeoff marker for the high jump. Linda Williams notes that rather than blame the breakup on "the pressures of competing in a patriarchal system of ruthless competition," *Personal Best* employs "the melodramatic contrivance" of such an accident to end the lesbian relationship. While Tingloff tells Chris that Tory moved the marker on purpose to hurt her, we see that the marker moved accidentally, yet the film never acknowledges how the idea of competition contributes to their separation. Instead, *Personal Best* simply shifts from the relationship between Chris and Tory to Chris's involvement with Denny.[87]

Christine Holmlund observes that while *Personal Best* includes both lesbian and heterosexual love scenes, the duration (longer) and placement (later) of the latter function to support the Chris character's shift from lesbianism to heterosexuality. This transition replaces the loving glances exchanged by Chris and Tory with Denny's voyeuristic looks, as when he first meets Chris at the pool or when he later looks up her shorts as she spots him in the weight room. While there are female point-of-view shots throughout the film, the end of *Personal Best* makes clear its interest in reclaiming Chris, the more feminine member of the lesbian couple, for heterosexuality. As Holmlund puts it: "The moral of the story is: a lesbian, and especially a femme, is not a lesbian when there's a man around."[88]

Holmlund points out, however, that despite this appeal to the heterosexual male viewer, *Personal Best* still retains its appeal to gay and lesbian audiences through its use of less butch, more conventionally feminine protagonists who could be read ambiguously as either lesbian or heterosexual. Like other mainstream "femme" films of the early to mid-1980s such as *Lianna* (1983), *Entre Nous* (1983), and *Desert Hearts* (1986), *Personal Best* employs femme lesbian lead characters to deny the conflation of lesbianism with the male as suggested by a butch appearance. Instead, according to Holmlund, the femme presents a "masquerade of femininity, not of masculinity." By "decking herself out as a girl," the femme lesbian character suggests that "femininity is neither necessarily heterosexual nor necessarily masochistic."[89]

Elizabeth Ellsworth supports Holmlund's analysis with documentation of how lesbian reception of *Personal Best* resisted the film's attempt at heterosexual containment. Lesbian reviewers reversed the return of Chris to heterosexuality by imagining that after the film's end she and Tory reestablished their sexual relationship, by privileging Patrice Donnelly as the star in opposition to the emphasis in the story and in promotional material on Mariel Hemingway, or by taking pleasure in what they saw as the film's unintentional lesbian verisimilitude. According to Ellsworth, such readings have often been part of lesbian communities' attempts to "carve out of dominant discourse space for their own sexualities, identities and existence."[90]

A fourth sports film about women, *Pumping Iron II,* combines conventional heterosexual objectification of the bodies of women athletes with the kind of critical masquerade of femininity similar to that which Holmlund observes in *Personal Best.* But in addition to how it shows a strategic use of a feminine appearance that heterosexuality accepts, *Pumping Iron II* also presents women athletes who successfully appropriate traits of masculinity. Especially when viewed in juxtaposition with subsequent television coverage of women's bodybuilding, one can see how one of the competitors in *Pumping Iron II* adopts a "mask" of traditional feminine characteristics that allows her to present a level of muscular development previously seen as "unfeminine." This masquerade reinforces Holmlund's point that a feminine look does not necessarily equate with weakness.

Pumping Iron II focuses on four women bodybuilders as they train and then compete in the 1983 World Cup Championship held at Caesar's Palace in Las Vegas. With her unprecedented muscularity, Australian powerlifter turned bodybuilder Bev Francis presents an aggressive challenge to the traditional notion of femininity that the judges seem intent on reinforcing. She represents what Mary Russo has called the "the female body . . . as unruly," not the passive, "to be looked at" sexual object described by Mulvey.[91] After a meeting with contest officials in which they make clear their intention to punish her challenge by enforcing a traditional notion of femininity, Francis parodies the fashion model poses of the more feminine contestants, who display vulnerability and availability rather than muscularity and self-confidence. Although she has muscular development that is clearly superior to that of any other woman in the contest, Francis finishes eighth in the competition. The film itself also displays a similar anxiety about female muscles in several scenes by fetishizing the bodies of some of the female bodybuilders as objects of heterosexual desire. We see them in the shower and in the pool at Caesar's Palace through voyeuristic shots that fragment and objectify their bodies. Despite the attempts at containment by the judges and the filmmakers, *Pumping Iron II* nevertheless shows Bev Francis as empowered by her muscularity, and it foregrounds as well the effectiveness of the combination of muscularity and feminine masquerade used by another bodybuilder, Carla Dunlap. Early in the film we see Francis winning a powerlifting competition back home in Australia. Friends and family, both men and women, cheer her on, and at a subsequent gathering, they listen attentively as she describes her plans and fears. Another example of the respect her muscular development has earned comes when Francis arrives in the United States and begins training with two male bodybuilders, Steve Michalik (a former Mr. America) and Steve Weinberger. The men show admiration and support for what Francis has achieved, as does Dunlap when she comments that Francis has a level of muscularity that most men would be proud to possess. We see another indication of how Francis's physical development has strengthened her sense of self-confidence when, even after finishing a disappointing eighth, she shows little reaction. Perhaps the unfair results were expected, but nonetheless Francis demonstrates emotional strength by not whining like a third participant, Rachel McLish, who is penalized for a padded swimsuit.

Moreover, *Pumping Iron II* focuses on how Carla Dunlap combines a muscularity second only to that of Francis with a mask of femininity. In one scene we see Dunlap practicing synchronized swimming in a Caesar's Palace pool to demonstrate her conventional beauty and grace. Yet in the next scene we also see and hear Bev and Carla discussing the arbitrariness and injustice of the "*Playboy* centerfold" notion of femininity used by most of the judges. Later, at a meeting of contest officials and contestants, Carla questions the standards of judgment. Official Oscar State responds: "The competitors must still look like women. . . . If they go to extremes and start looking like men, that's not what we're looking for in a women's contest." Dunlap's combination of a feminine appearance with her muscularity and assertiveness allays such fears and helps her win the contest.

The telecast in Spring 1994 on ESPN of the 1993 Ms. Universe bodybuilding contest shows that even Bev Francis herself later adopted a similar strategy of combining feminine masquerade with muscles. Before the individual routine of three-time defending champion Lenda Murray, a flashback shows her winning her first title in 1990, edging out none other than Bev Francis. In that 1990 contest Francis had attempted to look "feminine," appearing with permed, dyed-blond hair and make-up, but still as muscular as ever. Murray, too, combines impressive muscles with a feminine hair style and makeup. When the much less muscular but most conventionally pretty of the ten finalists in the 1993 competition, Sharon Bruneau, is the first to be eliminated, Carla Dunlap, now working as the color commentator for the ESPN telecast comments: "She [Bruneau] is a beautiful woman but that's not all it takes to be on the Olympia stage." This was just one of several occasions during the telecast when either Dunlap, or the other announcer, John Walls, commented on the shift that had taken place in judging criteria for women's bodybuilding to favor greater muscularity as well as feminine appearance. The combination of muscles and masquerade that Dunlap pioneered helped to redefine femininity in women's bodybuilding; but after she wins her fourth consecutive title, Lenda Murray in a postcompetition interview expresses concern that the larger society has not yet accepted such a change:

> Dunlap: Rachel McLish, movies. Corey Everson [six-time women's champion] movies. Carla Dunlap, television. What's going to happen with Lenda Murray?
> Murray: Television, that sounds really great. I don't know if I'm ready for that yet. . . . I'm going to take it one step at a time. The general public hasn't quite accepted female bodybuilders at this level of muscularity, so, let's see what happens.

Murray's reservations about mainstream acceptance of the level of muscularity she and other women bodybuilders achieved in the early 1990s proved well founded. Leslie Heywood has noted that when women's bodybuilding got started in the late 1970s it was modeled on beauty pageants. Contestants wore high heels and "were asked not to flex their muscles lest they appear too 'intimidating' or 'unfeminine.'"[92] Heywood credits Carla Dunlap with leading a "rebellion in which competitors kicked off their heels and began hitting front double-biceps poses," so that by the end of the 1980s a new kind of physical aesthetic had developed in women's bodybuilding, with "so much more muscle mass, vascularity, and striations that it made first wave bodies look tiny." Although Dunlap's skillful blending of intelligence, assertiveness, muscle, and femininity helped remove barriers, the pioneer in this new large look was Bev Francis, whose body Heywood describes as having "so much muscle mass and so little body fat that from the neck down it really was gender indeterminate." That type of muscular body became the standard in women's bodybuilding in 1990 when Lenda Murray won the first of her Ms. Olympia titles. Heywood designates the early 1990s as the second wave for women's bodybuilding, a time in which "really big women were the norm."[93]

A backlash against such muscularity would soon follow in the mid-1990s with the promotion of fitness training for women as an alternative to bodybuilding.[94] In contrast with the greater size and muscle definition of early-

1990s women's bodybuilding, fitness has emphasized less muscle mass and a return to the concern shown in *Pumping Iron II* with retaining traditional feminine looks. Like beauty contests, fitness contests often include swimsuit, evening gown, and interview rounds for participants. While Heywood in no way denies that fitness, like bodybuilding, demands extensive training and careful diet, she makes clear that its objectives are a traditional image of feminine beauty rather than muscle. The men who publish the influential magazines that have shifted their emphasis from women's bodybuilding to fitness claim that it is a decision influenced by an increase in reader interest in fitness and that they simply want to offer their readers a choice between the two. Heywood questions how much of a choice fitness represents for women, because she regards it as a notion of the female body defined by heterosexual male desire.[95] Her underlying assumption here is that a bodily aesthetic for women that advocates less muscularity confirms the masculinist belief that women should be physically weaker than men.

Viewed from this perspective, the reaction against women bodybuilders appears prompted by the challenge to male dominance they posed with their creation of female masculinity. As they achieved an unprecedented muscularity, female bodybuilders like Francis and Murray rejected the assumption that women are naturally soft and weak, instead demonstrating that "masculinity is a set of characteristics that women can possess as well as men."[96] In supporting this challenge, Heywood doesn't advocate a devaluation of women à la Camille Paglia, who has stated that "If civilization had been left in female hands, we would still be living in grass huts."[97] Heywood proposes instead that women participate in noncompetitive bodybuilding that doesn't pit them against each other, but rather allows women to build themselves up, to acquire traditionally masculine traits that help them maximize their potential and gain greater respect from others, especially men, many of whom have been socialized to value such physicality. Heywood gives personal testimony to the effectiveness of women's weightlifting: "One look at the way I carry myself and most people's response is, 'This chick don't take no shit.' Like affirmative action, like Title IX, like job opportunity, and all the other things that more traditional activisms opened up, this has affected me in daily, concrete ways."[98] While this endorsement of weight training for women may sound like another form of commodified self-improvement—and there is no denying that as consumers of weight training products and services, women to some degree are supporting male authority grounded in corporate profits— nonetheless Heywood argues persuasively that a prerequisite of unified action is for individual women to "change how they see themselves . . . and how they are seen by others."[99]

Acceptance of this strategy of women appropriating masculinity requires acknowledgment of how feminist film analysis has frequently pathologized normative masculinity. While Laura Mulvey, in her follow-up essay to "Visual Pleasure and the Narrative Cinema," advocates the "masculinization" of female film characters and viewers, Jane Gaines notes correctly that one of the most effective uses of the psychoanalytic approach Mulvey and other feminist scholars have employed is its ability to "make a stunning connection between aberrant eroticism and 'normal' male [hetero]sexual behavior." Gaines also notes, however, the danger of using such psychoanalytic readings, with their assumptions of active male desire for control and female passivity, to "arrive at the impossibility of female expression in male-dominated culture."[100] Without denying the importance of these feminist critiques, which identify some of the problems with conventional notions of sexual difference, scholars like Judith Halberstam and Leslie Heywood advocate that women appropriate aspects of masculinity—such as physical strength and self-confidence—not to replicate the controlling behaviors that characterize dominant masculinity, nor to accept the idea in *Personal Best* that competitive success precludes lesbian sexuality, but rather to protect themselves from being victims of patriarchy.

Gina Prince-Bythewood's film *Love and Basketball* doesn't shy away from its female protagonist's appropriation of masculine traits, but it also uses lighting and a general visual style to underscore the danger of adopting the wrong kind of masculine isolation. For much of this story of the on-again, off-again relationship between two young basketball players, Monica Wright (Sanaa Lathan) and Quincy McCall (Omar Epps), cinematographer Reynaldo Villalobos uses cooler lighting on Epps to show how he tries to emulate the "calculating personality" of his NBA player father. This very "blue" cool lighting conveys the emotional cost of such a self-absorbed identity when the father and son meet after the former's marital infidelities have become known. Describing this scene, Villalobos commented: "When his father comes in, it's very blue and cool—alien, uncomfortable and painful. I wanted a cold feeling so I took out the color."[101]

Villalobos and Prince-Bythewood then use this same cool light to represent negatively Monica's temporary adoption of a similar "masculine" self-interest. After her relationship with Omar falls apart, we see a scene of Monica playing in an international professional league in Barcelona, pictured with the same blue tones to emphasize her isolation.[102] This sequence contrasts with the warmer tones of the film's final scene in which Quincy, having given up his unsuccessful NBA career, holds their young daughter as they watch Monica play in the WNBA.

Girlfight also presents a young woman who suffers loneliness and disconnection because of her masculine toughness, but like *Love and Basketball* it differs from earlier films about women athletes by ending with an affirmative view of the benefits of female masculinity. *Girlfight* tells the story of a teenage Latina from the Red Hook projects in Brooklyn named Diana Guzmán (Michele Rodríguez) who channels her frustration and anger into boxing. The film shows that Diana's drive to fight comes in large part from an unhappy home life with an abusive single father, Sandro (Paul Calderón). As she trains hard with the help of a demanding but generous teacher, Hector (Jaime Tirelli), Diana develops enough strength and self-confidence to stand up to her father and hold her own in a relationship with another young fighter, Adrian (Santiago Douglas), whom she meets in the gym. In the film's riskiest but most impressive scene, Diana defeats her boyfriend to win an amateur tournament.

A big reason why critics have described *Girlfight* as a "knockout" and "a bravura reworking of the teenage rites-of-passage genre" is the presence of Michele Rodríguez, who with very little acting experience got the role of Diana by answering a casting call ad in *Backstage*. Rodríguez spent several months in the gym getting ready for the part, and her male trainers, who started out not believing that women should box, were impressed enough to think she justified the presence of female fighters in the ring.

The Sony Pictures Web site for *Girlfight* shows that the money behind the film seems comfortable with the marketing potential of such female masculinity. Beneath photos of a scowling Rodríguez dressed for battle, a synopsis describes *Girlfight* as "heralding a new femininity for the new century" and its

Female masculinity in *Girlfight* (1999).

Diana (Michele Rodríguez) defeats her boyfriend to win an amateur tournament in *Girlfight.*

star as "ferocious" and "fierce."[103] *Girlfight* goes beyond past sports movies about women by showing a female athlete who doesn't just overcome the constraints of traditional femininity to succeed in her chosen sport against other women but wins in competition with a man. Yet when asked whether the film therefore advocated a higher level of physical development for women, director Karyn Kusama, who has boxed herself, answered that the physical assertion Diana shows works for some women and not for others.[104] That's true as far as it goes, but it leaves unanswered the question of how important physical strength is to the achievement of equality for women.

Male Athletes As Erotic Spectacle

> *Japan takes what is best from other cultures and makes it her own.*
> —*Hiroko Uchiyama in* Mr. Baseball

Part of the containment of female athletes in sports films involves objectifying them. Hepburn shows a lot of leg playing tennis and is described by Tracy's character as "cherce [choice]" meat. *Pumping Iron II* presents numerous shots of female bodybuilders' buttocks and breasts. *Personal Best* offers similar voyeuristic looks representing Denny's desire for Chris, and the players in *A League of Their Own* complain about the short skirts that owners require them to wear, yet they appear in them in all the scenes of games. Even a less compromised movie such as *Love and Basketball* reassures us that Monica can still be feminine despite her masculine athleticism on the basketball court by showing her in one scene in a tight spandex dress.

While such sexual objectification is offered to us as reassurance that these athletes are still feminine, sexualized images of male bodies in sports films are less common, and when they do occur they are either disavowed by the film's emphasis on narrative action or else offered within the context of female desire.[105] Examples of narrative displacement can be found in two precode films, *Sports Parade* (1932) and *Winner Take All,* in which we see male athletes with very little on in locker rooms and female love interests who visit them there. In the 1980s and 1990s, such display of male athletes became more common, though movies such as *Pumping Iron II, Bull Durham, Mr. Baseball* (1922), and *Any Given Sunday* are still careful to offer male bodies within the framework of narrative competition or as the objects of female desire.

Steve Neale has argued that narrative film, especially masculine action genres, frequently eroticize the male body but disavow that representation by focusing on the narrative and the ideal male's performance in response to its challenges and conflicts. A similar disavowal occurs in sports films, even when there is some acknowledgment of female desire for the male athlete. *Bull Durham* offers an example of this, acknowledging the visual pleasure that the Annie Savoy character (Susan Sarandon) receives from looking at two players for a minor league baseball team (played by Kevin Costner and Tim Robbins). At several points in the film, we are asked to share her visual pleasure as the two players appear with very little on in the locker room and at Annie's home. Yet as the story in *Bull Durham* unfolds, it increasingly displaces this eroticized looking with questions of what will happen to the team (How will their season go?) and in particular the performance on the field of the two male leads (Will the young phenom, Robbins, make it to the big leagues? Will Costner's veteran catcher character succeed in molding the young player for success?). In its final scenes, the film also replaces Annie's eroticized looking at players' bodies with a more conventionalized romantic relationship with the Costner character focused on supporting his new career as a manager.

An important variation from this disavowal occurs in the film *Slap Shot* (1977), which instead acknowledges the commodification of the male body. *Slap Shot* tells the story of the Charlestown Chiefs, a minor league hockey team located in a Pennsylvania town where the biggest employer, a steel mill, has just laid off 10,000 workers. To keep the team from folding, the Chiefs' player-coach, Reggie Dunlop (Paul Newman), has his team adopt an aggressive, hypermasculine style of play to generate fan interest.

Several of Dunlop's players, including star forward Ned Braden (Michael Ontkean) resist the coach's call for such an exaggerated masculinity, prefer-

ring instead a more "dignified," less performative identity defined in a traditional manner through ideas of fair play and individual achievement within
a team context. Ned's insistence on a more traditional masculinity not only
costs him ice time, it creates problems in his personal life as well. His wife hates
being stuck in a small mill town, but Ned insists on his masculine prerogative
to decide where they should be and therefore what she should do.

Despite the reservations of Ned and a few other players, the Chiefs' fans,
in particular women, love the new "he-man" style of play, with its transcendence of the rules and limitations that Charlestown residents know all too
well. The stands fill up for games and the team is besieged by crowds of scream-
ing groupies. The Chiefs' new exaggerated masculinity is best represented by
the Hanson brothers, three anarchic young players who entertain themselves
with toys in their motel room but are the most aggressive players on the ice,
embodying a kind of adolescent outlaw masculinity.

Reggie clearly understands how the new style that the team has adopted is
about selling dreams of empowerment and sexual fantasy in a manner that
parodies more conventional notions of athletic masculinity. Just how objec-
tified the players have become, however, hits home when Reggie goes to see the
team's owner, a wealthy widow who tells him that she thinks of the Chiefs as
just another one of her properties, and that she can profit more by shutting
down the team at the end of the season and writing it off as a loss on her taxes.

The Chiefs nevertheless maintain an aggressive style and bully their way
to the championship game for the league title. Determined not to be outdone,
the other team matches the Chiefs' use of intimidation, and a bench-clearing
brawl breaks out. *Slap Shot* uses this "big game" scene to underline not only
the performative nature of its hypermasculinity, but also how the self-com-
modification of the players resembles the sexual objectification of women as
Ned decides to upstage the fight's male spectacle by taking off his clothes on
the ice. As he slowly removes his uniform and protective equipment, the
women in the crowd, including Ned's estranged wife, make clear with their
enthusiastic response that he is giving them what they really want. Neale
specifies that the eroticization of the male body in action films is frequently
disavowed by the violent conflict to which male characters are subjected within the narrative.[106] Ned's striptease to upstage the brawl literally reveals the
eroticized male body underneath that disavowal.

Toby Miller argues that such objectification of the male body in representations of men's sports works to undermine what he calls "the functionalist
world of total domination by straight, orthodox masculinity."[107] The representation of male bodies in sports films like *Slap Shot* and *Bull Durham* could
appeal to various forms of desire, not just those of heterosexual women as

Ned (Michael Ontkean) strips in *Slap Shot* (1977).

represented in the narratives, but also to gay viewers and to women who, recognizing the constructedness of masculinity as it is shown in these films, appropriate its strength and confidence for their own uses. Miller cites examples of how networks and corporations that mediate sports or use it to sell their products have begun "niche targeting" of men's sports to gay men and straight and lesbian women in ways that certainly complicate the assumption that male athletes offer only models of hegemonic masculinity.[108]

Regardless of such resistant appropriation, foregrounding the male body as visual spectacle may also work to support dominant masculinity. While the assumption based on Mulvey's work has been that the objectification of the body subordinates it to the control and definition of the gaze, within what Jim Collins calls the "perpetual circulation and recirculation of signs that form the fabric of postmodern cultural life," the ability to hold the attention of the viewing subject becomes a form of power.[109]

Seen this way, one might interpret the greater representation of the male body in sports film as another way that masculinity redefines itself in response to the changes of postmodern culture. Just as a racially in-between masculinity seeks to emulate the competitive excellence and appealing stylization of nonwhite athletes, this objectification diversifies the appeal and representational power of the male athlete beyond the role of protagonist in traditional narratives of self-assertion. Sports films therefore are responding to a culture of image flow in which holding the viewer's attention has become as important as being the bearer of the look. Yet there is also no denying the trend toward women and nonwhites increasingly asserting themselves in sports. And as recent films such as *Price of Glory, Love and Basketball,* and *Girlfight* show, these groups are not only buying these postmodern images of ideal athletic masculinity, but they are making them their own.

Notes

1. Arthur Brittan, *Masculinity and Power* (London: Blackwell, 1989), 78.

2. Michael Kimmel, *Manhood in America* (New York: Free Press, 1996), 82.

3. Richard L. McCormick, "Public Life in Industrial America, 1877–1917," in *The New American History,* ed. Eric Foner (Philadelphia: Temple University Press, 1990), 104.

4. Kimmel, *Manhood in America,* 84.

5. Burl Noggle, *Into the Twenties: The United States from Armistice to Normalcy* (Urbana: University of Illinois Press, 1974), 153.

6. Gail Bederman, *Manliness and Civilization: A Cultural History of Gender and Race in the United States, 1880–1917* (Chicago: University of Chicago Press, 1995), 12.

7. Kimmel, *Manhood in America,* 82–83.

8. Ibid., 83.

9. Ibid., 85–86.

10. Ibid., 86.

11. Lois Rudnick, "The New Woman," in *1915, the Cultural Moment,* ed. Adele Heller and Lois Rudnick (New Brunswick, N.J.: Rutgers University Press, 1991), 70.

12. Steven Mintz and Susan Kellogg, *Domestic Revolutions: A Social History of American Family Life* (New York: Free Press, 1988), 111.

13. Elliott Gorn and Warren Goldstein, *A Brief History of American Sports* (New York: Hill and Wang, 1993), 145.

14. Ibid.

15. Bederman, *Manliness and Civilization,* 15.

16. See Randy Roberts, *Papa Jack: Jack Johnson and the Era of White Hopes* (New York: Free Press, 1983); Al-Tony Gilmore, *Bad Nigger: The National Impact of Jack Johnson* (Port Washington, N.Y.: Kennikat Press, 1975); Jeffrey T. Sammons, *Beyond the Ring: The Role of Boxing in American Society* (Urbana: University of Illinois Press, 1990); and Dan Streible, "A History of the Boxing Film, 1894–1915: Social Control and Social Reform in the Progressive Era," *Film History* 3, no. 3 (1989): 243.

17. Streible, "History of the Boxing Film," 249.

18. Bederman, *Manliness and Civilization,* 17.

19. T. J. Jackson Lears, "From Salvation to Self-Realization: Advertising and the Therapeutic Roots of the Consumer Culture, 1880–1980," in *The Culture of Consumption: Critical Essays in American History, 1880–1980,* ed. Richard Wightman Fox and T. J. Jackson Lears (New York: Pantheon Books, 1983), 3–6.

20. Bederman, *Manliness and Civilization,* 11–12.

21. Ibid., 9.

22. Vito Russo, *Celluloid Closet: Homosexuality in the Movies* (New York: Harper and Row, 1987), 21.

23. Gorn and Goldstein, *Brief History of American Sports,* 129.

24. Ibid., 147–48.

25. Ibid., 148.

26. W. L. Umphlett, *The Movies Go to College* (Rutherford, N.J.: Fairleigh Dickinson University Press, 1984), 16.

27. Gerald Mast, *The Comic Mind: Comedy and the Movies,* 2d ed. (Chicago: University of Chicago Press, 1979), 127.

28. Ibid., 138.

29. Ibid., 283.

30. Ibid., 284.

31. *Variety,* June 2, 1937, rpt. in *Variety Film Reviews* (New York: Garland, 1983).

32. Ava Rose and James Friedman, "Television Sports As Mas(s)culine Cult of Distraction," in *Out of Bounds: Sports, Media, and the Politics of Identity,* ed. Aaron Baker and Todd Boyd (Bloomington: Indiana University Press, 1997), 6.

33. Steven A. Riess, "Sport and the Redefinition of American Middle-Class Masculinity," *International Journal of the History of Sport* 8, no. 1 (1991): 16.

34. Benjamin Rader, *American Sports: From the Age of Folk Games to the Age of Televised Sports* (Englewood Cliffs, N.J.: Prentice Hall, 1990), 90.

35. Bob Connell, "Masculinity, Violence, and War," in *Men's Lives,* 3d ed., ed. Michael S. Kimmel and Michael A. Messner (Boston: Allyn and Bacon, 1995), 127.

36. *Variety,* October 9, 1940, rpt. in *Variety Film Reviews.*

37. Quoted in Michael R. Steele, *Knute Rockne, a Bio-Biography* (Westport, Conn.: Greenwood Press, 1983), 44.

38. William Manchester, *The Glory and the Dream: A Narrative History of America, 1932–1972* (Boston: Little, Brown, 1974), 228.

39. David Karnes, "Hollywood Movie Premieres between the Wars," *American Quarterly* 38, no. 4 (Fall 1986): 565.

40. Murray Sperber, *Shake Down the Thunder: The Creation of Notre Dame Football* (New York: Henry Holt, 1993), 481.

41. Robert Buckner, *The Life of Knute Rockne,* original screenplay, University of Notre Dame Archives, 108. I would like to thank Murray Sperber for providing me with a copy of this script.

42. Charles Eckert, "The Carole Lombard in Macy's Window," in *Fabrications: Costume and the Female Body,* ed. Jane Gaines and Charlotte Herzog (New York: Routledge, 1990), 108.

43. Kimmel, *Manhood in America,* 236.

44. Marty Jezer, *The Dark Ages: Life in the United States, 1945–1960* (Boston: South End Press, 1982), 119.

45. Thomas Elsaesser, "Tales of Sound and Fury: Observations on the Family Melodrama," in *Movies and Methods,* ed. Bill Nichols, vol. 2 (Berkeley: University of California Press, 1985), 177.

46. Joan Mellen, *Big Bad Wolves: Masculinity in the American Film* (New York: Pantheon Books, 1977), 245–46.

47. Quoted in Kimmel, *Manhood in America,* 241.

48. Daniel Bernardi, "The Voice of Whiteness: D. W. Griffith's Biograph Films (1908–1913)," in *The Birth of Whiteness: Race and the Emergence of U.S. Cinema,* ed. Daniel Bernardi (New Brunswick, N.J.: Rutgers University Press, 1996), 107.

49. Churchill notes that Eldridge Cleaver's famous description of how white men have historically positioned themselves as "omnipotent administrators" and African American men as "ultramasculine menials" has applied equally well to filmic portray-

als of Native American men. See Ward Churchill, *Fantasies of a Master Race: Literature, Cinema, and the Colonization of American Indians* (San Francisco: City Lights Books, 1998), 190–92.

50. Quoted in ibid., 180.

51. Charles L. P. Silet and Gretchen Bataille, *The Pretend Indians: Images of Native Americans in the Movies* (Ames: Iowa State University Press, 1980), 57.

52. Bernardi, "Voice of Whiteness," 112.

53. Philip Deloria, "'I Am of the Body': Thoughts on My Grandfather, Culture, and Sports," *South Atlantic Quarterly* 95, no. 2 (Spring 1996): 329.

54. Ibid., 326.

55. Ibid.

56. Ibid., 330–31.

57. Ibid., 334.

58. Clive Barnes, "Howard Sackler's Play Given at Arena Stage," *New York Times,* December 14, 1967, 58.

59. Michael Ryan and Douglas Kellner, *Camera Politica: The Politics and Ideology of Contemporary Hollywood Film* (Bloomington: Indiana University Press, 1988), 23.

60. Robert Ray, *A Certain Tendency of the Hollywood Cinema, 1930–1980* (Princeton, N.J.: Princeton University Press, 1985), 299–300.

61. Vivian Sobchack, "Baseball in the Post-American Cinema; or, Life in the Minor Leagues," in *Out of Bounds: Sports, Media, and the Politics of Identity,* ed. Aaron Baker and Todd Boyd (Bloomington: Indiana University Press, 1997), 183.

62. Micaela di Leonardo, "White Ethnicities, Identity Politics, and Baby Bear's Chair," *Social Text* 41 (Winter 1994): 170.

63. Ibid., 176–77.

64. Stanley Aronowitz describes this loss of blue-collar jobs that began in the 1970s in his book *From the Ashes of the Old: American Labor and America's Future* (Boston: Houghton Mifflin, 1998), 238–44.

65. Judith Butler, *Gender Trouble: Feminism and the Subversion of Identity* (New York: Routledge, 1990), 9.

66. Susan K. Cahn, *Coming On Strong: Gender and Sexuality in Twentieth-Century Women's Sport* (New York: Free Press, 1994), 197.

67. Pat Jordan, "The Girls of Summer," *American Way* 25, no. 12 (June 15, 1992): 40.

68. Eve Kosofsky Sedgwick, "Axiomatic," in *The Cultural Studies Reader,* ed. Simon During (New York: Routledge, 1993), 243–68.

69. Judith Halberstam, *Female Masculinity* (Durham, N.C.: Duke University Press, 1998), 20.

70. Ibid., 41.

71. I estimate that only about thirty feature films have been made about female athletes since 1930.

72. Quoted in Wendy Dozoretz, "The Mother's Lost Voice in *Hard, Fast, and Beautiful,*" *Wide Angle* 6, no. 3 (1984): 52.

73. Susan E. Cayleff, *Babe: The Life and Legend of Babe Didrikson Zaharias* (Urbana: University of Illinois Press, 1995), 211.

74. Cahn, *Coming On Strong,* 214.

75. Emanuel Levy, *George Cukor* (New York: Morrow, 1994), 204.

76. Cayleff, *Babe,* 88.

77. Ibid., 156.

78. Ibid., 95.

79. Ibid., 248.

80. Cahn, *Coming On Strong,* 246.

81. Ibid., 250.

82. Ibid., 254, 259.

83. Ibid., 249, 255.

84. A recent study indicates that while the number of women's teams is at an all-time high, the percentage of those teams with women coaches is at a record low, having dropped from 90 percent when Title IX was enacted to 45.6 percent in 2000. "Women Playing More, but Coaching Less," *New York Times,* May 3, 2000, C31.

85. Cahn, *Coming On Strong,* 266.

86. Elizabeth Ellsworth, "Illicit Pleasures: Feminist Spectators and *Personal Best,*" *Wide Angle* 8, no. 2 (1985): 50.

87. Linda Williams, "*Personal Best* Women in Love," *Jump Cut* 27 (1982): 12.

88. Chris Holmlund, "When Is a Lesbian Not a Lesbian? The Lesbian Continuum and the Mainstream Femme Film," *Camera Obscura* 25–26 (1991): 154.

89. Ibid., 147–48.

90. Ellsworth, "Illicit Pleasures," 54.

91. Mary Russo, "Female Grotesques: Carnival and Theory," in *Feminist Studies/Critical Studies,* ed. Teresa de Lauretis (Bloomington: Indiana University Press, 1986), 214.

92. Leslie Heywood, *Bodymakers: A Cultural Anatomy of Women's Bodybuilding* (New Brunswick, N.J.: Rutgers University Press, 1998), 28.

93. Ibid., 28–29.

94. Ibid., 29.

95. Ibid., 44.

96. Ibid., 35.

97. Quoted in Marianna De Marco Togovnick, *Crossing Ocean Parkway* (Chicago: University of Chicago Press, 1996), 92.

98. Heywood, *Bodymakers,* 60.

99. Ibid., 57.

100. Laura Mulvey, "Afterthoughts on 'Visual Pleasure and Narrative Cinema' Inspired by *Duel in the Sun,*" in *Feminism and Film Theory,* ed. Constance Penley (New York: Routledge, 1988), 169–79; Jane Gaines, "Women and Representation: Can We Enjoy Alternative Pleasure?" in *Issues in Feminist Film Criticism,* ed. Patricia Erens (Bloomington: Indiana University Press, 1990), 77–78.

101. Andrew O. Thompson, "Love and Basketball," *ICG Magazine,* Mar. 2000, 50.

102. Ibid., 48–50.

103. This Web site is at <http://www.sonypictures2000.com/nav2000.html>.

104. Aaron Baker, "A New Combination: Women and Boxing Films, an Interview with Karyn Kusama," *Cineaste* 25, no. 4 (2000): 24.

105. In a recent article, Toby Miller describes how television representation of male athletes has begun to show them as the objects of the eroticized gaze of gay men as well as heterosexual women. See "Out at the Ball Game: The New Look of Sports," *Chronicle of Higher Education,* August 17, 2001, B14–15.

106. Steven Neale, "Masculinity As Spectacle," in *Screening the Male: Exploring Masculinities in Hollywood Cinema,* ed. Steven Cohan and Ina Rae Hark (New York: Routledge, 1993).

107. Toby Miller, "Commodifying the Male Body, Problematizing 'Hegemonic Masculinity'?" *Journal of Sport and Social Issues* (November 1998): 431–46.

108. Ibid.

109. Jim Collins, "Genericity in the Nineties: Eclectic Irony and the New Sincerity," in *Film Theory Goes to the Movies,* ed. Jim Collins, Hilary Radner, and Ava Preacher Collins (New York: Routledge, 1993), 246.

4   A Left/Right Combination: Class and American Boxing Films

Confidence, Ruben Luna believed, was the indispensable ingredient of success, and he had it in abundance—as much faith in his destiny as in the athletes he trained. In his own years of battling he had doubts which at times became periods of terror. With a broken jaw wired into silence, he had sucked liquid meals through a tube, wondering if he were even sane. After a severe body beating and bloody urination in the dressing room, he had wondered if the big fights and large sums he had thought would be coming but never came could be worth all that he endured.

—Leonard Gardner

Feature films about prizefighting speak more directly about capitalism and class than most other sports movies because they present both forceful representations of self-reliance and the drive for wealth, but they also mediate the material forces in the history of the fight game that have complicated such utopian optimism. In many boxing films the force of that material reality first manifests itself in the protagonist's decision to enter the ring. The conditions motivating this choice offer one of the least obfuscated representations of working-class life in American movies: a young man (or in a few recent films, a young woman) chooses to fight because it appears to be the best and sometimes only way to escape a life of hard work with little to show for it—what Stanley Aronowitz calls "the mode of surplus extraction" that operates in the ghetto or barrio.[1]

Professional boxing in the United States has always attracted youth from subordinate groups with limited opportunity for self-determination. As immigrants from Europe, African Americans, and Latinos settled in U.S. cities, young men from these communities would often learn to fight in order to protect their neighborhoods against incursions by other racial and ethnic groups. Because of the limited work opportunities available in urban slums, boys who showed special aptitude in street fighting, and were willing to undergo intense training and physical punishment, would perfect their pugilistic skills in the hope of becoming professionals.[2] From 1870 to 1920, the Irish dominated professional prizefighting, producing nine world champions during the 1890s and more title holders and contenders than any other group up until World War I. As their opportunities in other areas of the national economy improved, however, Irish dominance over the sport declined, and other ethnic groups gradually moved into professional prizefighting. After the turn of the century, Jewish fighters began to win titles; they were second only to the Irish in the number of champions they produced during the 1910s. Boxing also provided men of Italian and Eastern European extraction with their first major successes in professional sports during the same decade. Italian Americans retained their major role in prizefighting through the end of World War II; by that time the Jews had followed the Irish out of the inner-city neighborhoods, replaced as boxers by African Americans and Chicanos. While boxers of Jewish, Italian, and Eastern European backgrounds who fought before World War II were generally smaller, and therefore in lower weight classes, promoters could still generate a high degree of interest and draw large crowds by setting up fights between opponents from these ethnic groups and by billing the contests as struggles for national or religious pride.[3]

Only a select few who have entered the ring have attained wealth and fame, and even fewer have succeeded in overcoming the effects of crooked management. Steven Riess states that, given their tendency to overspend as a way of compensating for their poor background, their lack of any other marketable skills, and the often devastating effects of the punishment they took, boxers usually have had a bleak future. "Many retired fighters, especially the club boxers who didn't have any substantial fame, ended up about where they had started out," he concludes.[4] Joyce Carol Oates concisely describes the pyramidal structure of prizefighting when she says that it has "a limitless supply of losers, but . . . very few stars."[5]

While most prizefight films show the circumstances that motivate the choice to enter the ring, only a brave few trace the connection between the reification and exploitation of working-class labor common to prizefighting as a business and similar practices in the larger economy. Instead, the unfair remuneration and lack of guidance given to the young boxer often gets blamed on a criminal antagonist: the dishonest manager, gambler, or promoter whose charismatic characterization of evil and greed suggests that he alone is to blame for the difficulty the fighter has escaping the constraints of proletarian labor. In this way movies about boxing fit the tendency in the American social problem film whereby conflicts are individualized, therefore more easily overcome, and "never appear systemic."[6]

The most common narrative for the prizefight film involves the boxer's quick rise from disadvantage to the title, followed by a fall from grace, usually due to the seduction of wealth and fame, and some form of redemption in the third act. The heroic triumph over long odds implied in that bare-bones plot summary explains in part why so many boxing films have been made, and also probably why some of the biggest male stars in the movies have played boxers, including Jimmy Cagney, John Garfield, Errol Flynn, Kirk Douglas, Burt Lancaster, Paul Newman, Tony Curtis, Elvis Presley, James Earl Jones, Robert De Niro, Tom Cruise, Antonio Banderas, Denzel Washington, and the biggest box office boxer of all time, Sylvester Stallone, whose move onto the A list started with *Rocky* (1976).

Yet even the Hollywood fighter who overcomes the barriers of intense competition and criminal exploitation usually finds that, rather than escape the boundaries of class difference, his initial success in the ring simply makes him a better consumer, an identity consistent with the logic of a business in which he is as much a product as what he buys with his cut of the winnings. The clothes, cars, and nightlife that follow the fighter's initial success represent what Fredric Jameson calls the "embourgeoisment of the worker, or better still, the transformation of both bourgeois and worker into . . . the consumer" that has been an important part of liberalism's rejection of class difference in American society.[7]

Because he makes his living with his body, rather than through education and the upward mobility of professionalization, the movie prizefighter often lacks the knowledge of how to use his victories to gain greater self-determination. Leger Grindon refers to this fight film topos when he notes that the boxer embodies the physical in an environment in which power equals money, strategy, and social position that are controlled by the manager, promoter, or gambler.[8] Recognizing this, several of the more politically aware boxing films such as *Golden Boy* (1939), *City for Conquest* (1940), and *Body and Soul* (1947) present education and culture as preferable modes of social mobility.

The Price of Glory (2000) recalls an even more prominent response to the disadvantage of class in boxing films when it endorses, not individual empowerment through formal education, but the protection and support of family and community as the young fighter's best defense. *The Price of Glory* contrasts the self-interest represented by the investment advice of an accountant brother-in-law to a young boxer, Sonny Ortega (Jon Seda), with the instruction in class and racial self-defense offered by his ex-fighter father Arturo (Jimmy Smits)—himself a graduate from the school of hard knocks. *The Price of Glory* therefore shows how the unity of family and community in Chicano culture provides an effective response to the problems of class exploitation and racial discrimination for Sonny, as well as for his two younger brothers, who also want careers in prizefighting. Probably to appeal to a adolescent demographic, the film camouflages the father's cultural and class politics within a story of generational conflict in which two of the three sons resist Arturo's guidance because of their desire to act on their own in a way the larger society values (and exploits). To really make its point, *The Price of Glory* shows the youngest son, Johnny (Ernesto Hernández), who believes most strongly in the working-class and Chicano identity his father teaches him, dying as a result of his one attempt to go it alone against the predators who feed off young fighters.

Common to the redemption of the fighter in films as different as *Winner Take All* (1932), *Kid Galahad* (1937), *Spirit of Youth* (1938), *Keep Punching* (1939), *Golden Boy, Body and Soul, The Harder They Fall* (1956), *Girlfight* (2000), *Play It to the Bone* (2000), and *The Hurricane* (2000) is the realization that the individualized success of victory in the ring by itself doesn't allow the fighter to transcend the constraints of class, race, or gender. *The Price of Glory* is typical of these films in that it shows how the additional support the fighter needs takes the form of a family or familylike group. Moreover, these family structures often bring with them the baggage of racist and sexist ideas of white or male superiority. As Michael Rogin points out, even a politically aware film like *Body and Soul* "conditions Jewish/black solidarity on Jew knocking out black."[9] *The Price of Glory,* perhaps because it is so intent on celebrating the strength of the Ortega family, exaggerates the problematic, if standard, portrayal of the main female character as supportive and loyal by giving her four men to worry about. In other words, boxing films that avoid a simplistic utopian response to economic disadvantage often achieve only partial success in showing the relations with other forms of social identity that define class. To the degree that these films represent effective collectivity, they establish class identity in both senses described by Raymond Williams: as "including all who are objectively in that economic situation," and as "a formation in which, for historical reasons, consciousness of this situation and the organization to deal with it have developed."[10] In many of these films, however, class identity—like the boxer—tries unsuccessfully to stand alone.

Class and History

Terry Eagleton has written that the study of ideologies analyzes "the ideas, values and feelings by which [people] experience their societies at various times."[11] The historical variability of class identities implied in this statement is salient in boxing films, which from the 1930s to the present have responded to the influences of the Depression; changes in the Hollywood film industry and national and international politics after World War II; and the need to rethink ideas of class in relationship to other aspects of social identity that became apparent with the rise of the civil rights and women's movements.

Since this chapter emphasizes those boxing films that foreground working-class identity and its historical determinants in tension with the utopian self-determination that has characterized Hollywood cinema, it will focus on three groups of boxing movies. The first, made during the Depression years, serves as a metaphor for the society at large, attempting to resolve a contradiction between the values of rugged individualism and the values of community. Most boxing films of the 1930s celebrate a working-class hero who tries to beat the odds to escape the urban jungle and the exploitation of the fight game. In the spirit of the New Deal, however, these pictures also stress the importance of group support to help the protagonist succeed.

The second cycle analyzed here includes seven films released between 1947 and 1956. Three of these, *Body and Soul, The Set-Up* (1949), and *Champion* (1949), use a combination of noir and neorealist styles to criticize the exploitation of working-class fighters and capitalist culture in general. In reaction to the political repression of the blacklists and the increasingly nonwhite makeup of prizefighting, films from the 1950s such as *The Ring* (1952), *The Joe Louis Story* (1953), *The Harder They Fall,* and *Somebody Up There Likes Me* (1956) shift their focus to race and liberal models of assimilation as the best response to class and racial disadvantage.

Befitting its postmodern moment, the third cycle, which starts in 1976 and is ongoing, is the most diverse. *Rocky* and *Raging Bull* (1980) feature protagonists who believe passionately in their ability to single-handedly transcend social categories such as class and race. Stallone's film endorses that goal, while Scorsese's presents Jake LaMotta as achieving a kind of Christian transcendence for finally accepting its impossibility. I analyze also how several of these most recent films, including *Rocky, When We Were Kings* (1996), and *Don King: Only in America* (1997) represent Muhammad Ali, either to support his politics of anticolonialism and black unity, or to discredit his critique of whiteness to support the mythology of a self-reliant individualism. Finally, this chapter examines several of the most recent boxing films, including *The Great White Hype* (1996), *The Hurricane, Girlfight,* and *Play It to the Bone* for how they illustrate that issues of class, race, and gender are best understood by recognizing their tensions and interdependence.

The Populist Prizefighter As New Deal Hero

By pitting one fighter against another with only their hands to do battle, and by roping the combatants off from the rest of the world, boxing presents a dramatic metaphor for the rugged individualism that has traditionally been a central element of Hollywood's mythology. But while fight films celebrate the ideal of self-sufficiency, those made during the Depression era also question the sport's underlying myth of omnipotent individualism. Responding to the concerns that many in the United States felt about the country's future during the 1930s, these Depression-era boxing films endorsed a populist ideology, mythologizing the often ethnic or black fighter whose success depended upon group support and whose actions promoted traditional agrarian notions of the common good.

During the 1930s, jobless rates of 25 percent and higher for young people prompted an especially large number of working-class young men to try their hand at prizefighting.[12] Around eight thousand boxers entered the ring as professionals in the United States during that decade, although only a small percentage of those achieved title contender status.[13] The popularity of boxing as one of the few avenues to the American dream in those lean years may explain the large number of Hollywood films about prizefighting made during the 1930s. Such Depression-era films depict boxing as a means of advancement for disenfranchised urban youth and at the same time use the sport as a metaphor for the economic hard times.

Warner Brothers dominated the Depression cycle of boxing films, presenting them in the form of the aesthetically spare, "socially conscious" melodramas that were the hallmark of the studio in the 1930s. Not that other Hollywood studios left the making of boxing pictures entirely to Warner Brothers. MGM, Warner Brothers' political and stylistic opposite, made one of the most commercially successful boxing films of the decade, *The Champ* (1931). Unlike most of the later Depression-era films about boxing, *The Champ* makes a last-ditch effort to endorse the myth of individual self-reliance, essentially discounting any notion that social or economic forces might put limits on the rise to success.

Wallace Beery stars as Andy, a punch-drunk ex-heavyweight champion who lives a roller-coaster life in Tijuana with his young son Dink (Jackie Cooper). The ex-champ has occasional hot streaks at the craps table, but much of the time he is drunk and broke. Dink's mother, Linda (Irene Rich), and her wealthy second husband, Tony (Hale Hamilton), offer to take custody of the boy so as to give him a stabler home life and a chance to go to school, but Dink prefers to stay with his father, who loves him intensely. Anxious to better provide for Dink, Andy steers clear of the casinos and bars long enough to get a fight with the heavyweight champ of Mexico. For most of the bout the Mexican fighter punishes the out-of-shape American, but Andy somehow knocks out his opponent with a desperation punch. Despite his victory, the strain and punishment of the fight prove too much for Andy, and he dies of a heart attack in his dressing room. The film ends with Dink crying uncontrollably at the loss of his father and running into his mother's arms.

The Champ responds to concerns about the Depression through the class opposition between Andy and Tony as potential fathers for Dink. Meanwhile, the hard times that befall the Wallace Beery character are shown as resulting not from the general economy but from his weakness and lack of discipline. The film never acknowledges that Andy's problems with gambling and alcohol could be linked to his lack of marketable job skills, and it suggests that he is simply punchy from too many blows to the head. Because The Champ gives no institutional or social explanation for this vocational injury, it makes Andy seem like a big child—lovable, but physically and intellectually inferior to the successful Tony.

In his discussion of Hollywood's thematic paradigm, Robert Ray describes how American films often avoid taking sides in ideological debates, preferring instead to assert that an unlimited potential for new achievement and wealth in America can overcome contradictions or conflict.[14] According to Ray, classic Hollywood's avoidance of choice between conflicting value systems usually results in a narrative structure that splits the film's "moral center" from its "interest center." The Champ sets up this split by endorsing Tony as representative of family, traditional morality, and the work ethic (even though by his own account his status and wealth derive from inherited privilege), while casting Andy as an underdog for whom the audience roots despite his weaknesses. Sneak previews of The Champ confirmed Andy as the center of viewer interest. An initial version of the film in which he loses to the Mexican champion before dying received such a poor response from test audiences that MGM head of production Irving Thalberg ordered the last scene reshot so that the American wins the fight. At a second preview of the revised version in which Andy wins, the audience cheered the final scene.[15]

The Champ also avoids the need for choice by displacing the class conflict between Andy and Tony into frontier imagery of conquest presented in the defeat of the Mexican champion.[16] Jameson points to ideas of the frontier and its promise of new wealth as another of the arguments that liberalism has used to deny the existence of class.[17] Richard Slotkin describes how, as early as the 1870s, the newly developed mass-circulation press sought to effect a similar displacement of the class warfare that had erupted between workers and the corporate order. Even if the cause of the workers represented the "values of self-government and freedom of opportunity" on which the country was founded, such demands for political and economic self-determination threatened to undermine the profits of big business.[18] To avoid this obvious contradiction between corporate interests and egalitarian ideals, the press used the imagery of race war taken from the mythology of the frontier to describe the class conflict between workers and management. Working-class people were often likened to "redskin savages" as a way of undermining their ability to use democratic institutions in battles against landlords and employers. Such comparison recast class conflict in terms of "a choice . . . between 'savageism' and civilization."[19]

More than fifty years later, *The Champ* still employs this strategy by shifting its focus from the class conflict between Andy and Tony to the fight between the white American boxer and the Mexican champ. In making this shift, the film also counts on audience antagonism toward Mexico left over from a recent conflict with the United States. In 1927, after the Mexican Congress passed legislation claiming a bigger share of the profits from oil that American companies were pumping in Mexico, Washington had threatened military intervention.[20] The defeat of Mexico's heavyweight champion provides a convenient means by which domestic class anger, fueled in American society by the Depression, can be projected outward onto the racial other. As the two fighters represent their respective countries, the United States can also symbolically reassert its claim to new frontiers and natural resources that make class warfare unnecessary at home.[21] *The Champ* not only succeeds in performing this displacement but knocks out two of the inconvenient "lower" characters with one punch—defeating the Mexican and at the same time enabling Andy to die heroically. The film's last image of Dink in his mother's arms becomes a social Darwinist affirmation of "progress and right order" achieved through the removal of "inferior" peoples in favor of those better fit to survive the Depression.[22]

Another early 1930s film about prizefighting, Warner Brothers' *Winner Take All,* depicts a similar prizefight between a Mexican and a U.S. boxer, but with somewhat different implications. *Winner Take All* tells the story of an Irish fighter from New York, Jimmy Kane (Jimmy Cagney), who has ruined his health by fighting too often and therefore goes to a dude ranch in New Mexico for a rest cure. At the desert resort, he meets a young widow named Peggy (Marian Nixon), whose little boy Dickie (Dickie Moore) is also ill. Soon after meeting Jimmy, Peggy receives a letter from her insurance company stating that it will not honor her late husband's life insurance policy because he had missed several premium payments just before his death. To cover Peggy's and Dickie's expenses at the spa, Jimmy decides to go to Tijuana and win the money in a prizefight. Jimmy's victory over a Mexican boxer functions like the climactic fight in *The Champ,* displacing any stand the film might take against the insurance company with race war imagery of European American conquest of the West. By showing the greed and indifference of the insurance company, *Winner Take All* seems to be a relatively left-wing film; nevertheless, like most socially engaged Hollywood stories, it avoids an in-depth examination of class conflict, allowing the exploiters of the working class, in the words of Charles Eckert, "to recede like ghosts as quickly as they are glimpsed."[23]

This political waffling might be best explained by *Winner Take All*'s use of a populist ideology. Populism had a strong influence on Depression-era Hollywood—as it had during periods of economic crisis dating back to the nineteenth century—because it flattered the audience and at the same time preserved the essential values of capitalism. It had developed originally to articulate the support of middle-class rural Americans for the rights of the individual in the face of industrial revolution and growing corporate control of the economy. In all its later incarnations, populism nostalgically longed for a return to the land from big, immigrant-filled cities, and it sympathized with farmers or small-town mercantile capitalists rather than with the corporate executives, advocating local rather than federal government.[24]

The combination of progressive idealism and sentimental conservatism in populism made it appealing to both sides of the political debate. Its attacks on monopoly capital and its defense of the "common man" appealed to the Left, but the solutions it offered—free enterprise, the work ethic, return to the land—also fit the conservative agenda. Hollywood liked this broad appeal, its "safe patriotic cure-all which demanded change in the form of past achievement," because it combined "Depression cynicism with the American Dream."[25]

Winner Take All embodies this hybrid ideology. On the one hand, the insurance company's refusal to pay off on the policy of Peggy's late husband represents the type of corporate greed and indifference that from the left populist viewpoint was largely responsible for the economic hardship of the 1930s. On the other hand, Jimmy's solution to Peggy's financial problem also portrays a conservative response to this crisis: through the heroics of the small capitalist, the rugged individualist, who works not only for his own success but also for that of the community, the country will be saved.[26] His cure finished, Jimmy returns to New York to resume his boxing career, promising to send for Peggy and her son as soon as Dickie has finished his treatment. Jimmy, however, soon meets and becomes infatuated with an attractive young society woman, Joan Gibson (Virginia Bruce). As Joan and her friends make their rounds from ringside to nightclub table to her Park Avenue apartment, they embody another of the favorite populist villains, "the degenerate children of the wealthy class, spoiled and lazy wastrels who carelessly permit business affairs to deteriorate."[27] Joan interferes with Jimmy's business as a boxer by leading him on romantically. Although at first mildly excited by Jimmy's "primitive" energy, she never takes the boxer seriously as a lover. Jimmy, on the other hand, is obsessed with winning Joan, even going so far as to have plastic surgery to repair his broken nose and a cauliflower ear after she comments that he would be handsome without those battle scars. Despite warnings from his manager about Joan's insincerity, to protect his new face Jimmy abandons the aggressiveness in the ring that had earned him a shot at the lightweight title. When he learns, however, that she has skipped his title fight to go on a cruise to Cuba, Jimmy returns to his former style of all-out attack to finish off his opponent and win the championship just in time to board the ocean liner before it sails. Jimmy finds Joan with a blue-blood beau and exacts his revenge, knocking down the boyfriend and then Joan herself. His break with Joan not only removes her as the distraction that almost ruined his boxing career but also lets him be a hero whose title victory serves the film's populist "community"—in this case Jimmy's hardworking trainer, his honest manager, and Peggy, who agrees to marry him after all. In other words, individual assertiveness succeeds because of, and has value for, a supportive group—an idea consistent with the collectivist ideology of the New Deal, which provided Hollywood with still another way to attract a large audience by not aligning itself against capitalism.[28]

Differences between city and country life in several of these 1930s boxing films also functioned as a displacement for more troubling class conflicts. Populism depicted the city as the home of shysters and sharpies, the monopolists, and rich society snobs who have caused the Depression, a place where "the success ethic has given way to the jungle ethic."[29] Rural areas, on the other hand, recalled the country's agricultural past, its traditional values of self-help, its rugged individualism, yet also its good-neighborliness.

Even though prizefighters in the 1930s came largely from ethnic and racial groups who lived in large urban centers, several Depression-period films depict boxers who escape the city to find a better life in the country. Jimmy Key in *Winner Take All* finds his future family in the New Mexico desert. Ward Guisenberry (Wayne Morris), the boxer in *Kid Galahad,* is himself a farm boy who wins the heavyweight title with the help of his city-wise manager, Nick Donati (Edward G. Robinson), but finds true happiness by marrying Donati's sister Maria, who lives in the country with her mother. In *They Made Me a Criminal* (1939), the manager of city-bred boxer Johnny Bradfield (John Garfield) kills a reporter and then frames the fighter for the crime. To avoid the police, Johnny goes on the lam, winding up on a date farm in Arizona. The farm is a kind of reform school for a group of juvenile delinquents (the Dead End Kids) and for Johnny as well, as he soon becomes a positive role model for the boys and falls in love.

Whether or not the prizefighters in these films succeed in escaping to the country, their ability to survive the dangers of the city and the fight racket depends on the help of others. Although the boxers have plenty of rugged individualism, each of them also finds that he cannot make it to the top—or deal with the dangers and tragedies of the fight game—alone. For example, Ward Guisenberry in *Kid Galahad* relies on his manager Nick and Nick's girl-friend Louise (Bette Davis), to keep gangster Turkey Morgan (Humphrey Bo-gart) at bay and help him win the title. In *Knockout* (1941) the wife and train-er of Johnny Rocket (Arthur Kennedy) save him from killing himself in the ring. And after he is blinded in the ring, Danny Kenny (Jimmy Cagney) in *City for Conquest* relies on his trainer and manager to set him up with a newsstand business. As is evident from these examples, however, the people who help the boxer tend to be family members or friends. By such qualification of the individualism of the prizefighter, Hollywood carefully avoids endorsing col-lectivism of a more dangerous political stripe. One hundred years earlier, de Tocqueville had described this ideological compromise when he noted how "the circle of family and friends" fits well into the American mythology of individualism: "with this little society formed to his taste, [the individual] gladly leaves the greater society to look after itself."[30]

The critique of self-interest in these 1930s boxing films is generally limit-ed to the figure of the gangster or the crooked manager who seeks to exploit the prizefighter. These films avoided the idea that the rugged individualism celebrated by populism "had actually helped create the monopoly capitalism the populists resented," and that "laissez-faire had been more a cause of the Depression than its solution."[31] Therefore, in *Kid Galahad* and *Golden Boy,* gangsters try to take over control of the boxer's career for their own gain; in *They Made Me a Criminal,* a dishonest manager frames his fighter for murder; and in *City for Conquest* and *Knockout,* crooked managers use foreign sub-stances to cause the fighter/protagonist to lose.

The infiltration of organized crime into boxing during the 1930s resulted in part from economic forces set in motion by corporate interests and the free market. The temperance movement, which had succeeded in installing Pro-hibition in 1920, drew its support not only from rural Americans threatened by the growing number of immigrants settling in urban areas but also from industrialists concerned about the effects of alcohol on worker productivity. The enormous profits that Prohibition made available for bootleggers provid-ed the capital with which organized crime infiltrated the fight game, displac-ing the professional politicians who had largely controlled prizefighting up to that time.[32] Once on the inside, mobsters such as Frankie Carbo, a.k.a. Mr. Big, who was the prime mover in prizefighting from the mid-1930s until the late 1950s, made enormous profits from betting on fixed fights.

After mob control of prizefighting was established, its gambling opera-tions continued to function very much in accordance with the practices of capitalist entrepreneurship that had spawned it. As James Smith points out, "betting a known stake against the possibility of improving on it amid sometimes dangerous uncertainties" describes not only gambling but the mythology of "the whole American experience," from the opening of the West to European American settlement to the contemporary promise of economic opportunity through investment in business that forms an integral part of the American dream.[33] Realization of this similarity demonstrates, as Smith also notes, that while "gamblers are usually assumed to be alienated from traditional values," in fact "gambling is preeminently social, and goes so far as to echo prevailing cultural values."[34] Even though, as the 1930s boxing films show, the gamblers who controlled professional prizefighting used extreme measures—including intimidation and violence—to reduce the "uncertainties" threatening their investment, one need look no farther than the previously mentioned U.S. government threats to invade Mexico or the violent strikebreaking tactics of various industries in the early 1930s to see that such practices were common in American capitalism.

By adopting a populist view of the causes and solutions for the economic problems of the Depression, Hollywood boxing films could appear socially conscious while avoiding deep analysis of the real economic issues. Nonetheless, with the possible exception of *The Champ,* these films at least attempted to represent the problems of ethnic working-class youth, who saw boxing as a possible means of escape from the mean streets of America's urban slums. Moreover, while these films celebrate individuals of extraordinary physical strength, self-confidence, and tenacity, they also demonstrate that from the maze of forces at work in the business of professional boxing, no one makes it out on his own.

Race Films and "The Blues Hero"

> The world that the prizefighter comes from is one that understands the hypocrisy surrounding the commercialization of the body in a bourgeois, Calvinist-tinged culture.
>
> —Gerald Early

Like their Hollywood counterparts, the two prizefight pictures of the 1930s that featured African American boxers, *Spirit of Youth* (Grand National) and *Keep Punching* (M.C. Pictures), tell the stories of young fighters saved from the dangers of the big city through the guidance of friends and family who return them to rural populist values of hard work, self-discipline, and community. Following this narrative formula allowed the white producers of these "race" films to appeal to African American audiences without contradicting the bourgeois values endorsed by the Hollywood pictures that were shown most of the time in black theaters. Moreover, *Spirit of Youth* and *Keep Punching* starred real champions, Joe Louis and Henry Armstrong respectively, giving them a veneer of biographical realism that authenticated their populist stories as a historically valid response to the skepticism caused by the Depression.

Of course, for most African Americans, the limited economic opportunity of the 1930s was nothing new; Louis's management team was well aware that for a black man even to get a shot at the heavyweight title, he would have to reassure whites that he presented no threat to the racial status quo. That meant a change from the surly "jungle killer" image that white sportswriters had constructed for Louis to the "mother-loving, clean-living, humble young man" that is Joe Thomas, the lead character in *Spirit of Youth*.[35] Armstrong, because he fought in lighter weight classes, was affected less by the racial symbolism of beating white opponents. But, like Louis, he still had to overcome racist resistance to black champions as well as the general "pugilistic depression" of the 1930s resulting from a "rash of 'foul fights' and criminal dealings."[36]

The country/city opposition that structures both these films displaces racial conflict rather than the class difference avoided by the Hollywood boxing movies. As Daniel Leab notes, the majority of theaters for black audiences were located in the South, where on the screen, as in the ring, overt interracial conflict was taboo because of whites' fear that, in the words of James H. Stevenson, it "might upset the theory of [their] social superiority or imply social equality."[37] Furthermore, Hollywood operated under the assumption that the response of southern audiences to racial themes was a bellwether for audiences in the North.[38] Even a film made a decade later in 1947, *Body and Soul,* risked direct conflict between an African American boxer and his white promoter only when it was motivated by the black character's loyalty to a white friend. Instead, both *Spirit of Youth* and *Keep Punching* present segregated worlds and narrative conflicts that pit black against black: the young boxer and his supporters against the gambler and the sexualized woman who hope to lead him astray and then bet on his opponent.

While they ostensibly conform to dominant discourses of self-formation and segregation, both films also reverse the race film convention of casting dark-skinned blacks as the criminal heavies.[39] The gambler villains, as well as the women who plot with them, instead suggest "whiteness" through appearance, mannerisms, and speech patterns and therefore invoke the racial barriers that were a historical reality for both Louis and Armstrong. As a result, *Spirit of Youth* and *Keep Punching* make room for what Manthia Diawara has called the "resisting spectatorship" aware of "the impossibility of an uncritical acceptance" of Hollywood films and the influence they had on race films.[40]

Spirit of Youth and *Keep Punching* not only subvert their segregated worlds and black-on-black conflict by characterizing the villains in white cultural terms, they also reject the populist demonization of urban life altogether. While the young protagonists may return to the down-home values of hard work, self-discipline, and community, both films also concede that the city is a place of greater opportunity. Like the young blacks in Julie Dash's *Daughters of the Dust* (1991), who are reminded to take their African culture north with them, these two fighters survive because they retain their racial identity, yet they also know that the economic possibility of northern cities did not exist in the South.

The Henry Armstrong character's fictional middle-class southern family functions, then, more as part of the film's attempt to relieve white anxiety about a black champion than to dismiss the need for northern migration. In fact, *Keep Punching* pokes fun at black middle-class distaste for prizefighters as representatives of the race. When the Armstrong character's father complains to his wife that their son's prizefighting in the northern city "isn't respectable," she reminds him that he has not turned his nose up at the checks Henry has sent home. After Henry wins the title, the film's last scene refers again to the material base for middle-class morals as Fanny, Henry's hometown sweetheart, who also opposed his chosen career, concedes, "Maybe I was a little too fussy about what you ought to do."

Both Louis and Armstrong understood the contradiction between the need for bourgeois respectability to overcome racial prejudice and the realities of the prizefighting business in particular and life for a black male in white America in general. Before launching his career, Louis's two African American managers, Julian Black and John Roxborough, had earned their living as gamblers. Although he eventually became one of the best fighters of the decade and the only boxer ever to hold three titles simultaneously, Armstrong had started out on the club circuit in Los Angeles "winning, losing, or boxing to a 'draw' according to instructions."[41]

Spirit of Youth and *Keep Punching* acknowledge the importance of what Gerald Early means when he describes Joe Louis as a "blues hero" whose success should be measured less by the middle-class standards of respectability than by the simple fact that he "got over." Early calls such success a type of "underground victory," "used by both Black preachers and Black hustlers, the autobiographical summing up of both the sacred life and the profane life."[42] Henry Armstrong's success as a fighter, combined with his work as a minister after he left boxing, suggests that this description applies equally well to him.

While Early admits that such an idea of success may result in a "complex meshing of two distinct cultural attitudes, a meshing that is not always balanced and does not always work well," its ultimate defense must be that it produces something more than the "stereotypical put-upon and distressed Black American male."[43] Along these lines, *Spirit of Youth* and *Keep Punching* portray the trainers and managers who help the young protagonists succeed as by necessity just as skilled in the urban culture of nightclubs and gambling as those who seek to exploit them. The films avoid the simplistic message that "crime doesn't pay," which, as Thomas Cripps notes, often elicited laughter from black audiences.[44] Even the femme fatale character in both stories returns the fighter to his hometown girlfriend and thereby saves him from ruin, showing the interest both movies have in demonstrating the necessary coexistence of middle-class morality and a blues aesthetic for living.

Put simply, these films balance the abstraction of middle-class values with the economic reality of selling the black body. Rather than reveal middle-class hypocrisy about money, *Spirit of Youth* stays closer to the biographical truth of Louis's working-class background and never even raises bourgeois concerns about the respectability of prizefighting. The ring scenes in both films, along with narrative digressions for dance numbers and comic turns by Mantan Moreland or Hamtree Harrington, might have been misinterpreted to reinforce stereotypes of blacks as "rhythmic," "fun-loving," and an essentially physical rather than intellectual people. They are instead both a way of expressing individual and racial identity and a means of moving up.[45]

Knockouts and Nightmares

In 1949 Manny Farber reviewed two noir boxing films, *The Set-Up* and *Champion,* for *The Nation.* Farber saw them as inspired by the success two years earlier of another boxing film, *Body and Soul,* replicating its contradictory formula of a carefully arranged visual style "in which every effect is the $64 one, perfectly executed and dehumanized," and a "newsreel realism" of bouncing cameras and discontinuity editing, combined to tell what he calls "tightly humorless" stories "supersaturated with worn-out morality."[46]

The attributes Farber lists in his short but insightful review put these three films in the branch of noir, especially common in the years just after World War II, that James Naremore describes as characterized by "humanism and political engagement," as opposed to the "cynicism and misanthropy" of Alfred Hitchcock or Billy Wilder.[47] Since John Garfield's independent and ironically named Enterprise Productions made *Body and Soul* before the political repression of the HUAC investigations and the drop-off in box office in 1947, it could afford to present a stylized critique of capitalism.[48] Screenwriter Abraham Polonsky's working-class poetry and historical narrative, as well as the film's visual style, encourage viewers to question the values of middle-class American culture. Thom Andersen has remarked that the novelist and former English professor Polonsky "brought the street poetry Odets had synthesized in his plays of the thirties into the American cinema for the first time," and Robert Sklar places *Body and Soul* "as close to a work of the left as any produced to that time in Hollywood."[49] Andersen is right about Polonsky's debt to Odets, for *Body and Soul* bears a strong resemblance in setting, narrative conflict, and resolution to *Golden Boy*. In fact, all three prizefight films in Farber's review typify what Naremore calls the "proletarian concerns" of the Left during this period in movies "about middle-European or Mediterranean immigrants . . . dealing with the failure of the American dream in the big industrial centers."[50]

Body and Soul begins with prizefighter Charley Davis (John Garfield) waking from a nightmare the evening before a title fight. Davis has had a long and lucrative reign as middleweight champ, but he's haunted now by shame and guilt from his complicity with Roberts (Lloyd Goff), an exploitative promoter and gambler. Roberts has not only taken more than a fair share of the profits, he has also persuaded Charley to throw the upcoming fight and worst of all been responsible for the deaths of two of the champ's friends: his first manager, Shorty, and Ben, the former titleholder and later Charley's sparring partner, when they dared protest the dirty deals.

After waking from his nightmare, Charley drives frantically to see his mother (Anna Revere) and fiancée Peg (Lilli Palmer), both of whom are estranged from the fighter because of his selfish choices. The ensuing scene in the mother's cramped Lower East Side apartment uses shadow to represent the exploitation and violence that still cling to Charley. The mother's kitchen appears lit by a single bulb over the table at the center of the room, allowing darkness around the edges of the image to encroach on them as Charley tells her of his torment. Peg arrives from shopping, sees Charley, and runs into an adjoining small bedroom, turning off the light there so that when he enters and tries to embrace her, we see them surrounded by shadow and framed by a window separating the two rooms as the mother tells her son wearily, "Go away, Charley."[51]

In addition to such noir compositions that allegorize the greed and violence that encroach on Charley and his family, *Body and Soul* also relies on Polonsky's dialogue. In a 1962 interview, Polonsky commented that when he wrote for the movies, his intention was to create a language that could "play an equal role with the actor and the visual image."[52] He succeeds in *Body and*

Noir shadow and confinement in *Body and Soul* (1947).

Soul when, after the unsuccessful reconciliation with his mother and Peg, we next see Charley in his dressing room before the fight. Roberts enters, hears the champ angrily boast that he plans to win the fight, and responds: "What's wrong, Charley? The books are all balanced. The bets are in. You bet your purse against yourself. You gotta be business-like, Charley. . . . Everything is addition or subtraction, the rest is conversation." With lines like these, *Body and Soul* makes the point that "criminality can be businesslike," offering us "a critique of capitalism in the guise of an expose of crime."[53] The Roberts character combines criminality and traits of a successful businessman, as if to suggest the potential for the two to overlap. His lock on access to title fights allows Roberts to demand half Charley's earnings (the traditional manager's share is one-third), and like a company store, he consolidates his control over the fighter's services by advancing money that he calls "a little on account." Roberts's name, conservative suits, and public avoidance of alcohol and sex also make him look and act less like a gangster than the stereotype of a WASP businessman.

Moreover, consistent with Polonsky's literary aspirations, Roberts's colloquial directness articulates the motives behind his "legitimate" exterior, making clear his intention to manipulate fighters to maximize his profits and strongarm anyone who gets in the way. Roberts's colloquial language not only communicates directly his motives, it also reveals his own proletarian origins. Like Charley for much of the film, the gambler exemplifies a hardboiled response to disadvantage that pursues success by any means possible, even the ruthless destruction of those like him. Such a self-interested response to class disadvantage has been endemic to prizefighting throughout its history. Joyce Carol Oates describes this working-class cannibalism when she writes that "boxers fight one another because the legitimate objects of their anger are not accessible to them. . . . You fight what's nearest, what's available, what's ready to fight you. And, if you can, you do it for money."[54] *Body and Soul* uses Roberts's betrayal of his working-class origins and his influence on Charley to illuminate the ultimate goal in prizefighting and in the narrative of success frequently offered to those at the bottom: do what you gotta do to move up, and leave your people behind. That's exactly the notion of success that Charley's mother objects to when she first hears of his choice to fight: "Did you hurt the other boy good, Champion?" she asks her son.

Along with its colloquial dialogue and allegorical use of shadow, *Body and Soul* employs a realistic style. The film's cinematographer, James Wong Howe, had commented in a 1944 *American Cinematographer* article that during the war jerky hand-held motion photography had become equated in the minds of audiences with realism and made Hollywood films seem "artificial and therefore unbelievable" in comparison.[55] Guided by such thinking, Howe in the film's climactic fight scene used a subjective camera to convey the brutality of Charley's experience and its impact on his moral choice. Having been a boxer himself, Howe felt that the conventional way of shooting prizefights with a camera on a "big bulky dolly in the ring which can't move around and can only go up and down and sideways," couldn't convey the experience of a fighter. He therefore rented two lightweight Eyemo cameras and put on roller skates to shoot the fight. Using a handheld camera allowed him to move in closer to Charley when he gets hit and then quickly turn to show what the fighter saw—"nothing but hot light flashing down"—before cutting back to the boxer's face. Howe told the grip pushing him around in the ring not to worry about distance because he wanted the image to be out of focus at times to suggest the grogginess of a fighter who has been hit. Howe didn't let the fighter's glove actually hit the camera, however, because he wanted the audience to identify with the experience of being in the ring but not think about the fact that they were seeing a movie of it.[56]

The flashback used to narrate most of *Body and Soul* begins when Charley falls asleep in his dressing room before his title fight and ends when he wakes to enter the ring. It functions in part to explain the guilt and shame that plague Charley, but also to locate his moral corruption in the lack of economic opportunity that influenced his youth during the Depression. Robert Ray has described the historicizing function of the flashback in post–World War II noir: "The noir protagonists' relentless search for the moment where things had begun to go bad was an image of the American post-war mood—vaguely disillusioned, convinced that somewhere along the line the wrong turn had been taken, intuitively aware of the power of historical determinism for perhaps the first time in the nation's history."[57] During the flashback we see that a bomb thrown at a speakeasy inadvertently kills Charley's father in the family candy store next door. This tragedy forces Charley into the ring to provide for himself and his mother, and he becomes middleweight champ and a hero, especially to the working-class Jews of his neighborhood like the grocer Shimin, who tells Charley before the film's final fight that the whole neighborhood's counting on him: "Over in Europe the Nazis are killing people like us, just because of our religion. But here, Charley Davis is champeen. So you'll win, . . . and we are proud."[58]

Putting the flashback within Charley's dressing room nap allows *Body and Soul* to sum up the story contained within it as more noir nightmare than American dream. As he falls into sleep, we hear Charley mumbling about "All these years, everything down the drain." Fighters nap just before a fight to display their composure and self-confidence, as well as to get that little extra reservoir of energy needed to prevail in the grueling battle they're about to enter. The scene in which Charley wakes up refers to that optimistic approach to fighting and suggests that the upcoming fight will reverse his past as it was shown in the flashback. Just after he has gotten up, his new corner man, Ben's replacement, enters the dressing room and tells the fighter that he has bragged to reporters that the champ is sound asleep. Charley's response, "Yeah, dreaming," refers to his desire to break with the nightmare of his boxing career and follow the advice of his family and friends to stand up to Roberts rather than to embody the mythology of individualism with which the gambler has led him along.

The realistic style that *Body and Soul* uses in the big fight contributes to our understanding and identification with Charley's decision to reject the fix and hold on to his title and pride. Roberts had promised him a fifteen-round decision with the challenger Marlowe winning on points. In return for holding back, Charley would have had a big payday and avoided the physical and emotional pain of being knocked out. Yet after seeing how Roberts welshed on the same promise to Ben when Charley took the title and almost killed the African American champ, it's no surprise in the thirteenth round when Roberts gives the signal for Marlowe to go for the knockout. Howe's hand-held camera falls to the mat with Charley when Marlowe knocks him down, and we see in close-up the moral confusion on Garfield's face. Along with the bumpy, out-of-focus shots, this close-up conveys in a visceral way Charley's pain and confusion so that it makes sense when he decides to throw away the money and risk his life by winning the fight. The combination of Howe's newsreel style and the fight announcer's subdued description encourage viewer identification with Charley's situation, especially in the final round when the diegetic crowd goes nearly silent, transfixed by Charley's urgency to overcome his deficit in points and knock Marlowe out in the short time left. We see no reaction shots of Roberts during these last two rounds; Charley and the film have given up on what the gambler represents.

But as Charley heads to his dressing room after knocking Marlowe out, Roberts stops him. For once at a loss for words, the gambler angrily asks Charley how he thinks he'll get away with what he's done. Aware of the danger he's in but committed to his decision, Charley defiantly responds with his own question: "What are you going to do, kill me?" and then quickly answers with Roberts's callous maxim: "Everybody dies."

The "individual redemption" of Charley Davis represented a victory for Polonsky, who disagreed with director Robert Rossen about how *Body and Soul* should end. Rossen favored having Davis killed by Roberts for not throwing the climactic fight, but Polonsky's version prevailed. Robert Sklar argues that the screenwriter's choice of a more upbeat ending undercuts the social critique of the film by linking it with "the hundreds, if not thousands, of Hollywood movies [that] depict society's problems being solved by individuals triumphing over evil men." In Sklar's view, Rossen's ending might have been "truer to life" in that it would have illustrated that "protagonists caught in the nexus of capitalist forces find it less easy to escape them."[59]

While the ending of *Body and Soul* does depend on Charley's heroic choice, it by no means suggests that what he has done will solve the problem of exploitation of the working class by men like Roberts. Even though we don't see Charley die, the last shot after the conversation with Roberts shows him and Peg walking to his mother's apartment, choosing the unity of community, but still surrounded by the same dark shadows that have threatened them throughout the film. Moreover, *Body and Soul* is quite clear about the risks of getting in the way of gangsters: Charley's father, Shorty, and Ben all died for doing so. Charley's choice at the end of *Body and Soul* represents instead Polonsky's idea of the best option possible. Better for Charley to retain his self-respect and a feeling of pride knowing he offers an inspirational example to working-class people and Jews in particular. As Charley's mother told him when she first found out he wanted to be a fighter: "Fight for something, not for money." Although Polonsky didn't put his life on the line like his protagonist, the decision to hold onto his political convictions and be blacklisted in 1951 was a similar difficult but principled choice.

Because of the repressive political and economic climate in 1949 Holly-wood, the makers of *Champion* and *The Set-Up* were more careful in how they presented their prizefight stories as critiques of American society, relying on stylized lighting, camera work, and other formal devices rather than the ur-ban poetry and popular-front history in *Body and Soul.* Both later films avoid the big events (the Depression, the Holocaust) and ideological issues (racism, the choice of assimilation and quick money or cultural identity and commu-nity values) that structure *Body and Soul. Champion's* director Mark Robson and the director of *The Set-Up,* Robert Wise, had trained together as editors under Val Lewton at RKO, so they were experienced in a noir style, but nei-ther came out of the kind of literary and political culture that influenced Po-lonsky. By 1949 Wise and Robson had each invested almost two decades of hard work making their way up the Hollywood ladder—*Champion* in fact was Robson's first assignment as a director—and their films display a desire to pro-tect those careers.

Champion and *The Set-Up* therefore tell—if without much conviction—fair-ly conventional Hollywood stories focused on individuals. Midge Kelly, the selfish prizefighter played by Kirk Douglas in *Champion,* dies of a stroke in the film's last scene, conforming to the Production Code admonition that "No plot or theme should definitely side with evil and against good."[60] Screenwriter Carl Foreman's script includes a few lines about lack of opportunity, but, following the Ring Lardner story from which the film is adapted, it generally isolates the film's portrayal of greed and exploitation in its main character. *Champion* also neatly removes Midge in the last scene so as to confirm David Thompson's ap-praisal of Foreman: that he did "problem pictures for complacent audiences, films that voiced commitment but offered easy answers."[61] Just as incomplete is the characterization of Midge's brother, Connie (Arthur Kennedy), who has traveled the same rough road and has a lame leg to show for it, yet displays no hardheartedness and devotes himself to the fighter's wife, Grace (Ruth Roman), whom Midge abuses psychologically and physically.

The story in *The Set-Up* likewise focuses on the resolve and self-determi-nation of its main character, Stoker Thompson (Robert Ryan), a veteran box-er at the end of a not-very -successful career. Thompson's wife, Julie (Audrey Totter), fearing that her husband may be severely injured or even killed if he continues to fight, tries to convince him to quit boxing before a bout with a younger and stronger opponent in a town ironically called Paradise City. On that particular night, however, the strength and energy of his youth return to Stoker and for four rounds he endures tremendous punishment before knocking out the other fighter, Tiger Nelson (Hal Feberling). The problem with Stoker's surprising victory is that unknowingly he has spoiled a fix on the fight arranged by his dishonest manager Tiny (George Tobias). Nelson's gambler backers do not take kindly to this broken agreement, and they take out their displeasure on Stoker in an alley outside the arena. Julie sees Stoker stumble out of the alley after the beating and runs to his aid. His right hand broken, he tells her that he cannot fight anymore, to which she responds, "You won't have to. . . . We'll get that cigar stand you were telling me about, or maybe a piece of that fighter. It's going to be alright, you wait and see. . . . We both won tonight."

Despite the moral order established by Midge's death and the resolve for a better future shown in the last scene of *The Set-Up,* both films qualify these endings through their oppressive shadows, decaying settings, claustrophobic compositions, and "prowling" camera movements. Such formal devices suggest a feeling of menace and entrapment that the optimistic resolution of the events in the plot fails to offset.[62] In *The Set-Up* the main instance of such stylistic subversion occurs after Julie's encouraging words to her injured husband. From a closeup of the couple, the film cuts to a more objective long shot of Stoker and Julie amidst a small crowd that has gathered on the sidewalk. Above them and to their right a large neon sign in front of a nightclub flashes "Dreamland," dominating the composition and offering an ironic commentary on Julie's unjustified optimism. The camera then slowly pulls back further, in the process obscuring the Dreamland sign with a clock that reads 10:16 P.M., indicating that exactly one hour and twelve minutes of screen time have elapsed since a similar shot of the clock that opened the film. In a condensed version of the flashback in *Body and Soul, The Set-Up*'s exposition had shown how Stoker's world conspires against him while he naps before the fight, making clear that his life is also more noir nightmare than dreamland.

The clock's final reference to the real time in which *The Set-Up* unfolds also culminates a series of reminders of the tyranny of time in working-class life: an alarm clock jars Stoker from his prefight nap, and once in the dressing room at the arena we see the other fighters prepare quickly and hustle into the ring like workers on shifts. Stoker, made to wait because the main event has been moved up for radio coverage, recalls his twenty-one years as a fighter with little to show for it. He has no present means to escape this brutal routine except the future hope of the one big win, about which Julie says: "Stoker, you'll always be one big win away."

Even though on this night Stoker does get that big win, the noir mise-en-scène and cinematography of *The Set-Up* show how such modest success does little more than sustain his dream. We see the deep shadows of the streets and tawdry businesses of Paradise City, the run-down arena with its cramped dressing room and garbage strewn in the corridors, the ring itself enclosed by darkness once the round starts and the crowd lights go down, the fighters surrounded by the compensatory sadism of alienated spectators shown in repeated reaction shots. Joan Mellen describes how the careful depiction of environment in *The Set Up* debunks the "keep on punching" mythology implied by the film's upbeat ending: "*The Set-Up* bears the same relation to fight films as does its main character to the typical screen male. Ryan is not even a main-eventer. He is the average boxer fighting for peanuts under appalling conditions and suffering entirely unromantic damage in each encounter. The film shows how ninety-nine percent of fighters really live, debunking the myth of glamour, fortune, and fame that attaches to the very few."[63]

Robson's *Champion* also uses careful formal composition in its final scene—creating the $64 effects Farber mentioned—to make up for a story that stops short of identifying any structural causes for the individualist values the Douglas character represents. Early in the last scene Connie enters Midge's dressing room before a title fight to confront his brother about his mistreatment of Grace. Midge knocks Connie to the floor before leaving to enter the ring, where a radio announcer proclaims him "a popular champion." A low-angle shot of Midge belies that statement, its menace buttressed by a brass and percussion-heavy flourish from composer Dimitri Tiomkin's score that sounds more appropriate for King Kong entering Manhattan than the introduction of a sports hero.

After winning a tough fight in which he takes a great deal of punishment from his opponent, Midge returns to his dressing room and proclaims to his trainer Haley (Paul Stewart): "No fat bellies with big cigars are going to make a monkey out of me. I can beat 'em." In a story in which Midge has done most of the manipulating, and his rise from poverty to the championship has been almost entirely unimpeded by the greed of others, this statement sounds more like a defiant justification of his selfishness than a valid assertion of opportunity. While there is one fat belly with a cigar early in the film who inflates the expenses deducted from Midge's pay for a preliminary, once he becomes champ he deals only with an unimposing Broadway producer named Jerome Harris who wears a bow tie and tears up a contract for one-third of Midge's winnings to persuade the fighter to end his affair with Mrs. Harris.

Therefore the film's response to Midge's defiance after the fight is to impose poetic justice and strike him dead with a brain hemorrhage. When a reporter asks Connie for a statement about his brother's sudden death, he responds with the same generosity he has shown throughout the film, praising Midge as "a champion, . . . a credit to the fight game."

Our unrestricted view in this last scene of what happens in the dressing room, along with the ironic camerawork and music, make clear *Champion*'s attack on the selfish reality behind Midge's façade of sports stardom. More-over, Connie's tacked-on happy ending allows the film to parody the role of other movies in such false promotion. This self-reflexive commentary works most effectively, however, in *Champion*'s last shot, showing Connie and Grace as they walk away from Midge's dressing room down a long corridor, dark except for intermittent patches of light emitted by single bulbs suspended from the ceiling. The darkness on the margins of this metaphoric image of the filmic apparatus suggests what the story with its illumination of individual-ized evil leaves unexplored. By punishing Midge for his greed and violence, *Champion* exemplifies how even many social problem films made in Holly-wood conclude with the naive assumption that America is a place where any injustice can be fixed with only minor reform, offering the "pretense that the problems the film has raised are now resolved."[64]

The parallels between the work of Robson and Wise continued into the 1950s as they each directed a second boxing film released in 1956 (*The Harder They Fall* and *Somebody Up There Likes Me* respectively). Both films retained the shadow and tough existential choices of noir, combined with an imitation of Italian neorealism that dramatized social problems using the journalistic aura of black and white and some real settings, but with Hollywood production values in acting and narrative construction. *Somebody Up There Likes Me* add-

Noir shadow in *Champion* (1949).

ed the conventions of the biopic, using its realist elements not to counteract the utopian message of Rocky Graziano's overcoming an abusive father, a criminal record, and pressure from gamblers to become middleweight champion, but to make his success even more impressive. On the other hand, *The Harder They Fall* follows in the path of *Body and Soul* by exposing a rationalized, businesslike criminal operation exploiting prizefighters. Like Charley Davis, who rejects the fight business and a chance at a big payday for his working-class ethnic family and community, the lead in *The Harder They Fall,* a sportswriter turned publicist named Eddie Willis (Humphrey Bogart), risks violence from a crooked promoter by giving an exploited fighter enough money to escape the gangster's control.

Despite such similar responses to class exploitation in the two films, the more straightforward narrative structure of *The Harder They Fall,* and its revision of events from boxing history, softens the determinism found in *Body and Soul.* Rather than use a flashback structure to establish the influence of the past on its diegetic world, *The Harder They Fall* simply updates the story of Primo Carnera, a six-foot, six-inch former Italian circus strongman with little boxing ability who was imported in 1930 by management fronting for mobsters "Owney" Madden and "Dutch" Schultz. Carnera's handlers orchestrated his run to the heavyweight championship in 1933, demonstrating not only the influence of underworld money on the fight game, but also the collaboration of those "legitimate" interests that had a stake in renewing the popularity of prizefighting. Jeffrey Sammons refers to such collaboration when he notes that "Few of these fake fights could have occurred without the complicity of the boxing commissions and the press."[65]

While it represents such complicity, *The Harder They Fall* also operates with the liberal assumption that the journalistic documentation implied by its realist style can uncover injustice and prompt change. The film refers to this assumption in its final scene, in which Willis begins writing an exposé of the corruption he's witnessed and calls for congressional reform. There have been numerous attempts in Congress to clean up prizefighting, both before *The Harder They Fall* and since, but with little success. The issue was still alive more than four decades after the movie came out, when in 1999 the Muhammad Ali Boxing Reform Act was sponsored in the U.S. Senate. The long career of one-time journalist and later publicist Harold Conrad, on whom Budd Schulberg based the main character in his 1947 novel from which *The Harder They Fall* was adapted, shows the gap between the film's liberal idealism and the historical continuity of fighter exploitation. Conrad "beat the drums for champs and bums" well into the 1970s.[66]

"Don't Trade with 'Em, Box"

Punching is an exquisitely fascist means of self-expression.
—Benito Mussolini

By the time both *The Harder They Fall* and *Somebody Up There Likes Me* were made, the most important player in the partnership with the mob-controlled boxing business was the television industry. While prizefighting had for decades been plagued by the influence of organized crime, underworld infiltration of the fight game grew during the late 1940s and 1950s because of the massive infusion of television money. Boxing and wrestling dominated television sports during those years—both sports receiving weekly coverage on all four national networks by 1954—in part because the available camera technology at the time could better show the limited space of a ring than the much larger area of a baseball field.[67] Such technological limitations also made it difficult to appreciate the subtlety of a strategic style of boxing and, as a result, the big punch fighter became the norm.

Roland Barthes in a 1952 essay analyzed professional wrestling as a spectacle of masculinity that he interpreted as endorsing a fascistic ideology of might makes right. Wrestling in Barthes's view offers a "spectacle of excess" that presents the visual pleasure of "surface appearance" without the ambiguity and complexity of meaning. According to Barthes, the character of each wrestler can be read with total clarity from the bodily sign he presents as either a "perfect bastard" villain or a suffering hero who must forcibly reestablish the justice that the former has violated. Such reaffirmation of moral rectitude by the hero wrestler is achieved without the "ambiguity of everyday situations," but rather with "the perfect intelligibility of reality, . . . a univocal Nature."[68] Another French intellectual, Guy Debord, would later call this kind of spectacle "the existing order's uninterrupted discourse about itself, its laudatory monologue," that demands "passive acceptance . . . by its monopoly of appearance."[69] Barthes makes clear the political use of this might-makes-right style when he points out that in American wrestling the "bad" wrestler was "supposed to be a Red."[70]

Barthes contrasts wrestling understood in this way with boxing because in his view the latter sport requires the participants to prove their character during the contest. In fact, however, the slugger style of prizefighting popularized by television during the late 1940s and 1950s presented an uncritical spectacle of masculinity much like what Barthes describes in wrestling.

The Harder They Fall emphasizes how such a spectacle of self-determining masculinity represented by the slugger style is more mob and media product than social ideal. In the film's opening scene, gambler and promoter Nick Benko (Rod Steiger) tries to recruit veteran sportswriter Willis to help him sell the new fighter in his "stable," Argentine heavyweight Toro Moreno, by acknowledging that the public image fighters present is more performance than reality: "The fight game today is like show business, there's no real fighters anymore, they're like actors. The best showman becomes the champ." Moreno makes such performance necessary, as he is enormous and appears powerful but in fact has little force in his punches and even less ability to take punishment in the ring. Although Eddy obviously neither trŭsts Benko nor likes the idea of helping him put Moreno over on the public, his long career as a sportswriter has left him broke and taught him that the sports business—whether its crooked promotion or its media coverage—is about selling. Willis expresses this awareness as he defends his new job to his skeptical wife Beth (Jan Sterling): "You sell a fighter, you sell soap, what's the difference? It's all selling."

When the setup for Toro's first fight fails miserably, Willis must again defend himself, this time to television journalist Art Levitt (Harold J. Stone). After Levitt balks at Eddy's request not to tell the boxing commission that he thinks the fight was fixed, Eddy angrily asks him, "You never played ball with promoters who bought advertising in newspapers you wrote for?" Repeatedly throughout *The Harder They Fall* the film refers to this collaboration of the sports media—especially television—in Benko's scheme to promote and exploit Carnera. Benko boasts of this collaboration when Carnera arrives in Chicago after a successful bus tour across the West: "Not a kid in New York that wouldn't recognize him. That's the power of television today."

Liberal Assimilation and the Exception of Muhammad Ali

Battered by the blacklist and shaken by revelations about Stalinist repression, in particular against Jews and artists, left-wing novelists, playwrights, and filmmakers in the decade after the war "turned to themes of racism and anti-Semitism in more focused ways than before, when class had seemed to crowd out other issues."[71] Sports films from the early to mid-1950s about African American athletes—*The Jackie Robinson Story* (1950), *The Harlem Globetrotters* (1951), and *The Joe Louis Story*—and about Latinos—*Right Cross* (1950), *The Ring,* and *The Harder They Fall*—fit into this shift away from class as *the* issue. The movies about professional baseball and basketball responded to recent integration of those sports; those about boxing acknowledged the changing demographics of prizefighting. Historian Steven Riess notes that by 1948 nearly half of all contenders were African American, Italians were second, followed by Mexican Americans, a group he calls "new . . . to achieve prominence in boxing."[72]

Not that the racism central to these films precludes their representation of class issues as well. The African American and Latino athletes they feature all suffer the effects of discrimination in economic terms, and their success in overcoming mistreatment or exploitation caused by race improves their class status. Each of these films therefore presents a white character who models the benefits of self-determination and entrepreneurship and helps the nonwhite athlete improve his economic position. In *The Jackie Robinson Story* Branch Rickey invents the idea of giving the title character a chance to move up to the major leagues, and in fact Rickey chooses Robinson because he embodies the liberal ideal of hard work and belief in the ultimate fairness of American society. In *The Harlem Globetrotters* a similar story hinges on white largesse and entrepreneurial skill and the black athlete's determination to follow such a model and sacrifice to achieve success. *The Joe Louis Story* is told from the perspective of a white sportswriter, who presents Louis's story as a cautionary tale on the danger of not enough hard work and investment for the future. In *The Harder They Fall,* a similar liberal viewpoint is conveyed by Eddie Willis's success orchestrating Toro's run to a title fight, his resolve to make sure the fighter is fairly paid for his work, and the ending endorsing the power of the press used to prevent future exploitation of class and cultural difference.

As I noted in chapter 2, the films about Robinson and the Globetrotters include views of black style that imply skepticism about the rewards from deferred gratification. But on balance, like the other five stories analyzed here, they endorse gradual change for nonwhites based on individual achievement as the foundation for social equality. These movies therefore articulate an assimilationist theory of the role possible for professional sports in overcoming the double disadvantage of racial and class difference. Sports sociologists Merrill Melnick and Don Sabo call this thinking, "a pluralist conception of an American society that provides advancement opportunities for those who embrace the core value system and work hard to succeed."[73]

Such liberal attitudes in *Right Cross* and *The Ring* appealed to what Carlos Muñoz calls "the Mexican-American generation," which accepted that strategies of "political accommodation and assimilation were the only path toward equal status in a racist society."[74] In *The Ring,* a young Mexican American from East Los Angeles, Tomás Cantanios (Lalo Ríos), feels anger and resentment about harassment from the police and discrimination in hiring at white-run businesses. He expresses his anger through violence, attacking two white men he thinks have been looking at his girlfriend, Lucy (Rita Moreno). Chon Noriega notes how Tomás in this belligerent response to discrimination and disadvantage in *The Ring* fits the tendency in cultural representation from this period to show young Mexican American men as inherently violent.[75]

The Ring redirects such "unproductive" violence through the entrance of an Anglo fight manager named Pete (Gerald Mohr), who sees Tomás fleeing the police after the altercation with the two white men, and convinces the youth to try his hand at boxing. Although Tomás's career as a fighter doesn't pan out, Pete gets him $450 when a last-minute substitute is needed for a main event. With that money Tomás can bring economic stability to his family and hope for a better life by buying for his unemployed father a stand on Olvera Street to sell souvenirs to tourists.

As Manny Farber mentions in his review of the film, *The Ring* reverses several conventions of the fight film: Tomás isn't a success, he never even gets close to the welterweight title, and he also doesn't fall victim to exploitative management. *The Ring* uses such variation from convention to support its liberal optimism. Tomás's losses and the absence of exploitation (Farber comments that Pete handles the young fighter "with prudence and kindness") affirm the importance of merit: Tomás gets his chance, he simply doesn't have what it takes, while Pete's ability, as well as his liberal inclination to help Tomás and his family, are demonstrated by his quick thinking and forcefulness in getting the $450 when the opportunity presents itself.

Like the other five 1950s sports films about nonwhite athletes, *The Ring* doesn't hesitate to show the racist barriers the protagonists face, but it just as clearly endorses the view of America as a society that will reward hard work and excellence no matter who you are. It's ironic therefore that the King Brothers' independent production company that made the film was known during this period for hiring blacklisted talent, not for ideological reasons, but because they could get "top talent for minimal money."[76]

Between the late 1940s and the end of the 1960s not only prizefighting but also football, basketball, and even baseball became dominated by nonwhites, in particular African Americans, a trend that intensified in the last decades of the twentieth century.[77] Yet by the end of that initial period of integration, many African Americans questioned the idea that the integration of commercial sports symbolized social and economic progress for the race as a whole.[78] A lack of uniform economic progress fueled this skepticism; Manning Marable points out that income for African Americans as a group declined in the 1950s in relation to that of whites, and between 1959 and 1988 blacks as a percentage of Americans living in poverty increased from 25 to more than 30 percent.[79] David Rowe contends that entrance for blacks into a sports star system predicated upon "concentration of rewards and resources among an elite few athletes," rather than offering a viable model of economic empowerment for disenfranchised populations, has instead simply replicated the growing economic inequality in American society.[80]

The racial integration of professional athletics after World War II has also reinforced concentrations of corporate wealth as it has greatly expanded the market for sports products. If Fredric Jameson is right when he argues that both the civil rights and the women's movements fit the "ideology of capitalism itself . . . which has the fundamental interest in social equality . . . to transform as many of its subjects, its citizens into identical consumers," then the same can be said about the increased access of women to sports.[81]

The integration of sports as a strategy for creating new markets has also operated on a global level. Mark Naison points out that during the cold war "with the U.S. economy increasingly dependent on the penetration and control of emerging nations, racial segregation had become a political embarrassment that could be exploited by the Soviet bloc or anticolonial revolutionaries to mobilize resistance to U.S. aims."[82] By the 1970s, much publicized events such as Muhammad Ali fighting George Foreman in Zaire or Joe Frazier in Manila, or more recently Michael Jordan leading the Dream Team to an Olympic gold medal, attempted to respond to this vulnerability by presenting a façade of racial equality concealing global profits made from corporate sports products.

One exception to the self-interest that has accompanied the racial integration of sports was the religious and political activism of Muhammad Ali. In 1967 when Ali refused induction into the U.S. military, he acted not for selfish reasons (he probably would never have been in harm's way, and his defiance cost him the title and a long legal battle to stay out of jail), but instead to take a stand against racism in the United States and colonialism abroad. Ali refused to support U.S. involvement in Vietnam because it conflicted with his Muslim religious beliefs, but also because he regarded the war as colonialist. He saw no justification for American blacks to fight to preserve democratic rights abroad when many African Americans didn't have such rights in their own country. Ali summed up these beliefs in his now-famous response to a journalist's question about his decision to refuse induction by saying, "No Vietcong ever called me nigger."

The importance of Ali as a counterexample to the self-interest of professional sports can be seen in four films that represent or refer to him. Leon Gast's Academy Award–winning documentary, *When We Were Kings,* about Ali's fight in Kinshasa against George Foreman, shows how he became a symbol of racial unity and decolonization. Conversely, the HBO biopic *Don King: Only in America* presents a caricature of Ali as just another self-indulgent star athlete to support the view of its title character that "It ain't about this brotherhood crap." While the HBO film emphasizes the greed and survival-of-the-fittest mentality that governs prizefighting as a business and King's decision to adopt that ethos, *Rocky* and *Rocky II* (1979) endorse a mythology of utopian individualism by attempting to disprove the racial skepticism of an Apollo Creed character modeled after Ali. *Rocky* appeared at a time when a combination of events during the first half of the 1970s had served to undermine belief in the American dream. The military defeat in Southeast Asia demonstrated a loss in the stature of the United States as a world power; the Arab oil embargo showed that Americans could no longer count on unlimited cheap natural resources; the resignation of a president eroded public faith in government; stagflation hit with the combined effect of unemployment and rising prices; and the push for change from the civil rights and feminist movements challenged the social and political, if not economic, status quo.[83] The bicentennial celebration of 1976, however, offered a diversion from such assaults, and *Rocky* attempted to use the "determined optimism" generated by the celebration of the country's 200th birthday to reinforce belief in the continued viability of the American dream.

An unemployed actor named Sylvester Stallone wrote the screenplay for *Rocky*, inspired by the performance of veteran heavyweight Chuck Wepner, known as "The Bayonne Bleeder," in a March 1975 fight in which he knocked down and almost went the distance with Muhammad Ali. After United Artists approved financing for the project, Stallone refused to sell his script unless he played the lead. The lack of a major star caused United Artists to slash the film's budget, and Stallone was paid only one-fifth the money he could have made by merely selling the script; nevertheless *Rocky* won three Academy Awards (including best picture) on its way to becoming a box-office hit. Stallone himself attributed the success of the film to the desire to reaffirm the American dream: "I believe the country as a whole is beginning to break out of this . . . anti-everything syndrome," he stated.[84]

Rocky tells the story of a thirty-year-old club fighter named Rocky Balboa, who revives the slugger style of his 1950s namesakes Rocky Graziano and Rocky Marciano. Before Balboa becomes a success, Mick (Burgess Meredith), the owner of the gym where Rocky works out, disparages his style, but also previews its moral ascension when he comments: "You got heart, but you fight like a god damn ape." Rocky's big chance comes when the next scheduled opponent for heavyweight champion Apollo Creed (Carl Weathers) must pull out of the fight because of an injury. Without much time to find a new challenger, Creed picks Rocky because he wants to associate the fight with the patriotic hype of the bicentennial, giving an opportunity to a "snow white underdog" and playing on fans' desire to believe that such opportunity still exists in American society.

Unlike populist boxing films of the 1930s, *Rocky* does not portray the fight business as a corrupt jungle that the tough young pug must slug his way through with the help of a supportive woman and faithful trainer; nor does it, like *Body and Soul* and *The Harder They Fall,* parallel dishonest promoters and managers with "legitimate" capital interests in their exploitation of working people. Instead, *Rocky* indicts the African American Creed, who publicizes his title fight by playing on patriotic feeling without believing in the American dream himself. During a television interview before the fight, Creed explains that he chose to give Rocky a shot for "sentimental" reasons, as if to suggest that the champ believes that the opportunity that Rocky's big break represents is a thing of the past. Yet later in that same interview Creed carefully conceals his cynicism by describing Balboa as an example of how "American history proves that everybody's got a chance to win." "Haven't you ever heard of Valley Forge and Bunker Hill?" he asks the reporters.

Creed's doubt about the American promise of opportunity for all is apparent in his extravagant use of bicentennial imagery. Dressed as George Washington in a white wig and long overcoat, he enters the arena for the fight with Rocky atop a float decorated to represent the longboat on which the general crossed the Delaware. Upon reaching the ring, Creed takes off his wig and overcoat to reveal an elaborate red, white, and blue Uncle Sam costume. In obvious imitation of the wide-eyed proclamations of confidence for which Ali was known, he points first at the crowd and then at Balboa while yelling "I want you!" By making a charade of Uncle Sam, Creed, like Ali, questions the notion of patriotic duty. Meanwhile, Rocky jokes with his trainer Mick about the cost of such elaborate costumes, suggesting that Creed's doubt about the lack of opportunity for African Americans is disproven by the champion's own success.

Once the fight starts, Rocky's style of attack in the ring continues to affirm his unshakable faith in the rewards of dedication and sacrifice. He bores in on Creed, willing to take whatever punishment he has to, not sure he can beat the champion, but believing that a total effort will result in the best possible outcome. Creed, on the other hand, employs a more strategic defensive style of boxing, waiting for a clear opening before committing himself, confident of his ability, but guided by a healthy skepticism. Consistent with the film's interest in affirming the importance of believing in the promise of the American dream, Rocky's style proves the more effective; between rounds Creed's corner tells him to "quit shucking and jiving and fight," and the champion must adopt the slugging style of his challenger to win a narrow decision.

According to Daniel Leab, *Rocky*'s representation of Creed spoke to those white ethnics who believed that they had "'paid the costs' of American society's attempts to redress black grievances." Leab calls this part of the film's audience "'the poorest, least secure, least educated and least tolerant' in the white community [who] believe they have been sacrificed by a liberal elite anxious to insure 'responsible social change.'"[85] *Rocky* appeals to this audience through its assertion that the title character exemplifies a 200–year tradition of opportunity in America. By showing Creed as less political than self-serving, the film indirectly attacks Ali's skepticism about a lack of black access to opportunity and therefore rejects the necessity for the society to redress racial injustice.

While *Rocky* uses the hallowed iconography of the bicentennial and the landmarks of Philadelphia for all they are worth, it also revises or represses other aspects of history. Just after World War II, when Rocky Balboa's hero, Rocky Marciano, fought his way to the heavyweight crown, Italian Americans were frequently involved in prizefighting. By the mid-1970s, however, many Italians, like the Irish and Jews before them, had gained greater affluence and moved out of the tough inner-city neighborhoods from which boxing had been one of the few means of escape, leaving blacks and Latinos to dominate the sport. By the time of *Rocky*'s release in 1976, increased Italian American social and economic status had begun to manifest itself in the movies, with the success of actors such as Al Pacino and Robert De Niro, and filmmakers Francis Ford Coppola and Martin Scorsese. Andrew Ross points out that Spike Lee's 1989 film *Do the Right Thing* challenges "the reign of Italian-American figures as the favoured, semi-integrated ethnic presence in Hollywood film."[86] The conflict in that film between Buggin' Out (Giancarlo Esposito) and pizzeria owner Sal (Danny Aiello) about the lack of African Americans amongst the pictures of Italian American stars on the wall of the pizzeria in a predominately black part of Brooklyn vividly dramatizes this challenge. Taken in this context, the degree to which *Rocky*'s affirmation of the continued viability of the American dream rings true for certain parts of the audience may depend on their ethnic background or skin color. What is even more certain is that the model of success from the film is less the working-class protagonist Rocky Balboa than Sylvester Stallone. The latter's rise to fame and fortune has proven the greater viability of the myth of working-class upward mobility rather than real working-class opportunity in America's postindustrial economy.[87]

• • •

Writing in 1992, John Fiske hypothesized that the popularity of British cultural studies in the United States during the 1980s, with its emphasis on analyzing social difference, resulted from "the rise of Reaganism." In Fiske's view, Reaganism "rolled back the progress made during the 1960s and 1970s toward reducing inequalities in gender, race, and class; it widened the gap between the privileged and deprived and concentrated power in the white male upper middle classes."[88] At the beginning of the twenty-first century, a similar hypothesis explained the renewed relevance of boxing films that focus on class and other identity issues. Sixteen American films about boxing came out between 1990 and 2001, representing continued growth in the gap between haves and have-nots in the United States as a result of the economic policies Fiske refers to, and the inflection of that division by racial and gender difference.

If the utopian formula for achieving the American dream in *Rocky* attempts to dismiss not just class but social identity in general, classic era boxing films practiced their own form of exclusion, focusing on class as the most important issue that explains all others. Following instead on the model of *Raging Bull* in which Jake LaMotta's social dysfunction arises from his confusion about his racial, class, and sexual identities, several boxing films made during the last decade attempt to illustrate how class is often best understood through its relationships to other forms of social identity.

Two recent boxing films, *The Great White Hype* and *The Hurricane,* use this structural approach to portray how race has often displaced a focus on class. In his 1935 book, *Black Reconstruction in America,* W. E. B. Du Bois wrote that during the era of Jim Crow, working-class whites in the American South accepted the economic oppression imposed on them by landowners because they were compensated with a psychological wage paid by the public deference that blacks were forced to show them. In other words, poor whites accepted the unfair monetary compensation they received in the South's mainly agricultural economy because they were allowed to position themselves as white and therefore, in their own minds, superior to African Americans.[89]

The Great White Hype and *The Hurricane* transplant this idea of a psychological and public wage to the urban North. *The Great White Hype* uses it to explain how an opportunistic African American promoter, Reverend Sultan (Samuel L. Jackson), a character modeled on Don King, makes millions by orchestrating a plan to stage a fight between the black heavyweight champion and an unknown challenger he promotes as the next great white hope. The film shows such promotion as directed primarily at a white audience willing to pay for the idea of racial superiority represented by the challenger. After showing Sultan successfully cater to this need, *The Great White Hype* proves the idea of white superiority to be all hype and no substance, as the film concludes with the African American champion easily knocking out the white challenger, and Sultan besting the attempts of a white promoter (Jeff Goldblum) to take over control of the heavyweight championship.

The Hurricane points to the refusal of its title character, Ruben "Hurricane" Carter (Denzel Washington), to show deference to white authority as the explanation for his unjust imprisonment. In 1966 Carter was the top middleweight challenger when he was convicted of the murders of three whites in a Paterson, New Jersey, bar. Although there were no eyewitnesses, and Carter's conviction was based on the testimony of two ex-cons with plea-bargain deals who later recanted their accusations, he served almost twenty years in prison before being freed. *The Hurricane* ignores how FBI surveillance of Carter for his civil rights activism and anger over his outspoken support for black self-defense against police violence, may have contributed to the conviction. Instead, the story focuses on a single Italian American detective character, Vincent Della Pesca (Dan Hedaya), whose anger that a young African American from the streets he has policed could use his skill in the ring to achieve social and economic status motivates him to frame Carter.

Two other recent boxing films, *Girlfight* and *Play It to the Bone,* also go beyond the standard emphasis on economic disadvantage in fight films and show how gender difference functions to validate hierarchical class relations. On the one hand, *Play It to the Bone* recalls the conservative gender roles of many boxing films, even those with fairly sophisticated views of class difference such as *Golden Boy, Body and Soul,* and *The Set-Up,* by again showing the main female character, Grace (Lolita Davidovich), as the main source of support for two male boxers, Vince (Woody Harrelson) and Cesar (Antonio Banderas). The film becomes more interesting, however, when it parallels Grace's economic disadvantage with that of the fighters. *Play It to the Bone* represents the effects on Grace, Vince, and Cesar of what economists Robert Frank and Philip Cook call the "winner-take-all" form of capitalism that has long governed boxing and now permeates many sectors of the American economy.[90] The film's opening shots of the Las Vegas skyline show the ever more spectacular hotels and casinos that stand as monuments to the corporate power that dominates the fastest-growing city in the United States, the boxing game located there, and American society in general. Both in their thirties and fearing they've missed any chance for a big payday, Vince and Cesar are training in a run-down LA gym when they get an offer to fight each other in Las Vegas as last-minute replacements on the undercard for a Mike Tyson pay-per-view event. As they drive from Los Angeles, Grace explains that she's going along to look for someone to invest in her inventions. "There's a lot of venture capital in Vegas," she states matter-of-factly.

The drive provides the opportunity to showcase the film's witty combination of monologue and repartee about working-class life, what one reviewer of *Play It to the Bone* sees as typical of writer/director Ron Shelton's "most successful blueprint—over the hill jock inspired by sexy oddball and screwed by corporate evil."[91] Each of the three main characters offers his or her own identity claims: Grace for her liberal feminist right to have her own career, Cesar to his cultural difference and bisexuality, Vince to his patriarchal masculinity and born-again Christianity. After the two fighters batter each other to a draw, they wind up with less than a quarter of the money they were promised and Grace is roughly expelled from the hotel owned by the fight's promoter (whose investment capital she had hoped to get) when she refuses to have sex with him. This parallel between Grace's experience and that of the men shows that Shelton, who reportedly studied numerous old boxing films while making *Play It to the Bone,* was intent on creating an homage to their emphasis on working-class experience, but also that he sought to move beyond the conservative ideas about gender in those earlier movies.

As we saw in chapter 3, *Girlfight* focuses on the self-confidence and physical skills that a young Latina, Diana Guzmán (Michele Rodríguez), acquires from boxing. These skills enable Diana to stop the abusive behavior of her father and challenge the thinking of her boyfriend, Adrian, that his plans for a career as a prizefighter should determine their relationship.

While *Girlfight* is upbeat about the value of boxing for women in putting them on a fairer footing with men, it is less sanguine about what fighting offers in response to class disadvantage. Writer and director Karyn Kusama points out that the focus in *Girlfight* on amateur boxing helped the story avoid the utopian perspective of many fight films, which promise riches from success in the ring. Kusama explains that she avoided "any triumph that was larger than life, . . . the kind of success that very few can attain."[92]

Girlfight therefore avoids presenting boxing as a way of escaping economic determination, what Grant Farrad calls "The Horatio Alger narrative . . . where . . . class roots are at once invoked and transcended."[93] It instead represents how the desperation of working-class life fuels the patriarchal behavior of Diana's father and Adrian's similar fantasies of control. In the process, *Girlfight* also illustrates that often only by including consideration of its relationships to other forms of social identity can class be adequately understood.

Notes

1. Stanley Aronowitz, *The Politics of Identity* (New York: Routledge, 1992), 19. I've avoided framing the analysis in this chapter as Marxist, for several reasons. First, while I employ Marxist ideas, primarily the concept of surplus value that Aronowitz claims Marx saw as "the fundamental structuring relation that determines all other social forms" (16), as Robin Wood points out, "there are as many Marxes as there are Freuds" (Robin Wood, "Cards on the Table," in *Hollywood from Vietnam to Reagan,* ed. Robin

Wood [New York: Columbia, University Press, 1986], 5). and besides the fact that I don't know all their intricacies, I don't want to be beholden to one or another version. The cultural studies approach that I prefer also shares the Marxist assumption of a divided society with different interests and views culture as a site of both hegemonic representation that attempts to discount those differences and contestation of dominant meanings. Another reason not to take on the label Marxist is to avoid the kind of kneejerk negative reaction the term creates from many readers who reject it out of hand without really considering its usefulness. As Wood notes, such closed-mindedness is part of "the widespread suppression—in a culture that calls itself democratic and advertises itself as based on principles of freedom of thought and freedom of speech—not only of Marxist theory but all coherent radical positions" (5). In regard to Marxism in particular, the lazy assumption that justifies excluding consideration of its ideas is that it is synonymous with, or leads to, Stalinist totalitarianism, which as Wood points out, is an equation "rather like blaming Christ for the Spanish Inquisition" (5).

2. Steven A. Riess, *City Games: The Evolution of American Urban Society and the Rise of Sports* (Urbana: University of Illinois Press, 1989), 109–10.

3. Ibid., 110–16.

4. Ibid., 113.

5. Joyce Carol Oates, *On Boxing* (New York: Doubleday, 1987), 36. David Rowe attributes the kind of pyramidal reward structure found in boxing to professional sports as a whole: "Elite sportspeople, along with owners of clubs and sponsors, media and advertising organizations, are . . . in receipt of rewards which vastly outweigh those gained by the great mass of non-elite performers and would-be performers." See *Popular Cultures: Rock Music, Sport, and the Politics of Pleasure* (London: Sage Publications, 1993), 106–7.

6. James Naremore makes this observation about social problem films in his book *More Than Night: Film Noir in Its Contexts* (Berkeley: University of California Press, 1998), 120.

7. Fredric Jameson, *Signatures of the Visible* (New York: Routledge, 1990), 36.

8. Leger Grindon, "Body and Soul: The Structure of Meaning in the Boxing Film Genre," *Cinema Journal* 35, no. 4 (1996): 60.

9. Michael Rogin, *Blackface, White Noise: Jewish Immigrants in the Hollywood Melting Pot* (Berkeley: University of California Press, 1996), 216.

10. Raymond Williams, "Class," in *Keywords,* ed. Raymond WIlliams (New York: Oxford University Press, 1983), 68.

11. Terry Eagleton, *Marxism and Literary Criticism* (Berkeley: University of California Press, 1976), viii.

12. Otis L. Graham Jr. provides the statistic that 50 percent of Americans between the ages of 15 and 19 were unemployed in 1933. He also notes that "young people waited an average of two years after schooling before finding a job in the 1930s, and about 25 percent never found employment until the war." "Years of Crisis: America in Depression and War, 1933–1945," in *The Unfinished Century,* ed. William E. Leuchtenburg (Boston: Little, Brown, 1973), 381.

13. Riess, *City Games,* 112.

14. Robert Ray, *A Certain Tendency in the Hollywood Cinema, 1930–1980* (Princeton, N.J.: Princeton University Press, 1985), 55–69.

15. A description of these test screenings and the change in the ending of *The Champ*

appears in Samuel Marx, *Mayer and Thalberg: The Make-Believe Saints* (New York: Random House, 1975), 170.

16. I am using here Charles Eckert's idea of displacement as he describes it occurring in "proletarian" or "socially conscious" films of the 1930s and 1940s. Using both Freudian psychoanalysis and Lévi-Strauss's study of myth, Eckert sums up this process as a combination of displacement "as Freud defines this term (the substitution of an acceptable object of love, hate, etc., for a forbidden one)," and the transformation of unsolvable dilemmas like that in myths in order to "resolve the dilemma at another level, or to somehow attenuate its force." See "The Anatomy of a Proletarian Film: Warner's *Marked Woman*," in *Movies and Methods*, ed. Bill Nichols (Berkeley: University of California Press, 1985), vol. 2, 420.

17. Jameson, *Signatures of the Visible*, 36.

18. Richard Slotkin, *Gunfighter Nation: The Myth of the Frontier in Twentieth-Century America* (New York: Atheneum, 1992), 19.

19. Ibid., 20.

20. Josefina Zoraida Vázquez and Lorenzo Meyer, *The United States and Mexico* (Chicago: University of Chicago Press, 1985), 134–38.

21. Slotkin, *Gunfighter Nation*, 13.

22. Ibid., 21.

23. Eckert, "Anatomy," 415.

24. Peter Roffman and Jim Purdy, *The Hollywood Social Problem Film* (Bloomington: Indiana University Press, 1981), 46–47.

25. Ibid., 64.

26. Ibid., 47–48.

27. Ibid.

28. As Mark Roth has shown, Warner Brothers celebrated this same social model in backstage musicals such as *42nd Street* (1933), in which the director plays an FDR-like figure "both inducing and supported by a strong sense of community." "Some Warners Musicals and the Spirit of the New Deal," in *Genre: The Musical*, ed. Rick Altman (Boston: Routledge and Kegan Paul, 1981), 41.

29. Roffman and Purdy, *Hollywood Social Problem*, 60.

30. Alexis de Tocqueville, *Democracy in America*, ed. J. P. Mayer, trans. George Lawrence (Garden City, N.Y.: Anchor/Doubleday, 1969), 506, quoted in Ray, *Certain Tendency*, 61.

31. Roffman and Purdy, *Hollywood Social Problem*, 63. My point that these films condense the trait of extreme self-interest into criminal characters so as to mark it as an aberration and therefore avoid examination of the role of individualism in larger social problems is again indebted to Eckert's description of a similar process in "Anatomy," 420–24.

32. Riess, *City Games*, 171–72, 177–81.

33. James F. Smith, "Where the Action Is: Images of the Gambler in Recent Popular Films," in *Beyond the Star: Studies in American Popular Film*, ed. Paul Loukaides and Linda Fuller (Bowling Green, Ohio: Bowling Green State University Popular Press, 1990), 178.

34. Ibid., 181.

35. Jeffrey T. Sammons, *Beyond the Ring: The Role of Boxing in American Society* (Urbana: University of Illinois Press, 1988), 97.

36. Ibid., 96, 80.

37. Daniel J. Leab, *From Sambo to Superspade: The Black Experience in Motion Pictures* (Boston: Houghton Mifflin, 1976), 181. This quote describing southern white attitudes toward blacks is from James H. Stevenson's unpublished master's thesis, Howard University, 1948, reprinted in Sammons, *Beyond the Ring,* 100.

38. Thomas Cripps, *Slow Fade to Black: The Negro in American Film, 1900–1942* (New York: Oxford University Press, 1977), 110.

39. Ibid., 329.

40. Manthia Diawara, "Black Spectatorship: Problems of Identification and Resistance," in *Black American Cinema,* ed. Manthia Diawara (New York: Routledge, 1993), 212, 219.

41. Gilbert Odd, *Encyclopedia of Boxing* (New York: Crescent Books, 1983), 12.

42. Gerald Early, *Tuxedo Junction: Essays on American Culture* (New York: Ecco Press, 1989), 178.

43. Ibid.

44. Cripps, *Slow Fade,* 342.

45. Michael Eric Dyson describes a similar dual meaning for black sports heroes in his essay "Be like Mike?: Michael Jordan and the Pedagogy of Desire," in *Reflecting Black: African-American Cultural Criticism,* ed. Michael Eric Dyson (Minneapolis: University of Minnesota Press, 1993), 67.

46. Manny Farber, "Fight Films," in *Movies,* ed. Manny Farber (New York: Hillstone, 1971), 64–67.

47. Naremore, *More Than Night,* 125.

48. Movie attendance dropped in 1947 and kept falling for the next six years; by 1953 nearly half the postwar peak of 90 million weekly viewers had stopped going to the movies. See Robert Sklar, *Movie-Made America* (New York: Vintage, 1994), 272.

49. Thom Andersen, "Red Hollywood," in *Literature and the Visual Arts in Contemporary Society,* ed. Suzanne Ferguson and Barbara Groseclose (Columbus: Ohio State University Press, 1985), 186; Robert Sklar, *City Boys: Cagney, Bogart, Garfield* (Princeton, N.J.: Princeton University Press, 1992), 183.

50. Naremore, *More Than Night,* 125.

51. Todd Rainsberger, *James Wong Howe, Cinematographer* (San Diego: A. S. Barnes, 1981), 216.

52. Jim Cook and Alan Lovell, "Aesthetics," in *Coming to Terms with Hollywood,* ed. Jim Cook and Alan Lovell (London: British Film Institute, 1981), 41.

53. Andersen, "Red Hollywood," 186–87.

54. Oates, *On Boxing,* 63.

55. Quoted in Douglas Gomery and Robert Allen, *Film History: Theory and Practice* (New York: Alfred A. Knopf, 1985), 221.

56. Rainsberger, *James Wong Howe,* 217–18.

57. Ray, *Certain Tendency,* 160.

58. In recent versions of *Body and Soul* available on video and DVD, Shimin's reference to the Holocaust has been omitted.

59. Sklar, *City Boys,* 186.

60. "The Motion Picture Production Code of 1930," in *The Movies in Our Midst,* ed. Gerald Mast (Chicago: University of Chicago Press, 1982), 325.

61. David Thompson, *A Biographical Dictionary of Film,* 3d ed. (New York: Alfred A. Knopf, 1996), 258.

62. Ray, *Certain Tendency,* 159–60.

63. Joan Mellen, *Big Bad Wolves: Masculinity in the American Film* (New York: Pantheon Books, 1977), 166–67.

64. Robin Wood, "Ideology, Genre, Auteur," in *Film Genre Reader 2,* ed. Barry Keith Grant (Austin: University of Texas Press, 1995), 61.

65. Sammons, *Beyond the Ring,* 87.

66. Robert H. Boyle, "Man of Style," *Sports Illustrated,* June 3, 1991, 18.

67. The first television broadcast of wrestling took place in 1945 from a Paramount soundstage in Los Angeles. By 1948 three of the four national networks televised wrestling weekly; by 1950 the fourth network had joined the fray for wrestling viewers. Chad Dell, "'Lookit That Hunk of Man!': Subversive Pleasures, Female Fandom and Professional Wrestling," unpublished paper shared with me by author, 3–4. Prizefighting had developed a 31 percent share of television households for weekly national broadcasts by 1952; by 1954 all four networks (ABC, CBS, NBC, and Du Pont) had weekly boxing programs. See Randy Roberts and James S. Olson, *Winning Is the Only Thing: Sports in America since 1945* (Baltimore: Johns Hopkins University Press, 1989), 103, 107.

68. Roland Barthes, "The World of Wrestling," in *A Barthes Reader,* ed. Susan Sontag (New York: Hill and Wang, 1982), 29.

69. Guy Debord, *Society of the Spectacle* (Detroit: Black and Red, 1970), sections 3, 12, 24.

70. Barthes, "World of Wrestling," 27–28.

71. Paul Buhle and Dave Wagner, Introduction to *The World Above,* by Abraham Polonsky (Urbana: University of Illinois Press, 1999), xi.

72. Riess, *City Games,* 116.

73. Merrill J. Melnick and Donald Sabo, "Sport and Social Mobility among African-American and Hispanic Athletes," in *Ethnicity and Sport in North American History and Culture,* ed. George Eisen and David K. Wiggins (Westport, Conn.: Greenwood Press, 1994), 222.

74. Carlos Muñoz Jr., "From Segregation to Melting Pot Democracy: The Mexican-American Generation," in *Youth, Identity, Power: The Chicano Movement,* ed. Carlos Muñoz Jr. (London: Verso, 1989), 49.

75. Chon A. Noriega, "Citizen Chicano: The Trials and Titillations of Ethnicity in the American Cinema, 1935–1962," *Social Research* 58, no. 2 (Summer 1991): 424–25.

76. Victor S. Navasky, *Naming Names* (New York: Viking Press, 1980), 155.

77. Melnick and Sabo, "Sport and Social Mobility," 230.

78. Sammons, *Beyond the Ring,* 191.

79. Manning Marable, *Race, Reform, and Rebellion: The Second Reconstruction in Black America, 1945–1990* (Jackson: University of Mississippi Press, 1991), 54; Christopher Jencks, "Is the American Underclass Growing?" in *The Urban Underclass,* ed. Christopher Jencks and Paul E. Peterson (Washington, D.C.: Brookings Institution, 1991), 33.

80. Rowe, *Popular Cultures,* 110.

81. Jameson, *Signatures of the Visible,* 36.

82. Mark Naison, "Sports and the American Empire," in *American Media and Mass Culture: Left Perspectives,* ed. Donald Lazere (Berkeley: University of California Press, 1987), 502–3.

83. Daniel J. Leab, "The Blue Collar Ethnic in Bicentennial America: *Rocky,*" in *American History/American Film,* ed. John E. O'Connor and Martin A. Jackson (New York: Continuum, 1988), 258.

84. Ibid., 265.

85. Ibid., 266–67.

86. Andrew Ross, "Ballots, Bullets, or Batmen: Can Cultural Studies Do the Right Thing?" *Screen* 31, no. 1 (Spring 1990): 40.

87. Robert H. Frank and Phillip J. Cook point out that between 1979 and 1989 "the incomes of the top 1 percent [in the U.S.] more than doubled in real terms," while "the median income was roughly stable" and "the bottom 20 percent saw their incomes actually fall by 10 percent." See *The Winner-Take-All Society* (New York: Free Press, 1995), 5.

88. John Fiske, *Channels of Discourse* (Chapel Hill: University of North Carolina Press, 1992), 320.

89. W. E. B. Du Bois, *Black Reconstruction in America* (New York: Harcourt, Brace, 1935), 130.

90. Frank and Cook, *Winner-Take-All Society*.

91. Dennis Lim, "Ron Shelton Hits below the Belt," *Village Voice*, January 12–18, 2000, accessed at <http://www.rottentomatoes.com/author.124/?.letter=p>.

92. Aaron Baker, "A New Combination: Women and Boxing, an Interview with Karyn Kusama," *Cineaste* 25, no. 4 (2000): 24.

93. Grant Farrad, "Feasting on Foreman: The Problematics of Postcolonial Identification," *Camera Obscura* 39 (1996): 53.

CONCLUSION: THE BIG GAME

Any Given Sunday (1999) sums up the conflicting tendencies that mark the portrayal of identity in the American sports film. Through the success of its central character, professional football coach Tony D'Amato (Al Pacino), it upholds the convention of celebrating utopian self-determination while avoiding the potential for D'Amato's victory to appear selfish by having it advance the interests of others on his team. *Any Given Sunday* therefore adopts the nostalgia of a large number of movies about sports made in the last twenty-five years that relive the past to avoid the social complexities of what Fredric Jameson calls "our current experience."[1] The film uses this focus on the past—articulated by D'Amato's obsession with tradition—to minimize the challenge to individualized athletic identity presented by the growth of greed, and by the increased presence of women and nonwhite men, in contemporary college and professional sports.

Although *Any Given Sunday,* like many recent sports films, maintains the conservative narrative conventions of the past, it also shares with earlier films the need to ground utopian stories in a realist style, inadvertently allowing for a historical complexity that shows identity as relational, even hybridized, and defined by contests between different ideological discourses. Working with cinematographer Salvatore Totino, whose career has been in commercials and music videos, writer/director Oliver Stone combines a rapid flow of imagery and a pounding soundtrack to suggest the speed and violence of professional football. This MTV aesthetic also juxtaposes images that show cultural difference—and are at times so discontinuous that they suggest the impossibility of unified subjectivity—with others that offer commodified representations of individual empowerment.

Most sports films made in the last twenty-five years have continued to tell the stories of white male protagonists, insisting on hard work and determination as the only ingredients that matter for athletic achievement. The bicentennial success of *Rocky* (1976) demonstrated a desire to dismiss the inequalities that the counterculture had identified in American society and gave new life to utopian sports movies such as *The Natural* (1984), *Hoosiers* (1986), *Field of Dreams* (1989), *Mr. Baseball* (1992), *Rudy* (1993), *Angels in the Outfield* (1994), *The Air Up There* (1994), and *The Replacements* (2000). These nostalgic films not only remember the mythology of white male protagonists but also reassert the old portrayals of nonwhites and women as either obstacles that define the hero or faithful supporters of his achievement.

A second group of recent films with a less nostalgic inclination demonstrate greater acceptance of the increase in social diversity in the sports world, but they still contain constrain its potential for change within another idea from earlier movies about athletics by way of liberal political discourse: that even for women and nonwhite athletes success comes from simply emulating the achievement of white men. Films such as *Personal Best* (1982) and *Pumping Iron II* (1985)—and two of the top box office hits amongst sports movies, *Space Jam* (1996) and *Jerry Maguire* (1996)—update the message films of the late 1940s and early 1950s by modifying the utopian ethos of Hollywood films to say, not that social difference doesn't exist, but that it needn't be a barrier to success with the necessary individual initiative. *Any Given Sunday* overlaps with this group of films when it shows D'Amato encouraging his African American quarterback Willie Beamen (Jaime Foxx) to assimilate into a team run by white people, while at the same time implying that there is room for cultural pluralism.

There are several possible explanations for this dogged insistence in many recent sports films on the conventions from earlier movies. Hollywood has always recycled what it regards as a successful formula, though just a handful of sports films have earned over $100 million in ticket sales. The success of the conservative sports film is therefore as much ideological as financial, measured by its affirmation of the idea of self-determination. In this sense, the sameness of message in sports stories exemplifies the role of popular culture in convincing people of hegemonic truths through the sheer weight of repetition.

The casting and characterization in *Any Given Sunday* provide examples of how economic and ideological motivations coincide. One reviewer puzzled over what he regarded as the odd choice of Cameron Diaz to play the owner of a professional football team, but he concluded that she was chosen because of her bankable star appeal.[2] True as that may be, her role, and the aggression with which she plays it, also sets up a feminist foil for Tony D'Amato that contributes to his reassertion of male self-reliance.

The conflicts between D'Amato, the team's female owner, and its African

American quarterback represent how the "current experience" that nostalgic sports films like *Any Given Sunday* seek to contain is one characterized by the growing involvement of women and nonwhites and by the pressures of an increasingly corporatized sports world that makes self-determination harder to portray plausibly. Nearly two-thirds of the players in the NFL and more than three-quarters of those in the NBA are African American; prizefighting has been dominated by blacks and Latinos for decades; and even in baseball an increasing number of the top stars are African American, Latino, or Asian. The presence of women in college and professional sports has also grown dramatically in recent years, the result both of greater access since the enactment of Title IX in 1972 and of changing notions of normative femininity to include physical strength and self-assertion. Such athletic femininity has been defined by an odd alliance of feminist ideas and corporate commodification—the latter exemplified by ESPN's plans for a women's sports network and Nike's growing interest in female consumers as an important new market. That the Center for the Study of Sport in Society at Northeastern University issues an annual report covered in the national media evaluating the access of women and nonwhites to decision-making positions in college and professional sports indicates how expectations about diversity are changing.

Any Given Sunday shows this increasing diversity, but it ultimately oversimplifies issues of social identity by asserting that ability and a willingness to fit in are all that matter. The story covers the later half of a season in which D'Amato struggles to guide his Miami Sharks to the playoffs under the dual pressures of the demanding owner, Christina Pagniacci (Diaz), and the need to play his third-string quarterback, Beamen. Beamen's run-and-shoot style produces yardage and victories, but the young quarterback at first doesn't buy D'Amato's Vince Lombardi–inspired speech about the need to show leadership by sacrificing his individual achievement for the good of the team. Beamen sums up his skepticism—based on his experience with the rules of amateur eligibility in college football that disadvantage working-class black players and the reluctance of white coaches to rely on an African American quarterback—when he tells D'Amato "Maybe it's not racism, maybe it's placism." But, like Apollo Creed's lack of faith in equality for African Americans in *Rocky,* Beamen's doubts about the degree of opportunity and rewards for blacks are answered by an Italian American protagonist who never questions the promise of the American dream and leads his team to victory.

To demonstrate the coach's commitment to his team and make clear that he isn't asking Beamen to give up his cultural identity, the film associates D'Amato with African American culture through his visits to the bar with his black assistant (Jim Brown), his knowledge of jazz, and his facility with hip-hop language. During one of his Lombardi-like speeches to a team of mostly African American players, D'Amato asks, "Are we gonna let them fuck with us in our house?" As the story unfolds, however, it becomes increasingly clear that Oliver Stone also wants to portray D'Amato as less sexist and self-serving than the African American players. We see repeated instances of their objectification of women, while the coach offers commitment to a young prostitute and takes the time for conversation with Christina Pagniacci's alcoholic mother.

Like the African American quarterback, Christina Pagniacci is selfish and controlling, blaming D'Amato for the team's failures and denying him any credit for its successes. As the film masculinizes her, it also shows D'Amato to be nurturing and patient. He encourages his players, especially Beamen, by both insisting on his belief in their ability and urging them to put the team first. While D'Amato's strategy of teamwork aligns him with a working-class ethos of group solidarity, the movie measures the success of this team unity in individual rewards: Beamen has his best game once he subordinates his outward assertion of ego, and in the last scene we learn that both he and his coach jump ship for big contracts with another team. *Any Given Sunday* ends with D'Amato striding out of the postseason news conference where he unexpectedly announced his new job, and the subsequent credit sequence shows Beamen visiting his old Dallas neighborhood in a gleaming red Mercedes.

Several other recent sports movies, including *Slap Shot* (1977) and the first two *Major League* films (1989, 1994), have also vilified female owners. Such castrating characters are less an accurate representation of how women run teams (very few do), than an example of what Susan Faludi calls "the backlash against women's rights" that blames women for the inequities they face.[3] In these four films female owners vilify feminism through their selfish, controlling behavior, yet much of what they do is typical of the business of sports when it is run by men. In *Any Given Sunday, Slap Shot,* and the *Major League* films, each of the female owners wants to micromanage the team or sell or move it to maximize their profits; such practices, combined with the extortion of publicly funded stadiums or arenas from local governments, have been pervasive practices in men's professional sports during the last twenty-five years.

While female owners appear as uniformly greedy, only a few films give male owners the same treatment, and when they do, their self-serving behavior is shown as easily offset by a heroic individual (*The Last Boy Scout,* 1991, *Eddie,* 1996) or as safely removed into the past (*Eight Men Out,* 1988). Such representation of the greed in men's professional sports as the fault of a few players and even fewer owners ignores how fan alienation, because of big increases in player salaries, revenues, and the value of teams in the last twenty-five years, has coincided with a growth in the gulf between haves and have-nots throughout American society. While since the 1970s players in professional basketball, baseball, hockey, and football receive six- and seven-figure average salaries and owners (especially those with new venues) have seen the value of their teams increase dramatically, "the incomes of a majority of men under 35 rose about half as fast as they did in earlier decades and the incomes of a majority of men aged roughly 35 and older essentially stagnated or fell."[4]

Nonetheless, several other sports films even show team owners as colorful, benevolent, and representing positions that we are asked to adopt. Owner Edward O'Neill (Jack Warden) in *The Replacements* voices disgust with overpaid prima donna players who won't sacrifice their bodies for the team and who go on strike for even more money. If we are to identify with and root for the replacement players, "because they love to play," we must share his disdain. While *Celtic Pride* (1996) and *The Fan* (1996) show how fan anger toward greedy, self-absorbed players can bubble over into violence, both films also make the players either African American or Latino, suggesting another backlash—here to displace the growing economic inequity in American society onto multiculturalism.

To the credit of *Any Given Sunday,* there are only a few recent sports films that make as much room for dialogue about social identity as it does. *Eight Men Out* offers a revisionist view of the Black Sox scandal to show how, even when the working people follow the model of individual achievement, they often get caught in the web of class politics. *Girlfight* (2000) and *Love and Basketball* (2000) portray female athletes with plenty of determination and a taste for hard work who nevertheless need to adopt a more masculine version of femininity that forces the men in their lives to compromise. The latter two films also comment on class identity by the way their protagonists emphasize sports for how it boosts their confidence and self-image rather than as a marketable skill. Monica in *Love and Basketball* succeeds in part because of the education and nurturing provided by her middle-class family. Yet both she and the Michele Rodríguez character in *Girlfight* also recognize the limited chance of big paydays for female athletes. That these two films were directed by nonwhite women, yet emphasize gender and class issues more than race, demonstrates the need to avoid easy assumptions about the specific circumstances that influence the filmic representation of identity, as well as the importance of seeing how the various social categories that structure it are often multiple and interrelated.

Any Given Sunday makes room for such a hybrid conception of identity, although it is presented in cultural terms rather than through acceptance of variation in social experience. This interest in affirming cultural rather than social difference may explain Stone's choice of an Italian American protagonist. On the one hand, by making three very different characters—the team's owner, a dumb jock player, and D'Amato—Italian American, Stone seems to deny that ethnicity has much to do with who they are. At the same time, however, D'Amato's characterization clearly borrows well-established traits of Italian American masculinity: Pacino's character is expressive both verbally and through a body language of touching and kissing that he uses to establish his commitment to others. Also, like Italian American males in movies and television from Beppo Donnetti in the 1915 film *The Italian* to Tony Soprano, D'Amato feels his emotions with such intensity that he will resort to violence to protect those near and dear to him. This becomes apparent when D'Amato attacks a television commentator who has built up Beamen's ego, and more generally by the coach's compliance with the idea that the violence of football distinguishes the good guys from the enemy.

Besides these standard traits, *Any Given Sunday* also incorporates three revisionist ideas found in recent films about Italian American identity: first, like *Raging Bull* (1980) and *A Bronx Tale* (1993), it makes its protagonist somewhat less than white; second, by characterizing D'Amato as driven by both populist working-class sympathies and also by bourgeois ambition, *Any Given Sunday* resembles films as different as *Rocky* and *Mac* (1992); finally, Pacino's character is feminized to a degree, as were the Italian American leads in *Saturday Night Fever* (1977) and *Kiss Me Guido* (1997). Yet, despite all this hybridization of D'Amato's identity, *Any Given Sunday* ultimately uses Pacino's character to emphasize a white notion of self-reliant masculinity.

Any Given Sunday's conclusion demonstrates how it veers away from dialogic identity. Beamen accepts D'Amato's exhortation that faith in his coach and team will pay off, and it does. This choice and its success endorse the idea that race presents no more of a barrier to achievement than ethnicity as the latter has been defined within the European American experience of social and economic mobility through assimilation. The racial hybridity of Pacino's Italian American character throughout the film has helped set us up for that equation. Likewise, D'Amato's nurturing side implies that his victory over Christine Pagniacci results from his superior character and has nothing to do with gender.

In contrast to this dismissal of the importance of social identity, consider a very different response to racial difference in another football film, *Remember the Titans* (2000). Like *Any Given Sunday*, *Remember the Titans* wants to assert the importance of team unity on the football field as a metaphor for the significance of overcoming racial division in American society. Yet unity is a one-way street in Oliver Stone's film: it requires the marginalization of the

Cameron Diaz character's feminism, and the acceptance by Willie Beamen of his coach's idea that African Americans must emulate the assimilation of white ethnics. In contrast, *Remember the Titans* is much more dialogic in how it portrays the successful integration of blacks and whites as requiring something from both sides. Set in Alexandria, Virginia, in the early 1970s, the film tells of an African American coach, Herman Bone (Denzel Washington), who risks his coaching career, and even the physical safety of his family, to unite a high school football team of black and white players. Likewise, the white coach, Bill Yoast (Will Patton), who agrees to assist Bone, gives up an opportunity to enter the Virginia High School Football Hall of Fame because of the racism of the white men who decide admission. This choice to sacrifice such a long-anticipated honor for the larger goal of racial unity on the team presents an example of what Noel Ignatiev calls race treason, an act by which someone defined as white rejects the unearned privilege of whiteness—specifically here the assumption that one's identity is constituted solely by what one does. The difficult choice of the white coach underlines an unavoidable reality that few sports films have the courage to acknowledge directly, but that often makes its way into their stories nonetheless: the social complexities of the identities that define us.

Notes

1. Fredric Jameson, "Postmodernism and a Consumer Society," in *Movies and Mass Culture,* ed. John Belton (New Brunswick, N.J.: Rutgers University Press, 1996).

2. Jeff Z. Klein, "On 'Any Given Sunday,' Salome Can Have Her Day," *New York Times,* January 16, 2000, 36.

3. Susan Faludi, *Backlash: The Undeclared War against American Women* (New York: Doubleday, 1991), xxii.

4. Jeff Madrick, "Economic Scene," *New York Times,* August 31, 2000, C2.

BIBLIOGRAPHY

Andersen, Thom. "Red Hollywood." In *Literature and the Visual Arts in Contemporary Society*, edited by Suzanne Ferguson and Barbara Groseclose, 141–96. Columbus: Ohio State University Press, 1985.

Aronowitz, Stanley. *From the Ashes of the Old: American Labor and America's Future*. Boston: Houghton Mifflin, 1998.

———. *The Politics of Identity*. New York: Routledge, 1992.

Baker, Aaron. "A New Combination: Women and Boxing Films, an Interview with Karyn Kusama." *Cineaste* 25, no. 4 (2000): 22–26.

Baker, Aaron, and Todd Boyd, eds. *Out of Bounds: Sports, Media, and the Politics of Identity*. Bloomington: Indiana University Press, 1997.

Barthes, Roland. "The World of Wrestling." In *A Barthes Reader*, edited by Susan Sontag, 18–30. New York: Hill and Wang, 1982.

Bederman, Gail. *Manliness and Civilization: A Cultural History of Gender and Race in the United States, 1880–1917*. Chicago: University of Chicago Press, 1995.

Bernardi, Daniel. "The Voice of Whiteness: D. W. Griffith's Biograph Films (1908–1913)." In *The Birth of Whiteness: Race and the Emergence of U.S. Cinema*, edited by Daniel Bernardi, 103–28. New Brunswick, N.J.: Rutgers University Press, 1996.

Bordwell, David, and Kristin Thompson. *Film Art*. New York: McGraw-Hill, 1997.

Boyd, Todd. *Am I Black Enough for You: Popular Culture from the Hood and Beyond*. Bloomington: Indiana University Press, 1997.

Boyle, Robert H. "Man of Style." *Sports Illustrated*, June 3, 1991, 18.

Brittan, Arthur. *Masculinity and Power*. London: Blackwell, 1989.

Brook, Peter. *The Melodramatic Imagination: Balzac, Henry James, Melodrama, and the Mode of Excess*. New Haven, Conn.: Yale University Press, 1976.

Buckner, Robert. *The Life of Knute Rockne*. Original screenplay. University of Notre Dame Archives.

Buhle, Paul, and Dave Wagner. Introduction to *The World Above*, by Abraham Polonsky. Urbana: University of Illinois Press, 1999.

Butler, Judith. *Gender Trouble: Feminism and the Subversion of Identity*. New York: Routledge, 1990.

Cahn, Susan K. *Coming On Strong: Gender and Sexuality in Twentieth-Century Women's Sport*. New York: Free Press, 1994.

Cayleff, Susan E. *Babe: The Life and Legend of Babe Didrikson Zaharias.* Urbana: University of Illinois Press, 1995.

Churchill, Ward. *Fantasies of a Master Race: Literature, Cinema, and the Colonization of American Indians.* San Francisco: City Lights Books, 1998.

Coakley, Jay. *Sport in Society: Issues and Controversies.* St. Louis: Times Mirror, 1998.

Collins, Jim. "Genericity in the Nineties: Eclectic Irony and the New Sincerity." In *Film Theory Goes to the Movies,* edited by Collins, Hilary Radner, and Ava Preacher Collins, 242–63. New York: Routledge, 1993.

Connell, Bob. "Masculinity, Violence, and War." In *Men's Lives.* 3d ed., edited by Michael S. Kimmel and Michael A. Messner, 125–30. Boston: Allyn and Bacon, 1995.

Cook, David. *A History of Narrative Film.* 3d ed. New York: W. W. Norton, 1996.

Cook, Jim, and Alan Lovell. "Aesthetics." In *Coming to Terms with Hollywood,* edited by Jim Cook and Alan Lovell, 28–48. London: British Film Institute, 1981.

Cripps, Thomas. *Black Film As Genre.* Bloomington: Indiana University Press, 1979.

———. *Making Movies Black.* New York: Oxford University Press, 1993.

———. *Slow Fade to Black: The Negro in American Film, 1900–1942.* New York: Oxford University Press, 1977.

Custen, George. *Bio/Pics: How Hollywood Constructed Public History.* New Brunswick, N.J.: Rutgers University Press, 1992.

Debord, Guy. *Society of the Spectacle.* Detroit: Black and Red, 1970.

DeJonge, Peter. "Talking Trash." *New York Times Magazine,* June 6, 1993, sec. 6, pp. 34–38.

Dell, Chad. "'Lookit That Hunk of Man!': Subversive Pleasures, Female Fandom and Professional Wrestling." Unpublished paper shared with me by the author.

Deloria, Philip. "'I Am of the Body': Thoughts on My Grandfather, Culture, and Sports." *South Atlantic Quarterly* 95, no. 2 (Spring 1996): 321–38.

DeMott, Benjamin. *The Trouble with Friendship: Why Americans Can't Think Straight about Race.* New York: Atlantic Monthly Press, 1995.

Diawara, Manthia. "Black Spectatorship: Problems of Identification and Resistance." In *Black American Cinema,* edited by Manthia Diawara, 211–20. New York: Routledge, 1993.

Dozoretz, Wendy. "The Mother's Lost Voice in *Hard, Fast, and Beautiful.*" *Wide Angle* 6, no. 3 (1984): 50–57.

Du Bois, W. E. B. *Black Reconstruction in America.* New York: Harcourt, Brace, 1935.

Dyer, Richard. "Entertainment and Utopia." In *The Cultural Studies Reader,* edited by Simon During, 271–83. London: Blackwell, 1993.

———. *Heavenly Bodies.* New York: St. Martin's, 1986.

———. *White.* New York: Routledge, 1997.

Dyson, Michael Eric. "Be like Mike?: Michael Jordan and the Pedagogy of Desire." In Dyson, *Reflecting Black: African-American Cultural Criticism,* 64–75. Minneapolis: University of Minnesota Press, 1993.

Eagleton, Terry. *Marxism and Literary Criticism.* Berkeley: University of California Press, 1976.

Early, Gerald. *Tuxedo Junction: Essays on American Culture.* New York: Ecco Press, 1989.

Eckert, Charles. "The Anatomy of a Proletarian Film: Warner's *Marked Woman.*" In *Movies and Methods,* edited by Bill Nichols, vol. 2, 407–29. Berkeley: University of California Press, 1985.

———."The Carole Lombard in Macy's Window." In *Fabrications: Costume and the Female Body,* edited by Jane Gaines and Charlotte Herzog, 100–121. New York: Routledge, 1990.

Ellsworth, Elizabeth. "Illicit Pleasures: Feminist Spectators and *Personal Best." Wide Angle* 8, no. 2 (1985): 45–56.

Elsaesser, Thomas. "Tales of Sound and Fury: Observations on the Family Melodrama." In *Movies and Methods,* edited by Bill Nichols, vol. 2, 165–89. Berkeley: University of California Press, 1985.

Faludi, Susan. *Backlash: The Undeclared War against American Women.* New York: Doubleday, 1991.

Farber, Manny. "Fight Films." Reprinted in Farber, *Negative Space,* 64–67. New York: Praeger, 1971.

Farrad, Grant. "Feasting on Foreman: The Problematics of Postcolonial Identification." *Camera Obscura* 39 (1996): 53–77.

Fiske, John. *Channels of Discourse.* Chapel Hill: University of North Carolina Press, 1992.

Foner, Eric. "A Conversation between Eric Foner and John Sayles." In *Past Imperfect: History according to the Movies,* edited by Mark C. Carnes, 11–28. New York: Henry Holt, 1995.

Frank, Robert H., and Phillip J. Cook. *The Winner-Take-All Society.* New York: Free Press, 1995.

Franklin, John Hope. *From Slavery to Freedom: A History of Negro Americans.* 6th ed. New York: Knopf, 1988.

Gabler, Neal. *An Empire of Their Own: How the Jews Invented Hollywood.* New York: Anchor Books, 1988.

Gaines, Jane. "Women and Representation: Can We Enjoy Alternative Pleasure?" In *Issues in Feminist Film Criticism,* edited by Patricia Erens, 75–92. Bloomington: Indiana University Press, 1990.

Gardner, Leonard. *Fat City.* Berkeley: University of California Press, 1996.

Gates, Henry Louis, Jr. "New Worth: How the Greatest Player in the History of Basketball Became the Greatest Brand in the History of Sports." *New Yorker,* June 1, 1998, 48–61.

George, Nelson. *Elevating the Game: Black Men and Basketball.* New York: HarperCollins, 1992.

Gilmore, Al-Tony. *Bad Nigger: The National Impact of Jack Johnson.* Port Washington, N.Y.: Kennikat Press, 1975.

Goldberg, David Theo. "Call and Response: Sports, Talk Radio, and the Death of Democracy." In *Soundbite Culture: The Death of Discourse in a Wired World,* edited by David Slayden and Rita Kirk Whillock, 29–42. Thousand Oaks, Calif.: Sage Publications, 1999.

———. *Racial Subjects.* New York: Routledge, 1997.

Gomery, Douglas, and Robert Allen. *Film History: Theory and Practice.* New York: Alfred A. Knopf, 1985.

Gorn, Elliot, and Warren Goldstein. *A Brief History of American Sports.* New York: Hill and Wang, 1993.

Graham, Otis L., Jr. "Years of Crisis: America in Depression and War, 1933–1945." In *The Unfinished Century,* edited by William Leuchtenburg, 359–459. Boston: Little, Brown, 1973.

Grey, Herman. *Watching Race: Television and the Struggle for "Blackness."* Minneapolis: University of Minnesota Press, 1995.

Grindon, Leger. "Body and Soul: The Structure of Meaning in the Boxing Film Genre." *Cinema Journal* 35, no. 4 (1996): 54–69.

Guerrero, Ed. *Framing Blackness: The African American Image in Film.* Philadelphia: Temple University Press, 1993.

Halberstam, Judith. *Female Masculinity.* Durham, N.C.: Duke University Press, 1998.

Hall, Stuart. "Notes on Deconstructing 'The Popular.'" In *People's History and Socialist Theory,* edited by Raphael Samuel, 21–33. London: Routledge and Kegan Paul, 1981.

Hall, Stuart. "What Is This 'Black' in Black Popular Culture?" In *Black Popular Culture,* edited by Gina Dent, 21–33. Seattle, Wash.: Bay Press, 1992.

Harris, Mark. "Where Have You Gone, Jackie Robinson?" *The Nation,* May 15, 1995, 674–76.

Heywood, Leslie. *Bodymakers: A Cultural Anatomy of Women's Bodybuilding.* New Brunswick, N.J.: Rutgers University Press, 1998.

Holmlund, Chris. "Visible Difference and Flex Appeal: The Body, Sex, Sexuality, and Race in the *Pumping Iron* Films." In *Out of Bounds: Sports, Media, and the Politics of Identity,* edited by Aaron Baker and Todd Boyd, 145–60. Bloomington: Indiana University Press, 1997.

———. "When Is a Lesbian Not a Lesbian?: The Lesbian Continuum and the Mainstream Femme Film." *Camera Obscura* 25–26 (1991): 145–79.

hooks, bell. "Neo-Colonial Fantasies of Conquest: *Hoop Dreams.*" In hooks, *Reel to Reel: Race, Sex, and Class at the Movies,* 22–25. New York: Routledge, 1996.

Isenberg, Michael T. *John Sullivan and His America.* Urbana: University of Illinois Press, 1988.

Jameson, Fredric. "Postmodernism and a Consumer Society." In *Movies and Mass Culture,* edited by John Belton, 185–202. New Brunswick, N.J.: Rutgers University Press, 1996.

———. *Signatures of the Visible.* New York: Routledge, 1990.

Jencks, Christopher. "Is the American Underclass Growing?" In *The Urban Underclass,* edited by Christopher Jencks and Paul E. Peterson, 28–100. Washington, D.C.: Brookings Institution, 1991.

Jezer, Marty. *The Dark Ages: Life in the United States, 1945–1960.* Boston: South End Press, 1982.

Jordan, Pat. "The Girls of Summer." *American Way* 25, no. 12 (June 15, 1992): 38–41.

Karnes, David. "The Glamorous Crowd: Hollywood Movie Premieres between the Wars." *American Quarterly* 38, no. 4 (Fall 1986): 553–72.

Kimmel, Michael. *Manhood in America.* New York: Free Press, 1996.

Krase, Jerome, and Charles LaCerra, *Ethnicity and Machine Politics* (Lanham, Md.: University Press of America, 1991).

Leab, Daniel J. "The Blue Collar Ethnic in Bicentennial America: *Rocky.*" In *American History/American Film,* edited by John E. O'Connor and Martin A. Jackson, 257–72. New York: Continuum, 1988.

———. *From Sambo to Superspade: The Black Experience in Motion Pictures.* Boston: Houghton Mifflin, 1976.

Lears, T. J. Jackson. "From Salvation to Self-Realization: Advertising and the Therapeutic Roots of the Consumer Culture, 1880–1980." In *The Culture of Consumption: Crit-*

ical Essays in American History, 1880–1980, edited by Richard Wightman Fox and T. J. Jackson Lears, 3–38. New York: Pantheon Books, 1983.

Leonardo, Micaela di. "White Ethnicities, Identity Politics, and Baby Bear's Chair." *Social Text* 41 (Winter 1994): 165–91.

Levy, Emanuel. *George Cukor.* New York: Morrow, 1994.

Lim, Dennis. "Ron Shelton Hits below the Belt." *Village Voice,* January 12–18, 2000. <http://www.rottentomatoes.com/author.124/?.letter=p>.

Maharaj, Gitanjali. "Talking Trash: Late Capitalism, Black (Re)Productivity, and Professional Basketball." *Social Text* 50 (Spring 1997): 97–110.

Manchester, William. *The Glory and the Dream: A Narrative History of America, 1932–1972.* Boston: Little, Brown, 1974.

Marable, Manning. *Race, Reform, and Rebellion: The Second Reconstruction in Black America, 1945–1990.* Jackson: University of Mississippi Press, 1991.

Marx, Samuel. *Mayer and Thalberg: The Make-Believe Saints.* New York: Random House, 1975.

Mast, Gerald. *The Comic Mind: Comedy and the Movies.* 2d ed. Chicago: University of Chicago Press, 1979.

———, ed. *The Movies in Our Midst.* Chicago: University of Chicago Press, 1982.

McCormick, Richard L. "Public Life in Industrial America, 1877–1917." In *The New American History,* edited by Eric Foner, 93–117. Philadelphia: Temple University Press, 1990.

Mellen, Joan. *Big Bad Wolves: Masculinity in the American Film.* New York: Pantheon Books, 1977.

Melnick, Merrill J., and Donald Sabo. "Sport and Social Mobility among African-American and Hispanic Athletes." In *Ethnicity and Sport in North American History and Culture,* edited by George Eisen and David K. Wiggins, 221–41. Westport, Conn.: Greenwood Press, 1994.

Miller, Mark Crispin. "Advertising." In *Seeing through the Movies,* edited by Mark Crispin Miller, 186–246. New York: Pantheon Books, 1990.

Miller, Toby. "Commodifying the Male Body, Problematizing 'Hegemonic Masculinity'?" *Journal of Sport and Social Issues* 22 (November 1998): 431–46.

Mintz, Steven, and Susan Kellogg. *Domestic Revolutions: A Social History of American Family Life.* New York: Free Press, 1988.

Morse, Margaret. "Sports on Television: Replay and Display." In *Regarding Television: Critical Approaches—An Anthology,* edited by E. Ann Kaplan, 44–66. Frederick, Md.: University Publications of America, 1983.

Motion Picture Producers and Distributors of America." The Motion Picture Production Code of 1930." In *The Movies in Our Midst,* edited by Gerald Mast, 321–33. Chicago: University of Chicago Press, 1982.

Mulvey, Laura. "Afterthoughts on 'Visual Pleasure and Narrative Cinema' Inspired by *Duel in the Sun.*" In *Feminism and Film Theory,* edited by Constance Penley, 69–79. New York: Routledge, 1988.

———. "Visual Pleasure and Narrative Cinema." In *Issues in Feminist Film Criticism,* edited by Patricia Erens, 28–40. Bloomington: Indiana University Press, 1990.

Muñoz, Carlos, Jr. *Youth, Identity, Power: The Chicano Movement.* London: Verso, 1989.

Musser, Charles. *The Emergence of Cinema: The American Screen to 1907.* New York: Charles Scribner's Sons, 1990.

Muwakkil, Salim. "Letting Go of the Dream." *In These Times,* November 2, 1997, 13–15.

Naison, Mark. "Sports and the American Empire." In *American Media and Mass Culture: Left Perspectives,* edited by Donald Lazere, 499–515. Berkeley: University of California Press, 1987.

Naremore, James. *More Than Night: Film Noir in Its Contexts.* Berkeley: University of California Press, 1998.

Navasky, Victor S. *Naming Names.* New York: Viking Press, 1980.

Neale, Steven. "Masculinity As Spectacle." In *Screening the Male: Exploring Masculinities in Hollywood Cinema,* edited by Steven Cohan and Ina Rae Hark, 9–20. New York: Routledge, 1993.

Noggle, Burl. *Into the Twenties: The United States from Armistice to Normalcy.* Urbana: University of Illinois Press, 1974.

Noriega, Chon A. "Citizen Chicano: The Trials and Titillations of Ethnicity in the American Cinema, 1935–1962." *Social Research* 58, no. 2 (Summer 1991): 413–38.

Oates, Joyce Carol. *On Boxing.* New York: Doubleday, 1987.

Odd, Gilbert. *Encyclopedia of Boxing.* New York: Crescent Books, 1983.

Orsi, Robert. "The Religious Boundaries of an Inbetween People: Street Feste and the Problem of the Dark-Skinned Other in Italian Harlem, 1920–1990." *American Quarterly* 44, no. 3 (September 1992): 313–47.

Pope, S. W. "Introduction: American Sport History—Toward a New Paradigm." In *The New American Sport History: Recent Approaches and Perspectives,* edited by S. W. Pope, 1–30. Urbana: University of Illinois Press, 1997.

Rader, Benjamin G. *Baseball: A History of America's Game.* Urbana: University of Illinois Press, 1992.

Rader, Benjamin G. *American Sports: From the Age of Folk Games to the Age of Televised Sports.* Englewood Cliffs, N.J.: Prentice Hall, 1990.

Rafferty, T. "Boys' Games." *New Yorker,* June 6, 1992, 80–82.

Rainsberger, Todd. *James Wong Howe, Cinematographer.* San Diego: A. S. Barnes, 1981.

Rampersad, Arnold. *Jackie Robinson.* New York: Knopf, 1997.

Ray, Robert. *A Certain Tendency of the Hollywood Cinema, 1930–1980.* Princeton, N.J.: Princeton University Press, 1985.

Riess, Steven A. *City Games: The Evolution of American Urban Society and the Rise of Sports.* Urbana: University of Illinois Press, 1989.

———. "Sport and the Redefinition of American Middle-Class Masculinity." *International Journal of the History of Sport* 8, no. 1 (1991): 5–27.

Roberts, Randy. *Papa Jack: Jack Johnson and the Era of White Hopes.* New York: Free Press, 1983.

Roberts, Randy, and James S. Olson. *Winning Is the Only Thing: Sports in America since 1945.* Baltimore, Md.: Johns Hopkins University Press, 1989.

Roffman, Peter, and Jim Purdy. *The Hollywood Social Problem Film.* Bloomington: Indiana University Press, 1981.

Rogin, Michael. *Blackface, White Noise: Jewish Immigrants in the Hollywood Melting Pot.* Berkeley: University of California Press, 1996.

Rose, Ava, and Jim Friedman. "Television Sports As Mas(s)culine Cult of Distraction." In *Out of Bounds: Sports, Media, and the Politics of Identity,* edited by Aaron Baker and Todd Boyd, 1–15. Bloomington: Indiana University Press, 1997.

Rosenstone, Robert. *Visions of the Past.* Cambridge, Mass.: Harvard University Press, 1995.

Ross, Andrew. "Ballots, Bullets, or Batmen: Can Cultural Studies Do the Right Thing?" *Screen* 31, no. 1 (Spring 1990): 26–44.

Roth, Mark. "Some Warners Musicals and the Spirit of the New Deal." In *Genre: The Musical,* edited by Rick Altman, 41–56. Boston: Routledge and Kegan Paul, 1981.

Rowe, David. *Popular Cultures: Rock Music, Sport, and the Politics of Pleasure.* London: Sage Publications, 1993.

Rudnick, Lois. "The New Woman." In *1915, the Cultural Moment,* edited by Adele Heller and Lois Rudnick, 69–81. New Brunswick, N.J.: Rutgers University Press, 1991.

Russo, Mary. "Female Grotesques: Carnival and Theory." In *Feminist Studies/Critical Studies,* edited by Teresa de Lauretis, 213–29. Bloomington: Indiana University Press, 1986.

Russo, Vito. *Celluloid Closet: Homosexuality in the Movies.* New York: Harper and Row, 1987.

Ryan, Michael, and Douglas Kellner. *Camera Politica: The Politics and Ideology of Contemporary Hollywood Film.* Bloomington: Indiana University Press, 1988.

Sammons, Jeffrey T. *Beyond the Ring: The Role of Boxing in American Society.* Urbana: University of Illinois Press, 1990.

Schor, Juliet B. *The Overworked American: The Unexpected Decline of Leisure.* New York: Basic Books, 1991.

Schulze, Laurie. "The Made-for-TV Movie: Industrial Practice, Cultural Form, Popular Reception." In *Television: The Critical View,* edited by Horace Newcomb, 155–74. New York: Oxford University Press, 1982.

Sedgwick, Eve Kosofosky. "Axiomatic." In *The Cultural Studies Reader,* edited by Simon During, 243–68. New York: Routledge, 1993.

Shropshire, Ken. *In Black and White: Race and Sports in America.* New York: New York University Press, 1996.

Silet, Charles L. P., and Gretchen Bataille. *The Pretend Indians: Images of Native Americans in the Movies.* Ames: Iowa State University Press, 1980.

Sklar, Robert. *City Boys: Cagney, Bogart, Garfield.* Princeton, N.J.: Princeton University Press, 1992.

———. *Movie-Made America.* New York: Vintage, 1994.

Slotkin, Richard. *Gunfighter Nation: The Myth of the Frontier in Twentieth-Century America.* New York: Atheneum, 1992.

Smith, James F. "Where the Action Is: Images of the Gambler in Recent Popular Films." In *Beyond the Stars: Studies in American Popular Film,* edited by Paul Loukaides and Linda Fuller, 177–86. Bowling Green, Ohio: Bowling Green State University Popular Press, 1990.

Sobchack, Vivian. "Baseball in the Post-American Cinema; or, Life in the Minor Leagues." In *Out of Bounds: Sports, Media, and the Politics of Identity,* edited by Aaron Baker and Todd Boyd, 175–97. Bloomington: Indiana University Press, 1997.

Sollors, Werner. *Beyond Ethnicity: Consent and Descent in American Culture.* New York: Oxford University Press, 1986.

Sperber, Murray. *Shake Down the Thunder: The Creation of Notre Dame Football.* New York: Henry Holt, 1993.

Staiger, Janet. "The Director System: Management in the First Years." In *The Classical Hollywood Cinema: Film Style and Production to 1960,* edited by David Bordwell, Kristin Thompson, and Janet Staiger, 113–27. New York: Columbia University Press, 1985.

Stam, Robert. "Bakhtin, Polyphony, and Ethnic/Racial Representation." In *Unspeakable Images: Ethnicity and the American Cinema,* edited by Lester D. Friedman, 251–76. Urbana: University of Illinois Press, 1991.

Steele, Michael R. *Knute Rockne, a Bio-Biography.* Westport, Conn.: Greenwood Press, 1983.

Streible, Dan. "A History of the Boxing Film, 1894–1915: Social Control and Social Reform in the Progressive Era." *Film History* 3, no. 3 (1989): 235–57.

Thompson, Andrew O. "Love and Basketball," *ICG Magazine,* March 2000, 48–50.

Thompson, David. *A Biographical Dictionary of Film.* 3d ed. New York: Alfred A. Knopf, 1996.

Thompson, Kristin. *The Classical Hollywood Cinema.* New York: Columbia University Press, 1985.

Thompson, Kristin, and David Bordwell. *Film History, an Introduction.* New York: McGraw-Hill, 1994.

Tocqueville, Alexis de. *Democracy in America,* edited by J. P. Mayer, Translated by George Lawrence. Garden City, N.Y.: Anchor/Doubleday, 1969.

Togovnick, Marianna De Marco. *Crossing Ocean Parkway.* Chicago: University of Chicago Press, 1996.

Tomasulo, Frank P. "Italian Americans in the Hollywood Cinema: Filmmakers, Characters, Audiences." *Voices in Italian Americana* 7, no. 1 (1996): 65–77.

Umphlett, W. L. *The Movies Go to College.* Rutherford, N.J.: Fairleigh Dickinson University Press, 1984.

Variety Film Reviews. New York: Garland, 1983.

Vázquez, Josefina Zoraida, and Lorenzo Meyer. *The United States and Mexico.* Chicago: University of Chicago Press, 1985.

West, Cornel. *Race Matters.* New York: Vintage, 1994.

Wideman, John Edgar. "Michael Jordan Leaps the Great Divide." *Esquire,* November 1990, 143–45, 210–16.

Williams, Linda. "*Personal Best* Women in Love." *Jump Cut* 27 (1982): 1, 11–12.

Williams, Raymond. "Class." In Williams, *Keywords,* 60–69. New York: Oxford University Press, 1983.

Wolff, Edward N. *Top Heavy: The Increasing Inequality of Wealth in America and What Can Be Done about It.* New York: New Press, 1995.

Wood, Robin. "Cards on the Table." In Wood, *Hollywood from Vietnam to Reagan,* 1–10. New York: Columbia University Press, 1986.

———. *Hollywood from Vietnam to Reagan.* New York: Columbia University Press, 1990.

———. "Ideology, Genre, Auteur." In *Film Genre Reader 2,* edited by Barry Keith Grant, 59–73. Austin: University of Texas Press, 1995.

Zucker, Harvey Marc, and Lawrence J. Babich. *Sports Films: A Complete Reference.* Jefferson, N.C.: McFarland, 1987.

INDEX

AARON BAKER is an assistant professor at Arizona State University. He coedited the volume *Out of Bounds: Sports, Media, and the Politics of Identity.*

The University of Illinois Press
is a founding member of the
Association of American University Presses.

_____

Composed in 9/13 Stone Serif
with Stone Sans display
by Jim Proefrock
at the University of Illinois Press
Manufactured by Thomson-Shore, Inc.

University of Illinois Press
1325 South Oak Street
Champaign, IL 61820-6903
www.press.uillinois.edu